# Getting Started with Visual Studio 2022

## Learning and Implementing New Features

## Second Edition

**Dirk Strauss**

Apress®

*Getting Started with Visual Studio 2022: Learning and Implementing New Features*

Dirk Strauss
Uitenhage, South Africa

ISBN-13 (pbk): 978-1-4842-8921-1                    ISBN-13 (electronic): 978-1-4842-8922-8
https://doi.org/10.1007/978-1-4842-8922-8

Managing Director, Apress Media LLC: Welmoed Spahr
Acquisitions Editor: Smriti Srivastava
Development Editor: Laura Berendson
Coordinating Editor: Mark Powers

Cover designed by eStudioCalamar

Cover image by Pawel Czerwinski on Unsplash (www.unsplash.com)

Distributed to the book trade worldwide by Apress Media, LLC, 1 New York Plaza, New York, NY 10004, U.S.A. Phone 1-800-SPRINGER, fax (201) 348-4505, e-mail orders-ny@springer-sbm.com, or visit www.springeronline.com. Apress Media, LLC is a California LLC and the sole member (owner) is Springer Science + Business Media Finance Inc (SSBM Finance Inc). SSBM Finance Inc is a **Delaware** corporation.

For information on translations, please e-mail booktranslations@springernature.com; for reprint, paperback, or audio rights, please e-mail bookpermissions@springernature.com.

Apress titles may be purchased in bulk for academic, corporate, or promotional use. eBook versions and licenses are also available for most titles. For more information, reference our Print and eBook Bulk Sales web page at http://www.apress.com/bulk-sales.

Any source code or other supplementary material referenced by the author in this book is available to readers on GitHub (https://github.com/Apress). For more detailed information, please visit http://www.apress.com/source-code.

Printed on acid-free paper

*To Adele, Tristan, and Irénéé. My everything for you, always!*

# Table of Contents

# About the Author

**Dirk Strauss** has over 17 years of experience programming with C# and Visual Studio. Working for various companies throughout his career, he has been privileged to work with and learn from some of the most brilliant developers in the industry. He has authored several books on topics ranging from Visual Studio and C# to ASP.NET Core. Passionate about writing code, he loves learning new tech and imparting what he learns to others.

# About the Technical Reviewer

**Sanjaya Prakash Pradhan** is a Microsoft Dynamics 365 and Power Apps Business Applications MVP and, at the same time, a Microsoft Certified Trainer (MCT) in Dynamics 365 CE and Power Apps. He is an experienced senior technical consultant with 13+ years of experience in consulting and training who has worked on numerous business system implementations. Sanjaya is currently working as the research and development industry solutions lead in an established worldwide business applications practice. Having led software projects in numerous industries including BFS, health care, retail, and the public sector, he works across all areas of the project life cycle from demonstrations, design, architecture, documentation, customization, and development. Sanjaya gets involved in the technical community through leading the Power Platform and Dynamics 365 user group in India, running technical events, and presenting on technical and functional topics at conferences around the world. In one line, he is an MVP, MCT, community director, UG lead, speaker, trainer, blogger, author, podcaster, business advisor, and senior solution architect.

# Acknowledgments

I would like to thank my wife and children for their support while writing this book. I would not have been able to do it without you by my side.

I would also like to thank the Apress team for supporting this book and for turning my vision into reality. It is a topic I have wanted to write about for a long time.

I also want to thank Sanjaya Prakash for his help during the review of this book.

Last but not least, I want to thank you for reading this book. Your passion for knowing more drives me to learn more and impart what I learn. It's a symbiotic relationship that benefits us as we grow and become better at what we do.

# Introduction

Visual Studio 2022 is the next version of the stellar development tool we love to use. This book is for developers ready to get to know the IDE better. It aims to get you started on the road to exploring Visual Studio 2022, beyond what you are already comfortable with.

The book starts with installing Visual Studio and adding workloads. Then you explore the IDE a bit more before looking at the existing (and some new) features in Visual Studio 2022. After that, a few productivity tips are included for good measure.

Being able to effectively work with different project types and knowing when to use them are explored in a bit more detail in Chapter 2. We will look at the new MAUI project template and how to create cross-platform applications. We then see how to create project templates and then explore using and creating code snippets. This chapter covers many of the basics essential to working with Visual Studio, including using bookmarks, code shortcuts, the Server Explorer, and other Visual Studio Windows.

In Chapter 3, we look at debugging techniques such as using breakpoints, setting conditional breakpoints, breakpoint actions, temporary breakpoints, dependent breakpoints, and labels. We see how to use data tips as well as the DebuggerDisplay attribute. We then take a closer look at Diagnostic Tools and the Immediate Window. Finally, to close off the debugging chapter, we see how to attach to a running process and how to use remote debugging.

The next chapter introduces you to creating and running unit tests. You learn how to create live unit tests, use IntelliTest to generate unit tests, and measure code coverage in Visual Studio.

Finally, we look at working with Git and GitHub. We see how to create a GitHub account and what creating and cloning a repository involves. The new Git features in Visual Studio 2022, such as multi-repo branching, comparing branches, and line staging, are also discussed.

You learn how to commit changes in code to the repository and create a branch of your code when you need to work on a new feature in isolation. Then we look at creating a pull request and how these pull requests are managed. Lastly, we have a look at the benefit of working with stashes.

If you need an excellent reference book that deals exclusively with (and only with) Visual Studio, then look at what this book has to offer you. If you spend any time using Visual Studio or want to learn how working with Visual Studio 2022 can increase your productivity, then this book makes a perfect reference book for your office.

# CHAPTER 1

# Getting to Know Visual Studio 2022

Visual Studio is an amazing bit of software. If you have been using Visual Studio for a number of years, you will certainly agree that the IDE offers developers a host of tools and features to make them more productive. You will also be aware that it has grown a lot during the past couple of years and is an absolute powerhouse when it comes to providing tools to develop world-class software.

Initially released as Visual Studio 97 in February 1997, this was the first attempt at using a single development environment for multiple languages. The evolution of Visual Studio is detailed in Table 1-1.

© Dirk Strauss 2023
D. Strauss, *Getting Started with Visual Studio 2022*, https://doi.org/10.1007/978-1-4842-8922-8_1

**Table 1-1.**  *The Evolution of Visual Studio*

| Release | Version | .NET Framework | .NET Core | Release Date |
|---|---|---|---|---|
| Visual Studio 2022 | 17.0 | 3.5, 4.6.0–4.8 | 2.1, 3.1, 5.0, 6.0 | February 15, 2022 |
| Visual Studio 2019 | 16.0 | 3.5–4.8 | 2.1, 2.2, 3.0, 3.1, 5.0 | April 2, 2019 |
| Visual Studio 2017 | 15.0 | 3.5–4.7 | 1.0, 1.1, 2.0, 2.1 | March 7, 2017 |
| Visual Studio 2015 | 14.0 | 2.0–4.6 | 1.0 | July 20, 2015 |
| Visual Studio 2013 | 12.0 | 2.0–4.5.2 | | October 17, 2013 |
| Visual Studio 2012 | 11.0 | 2.0–4.5.2 | | September 12, 2012 |
| Visual Studio 2010 | 10.0 | 2.0–4.0 | | April 12, 2010 |
| Visual Studio 2008 | 9.0 | 2.0, 3.0, 3.5 | | November 19, 2007 |
| Visual Studio 2005 | 8.0 | 2.0, 3.0 | | November 7, 2005 |
| Visual Studio .NET 2003 | 7.1 | 1.1 | | April 24, 2003 |
| Visual Studio .NET 2002 | 7.0 | 1.0 | | February 13, 2002 |
| Visual Studio 6.0 | 6.0 | N/A | | June 1998 |
| Visual Studio 97 | 5.0 | N/A | | February 1997 |

There is so much to see and learn when it comes to Visual Studio. Therefore, in this chapter, we will start by having a look at the following:

- Installing Visual Studio

- What workloads are

- Exploring the IDE (integrated development environment)

- Existing and new features available in Visual Studio 2022

- Productivity tips

If you are using a macOS or a Windows machine, Visual Studio will happily run on both. Let us see where to find the Visual Studio Installer and get going.

# Installing Visual Studio

At the time of this writing, Visual Studio 2022 is available for Windows machines as well as for macOS machines. You can download Visual Studio 2022 for Windows from https://visualstudio.microsoft.com/vs/, and if you are on macOS, you will need to head on over to https://visualstudio.microsoft.com/vs/mac/ to download the installer.

Clicking the Download Visual Studio button, you will see a list drop-down with the options as displayed in Figure 1-1.

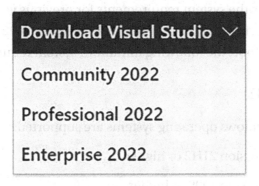

*Figure 1-1.* *Versions of Visual Studio available*

If you would like to compare the Visual Studio 2022 editions, you can have a look at https://visualstudio.microsoft.com/vs/compare/ for a detailed comparison. The bottom line is that if you want Visual Studio 2022 for free, download Visual Studio Community 2022.

Visual Studio Community 2022 is aimed at students, open source, and individual developers. The paid tiers include Visual Studio Professional 2022 which is aimed at small teams and Visual Studio Enterprise 2022 aimed at large development teams.

---

Microsoft specifies enterprise organizations as those having more than 250 PCs or more than 1 million US dollars in annual revenue.

---

Let us have a brief look at the recommended system requirements for installing Visual Studio on your machine. For a comprehensive list, browse to `https://docs.microsoft.com/en-us/visualstudio/releases/2022/system-requirements` and have a read through that.

# Visual Studio 2022 System Requirements

The system requirements for installing Visual Studio 2022 might differ from those of previous versions of Visual Studio. Refer to the documentation on `https://docs.microsoft.com` to review the system requirements for previous versions of Visual Studio.

Visual Studio Enterprise 2022, Visual Studio Professional 2022, and Visual Studio Community 2022 all support the following minimum system requirements.

## Operating Systems

The following 64-bit Windows operating systems are supported:

- Windows 11 version 21H2 or higher

- Windows 10 version 1909 or higher

- Windows Server 2022 – Standard and Datacenter

- Windows Server 2019 – Standard and Datacenter

- Windows Server 2016 – Standard and Datacenter

## Hardware

There is a line here that developers generally don't like to cross when it comes to the minimum hardware specs. Many developers I know will geek out on system RAM and favor SSDs over HDDs. Nevertheless, here are the minimum recommended requirements:

- 1.8 GHz or faster 64-bit processor (quad-core or better recommended). ARM processors are not supported.

- 4 GB of RAM (16 GB of RAM recommended).

- Minimum 2 vCPU and 8 GB RAM. 4 vCPU and 16 GB of RAM is recommended.

- Minimum of 850 MB and up to 210 GB of available hard disk space (depending on installed features, 20–50 GB of free space is typically required).

- For improved performance, install Windows and Visual Studio on an SSD.

- Minimum display resolution of WXGA (1366 by 768) but works best at 1920 by 1080 or higher.

## Supported Languages

Visual Studio and the Visual Studio Installer are available in 14 languages as follows:

- English
- Chinese (Simplified)
- Chinese (Traditional)
- Czech
- French
- German
- Italian
- Japanese
- Korean
- Polish
- Portuguese (Brazil)
- Russian
- Spanish
- Turkish

## Additional Notes

There are several additional requirements to take note of that I will briefly list here. There are however other requirements that might be of importance to your unique development environment. For a full list, refer to the system requirements at the following link: `https://docs.microsoft.com/en-us/visualstudio/releases/2022/system-requirements`.

- Administrator rights are required to install Visual Studio.

- .NET Framework 4.5.2 or above is required to run the Visual Studio Installer and install Visual Studio.

- Visual Studio requires .NET Framework 4.8 and will be installed during setup.

## Visual Studio Is 64-Bit

Visual Studio 2022 on Windows will now run as a 64-bit application, which means that you can open, modify, and debug really large solutions without running out of memory. Being a 64-bit application, Visual Studio 2022 is no longer limited to just 4 GB of memory in the main devenv.exe process.

It is also important to note that even though Visual Studio 2022 is 64-bit, it will not change the types or bitness of the applications you create and that you can still build and deploy 32-bit apps.

## Full .NET 6.0 Support

Visual Studio 2022 has full support for .NET 6, and its unified framework is available for both Windows and Mac developers. This includes .NET MAUI which allows developers to develop cross-platform client apps on Windows, Android, macOS, and iOS. Visual Studio 2022 also allows developers to use ASP.NET Blazor to develop desktop apps via .NET MAUI.

## Using Workloads

After Visual Studio has been installed, you can customize the installation by selecting feature sets, also known as workloads. Think of workloads as a collection of individual features that belong together. This allows you to easily modify Visual Studio to include only what you need.

To launch the workloads screen, find the Visual Studio Installer as can be seen in Figure 1-2.

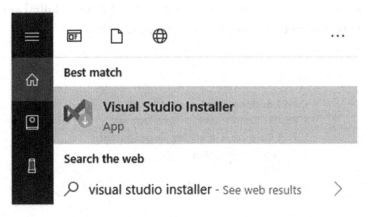

***Figure 1-2.*** *Find the Visual Studio Installer*

Clicking the Visual Studio Installer will launch the installer from where you can modify your installation of Visual Studio as seen in Figure 1-3.

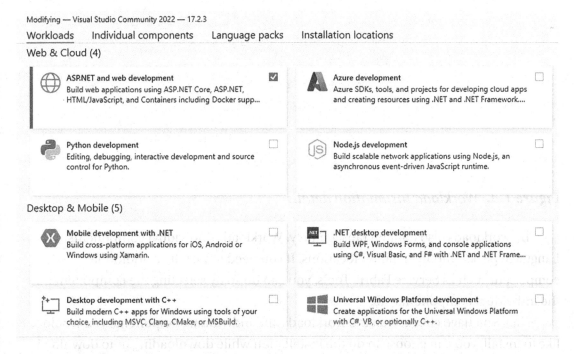

***Figure 1-3.*** *Installing additional workloads*

If you want to start doing Python development, you can simply check the *Python development* workload and install that. As can be seen in Figure 1-4, this will update the installation details section and show you exactly what is being installed and how much additional space you will need to install the selected workload.

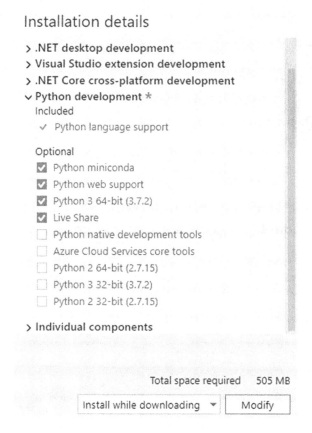

*Figure 1-4.* *Workload installation details*

The workloads also contain tabs, namely, Workloads, Individual components, Language packs, and Installation locations. If you need to install an additional component such as Service Fabric Tools, you can do so by selecting the component on the Individual components tab.

When you have checked all the workloads and individual components you would like to install, you can choose to do the installation while downloading or to download everything before installing as can be seen in Figure 1-5.

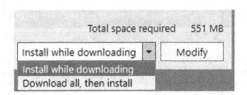

*Figure 1-5.* *Installation options*

This will modify your existing installation of Visual Studio 2022 and apply the changes you selected.

# Exploring the IDE

The Visual Studio IDE is full of features and tools that help developers do what they need to do, efficiently and productively. Developers start off creating one or more projects that contain the logic for their code. These projects are contained in what we call a solution. Let's have a look at the Solution Explorer first.

## The Solution Explorer

In Visual Studio, the notion of solutions and projects is used. A solution contains one or more projects. Each project contains code that runs the logic you need for your application to do what it does.

Consider the example of a Shipment Locator application as can be seen in Figure 1-6.

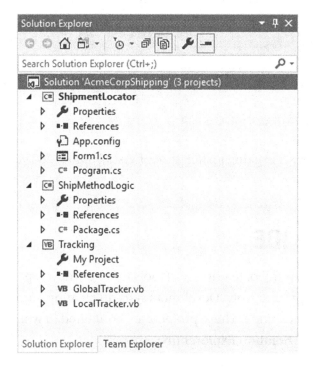

***Figure 1-6.*** *The Shipment Locator solution*

It is with this solution that you will add all the required projects to create your application. From the example in Figure 1-6, we can see that the solution contains three projects. The projects are as follows:

- ShipmentLocator – WinForms application – C#

- ShipMethodLogic – Class Library – C#

- Tracking – Class Library – VB.NET

Of particular interest, you will notice that you can have a solution that contains a mix of C# projects and VB.NET projects. The various project templates are discussed in Chapter 2 of this book, but if you would like to read more on creating a new project in Visual Studio, refer to the documentation at the following link: `https://docs.microsoft.com/en-us/visualstudio/ide/create-new-project?view=vs-2022`.

Take note that you do not need the AcmeCorpShipping source code for this chapter. The project is illustrative and is used to explain the concepts of Visual Studio solutions and projects. If, however, you would like to view the code, it is available from the GitHub repository for this book at the following URL: `github.com/apress/getting-started-vs2022.`

You are therefore not limited by a particular language and can create applications containing a mix of .NET languages.

The reason that we can mix .NET languages in the same solution is due to something we call IL (Intermediate Language). IL is used by the .NET Framework to create machine-independent code from the source code used in your projects.

The WinForms application will contain the UI needed to track and trace shipments. For the WinForms application to be able to use the logic contained in the other two class libraries, we need to add what is called a reference to the other projects.

This is done by right-clicking the project that you want to add the reference to and selecting *Add Reference* from the context menu (Figure 1-7).

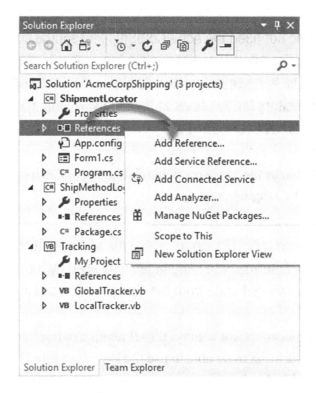

**Figure 1-7.** *Adding a project reference*

When you click the Add Reference menu item, you will be presented with the Reference Manager screen as seen in Figure 1-8.

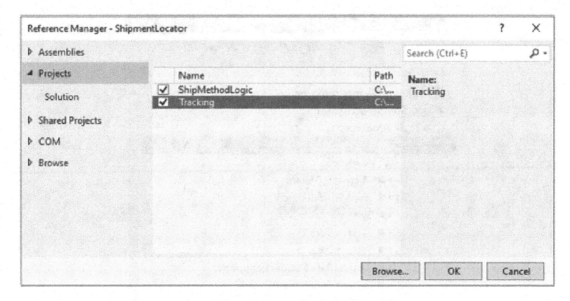

***Figure 1-8.***  *The Reference Manager screen*

Under the Projects tab, you will find the other two Class Library projects in your solution. By checking each one and clicking the OK button, you will add a reference to the code in these projects.

If you had to expand the References section under the ShipmentLocator project, you will see that there are two references to our Class Library projects ShipMethodLogic and Tracking as can be seen in Figure 1-9.

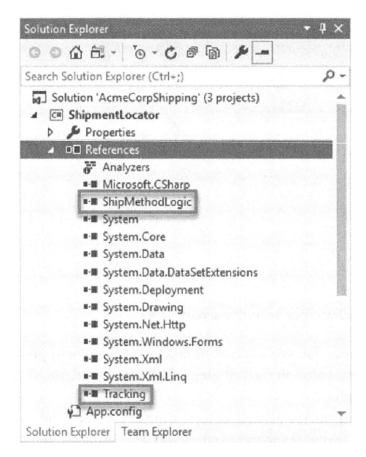

**Figure 1-9.** *Added references*

This will now make all the code you write in the ShipMethodLogic and Tracking projects available to the ShipmentLocator project. Having a look at the toolbar on the Solution Explorer (Figure 1-10), you will notice that it contains several buttons.

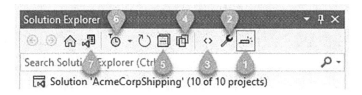

**Figure 1-10.** *The Solution Explorer toolbar*

The buttons contained here are displayed as needed. The View Code button, for example, will only show up in the toolbar when a file containing code is selected in the Solution Explorer. These buttons give you quick access to the following features as outlined in the following:

1. Preview Selected Items

2. Properties

3. View Code

4. Show All Files

5. Collapse All

6. Pending Changes Filter

7. Toggle between Solution and Folder views

I will not go through each one in detail, but of particular interest, you will notice that the Show All Files will display unnecessary files and folders such as the bin folder in your Solution Explorer. Go ahead and click the Show All Files button, and look at the Solution Explorer again.

By looking at Figure 1-11, you can see that it now displays the bin folder and the obj folder. These folders are not necessary for your code but are important to your solution.

---

The obj folder contains bits of files that will be combined to produce the final executable. The bin folder contains the binary files that are the executable code for the application you are writing.

---

Each obj and bin folder will contain a Debug and Release folder that simply matches the currently selected build configuration of your project.

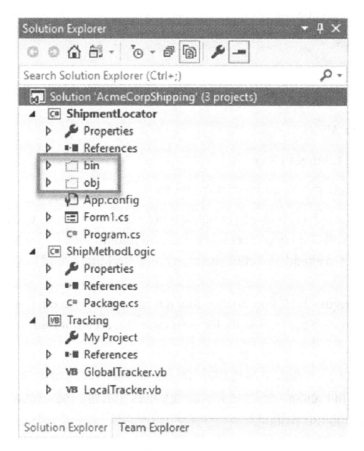

***Figure 1-11.*** *Solution Explorer displaying all files*

You can now right-click the bin folder as seen in Figure 1-12 and click the Open Folder in File Explorer menu to quickly have a look at the contents of the folder.

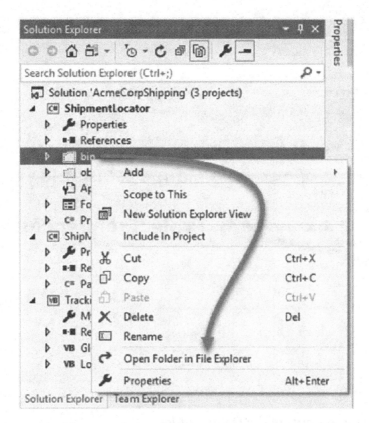

**Figure 1-12.**  *Open Folder in File Explorer*

This is a nice shortcut for anyone needing to navigate to the location of the Visual Studio files in the solution.

If you open the bin folder and click the Debug folder contained in the bin folder, you will see the main exe as well as any referenced dll files in the project (Figure 1-13).

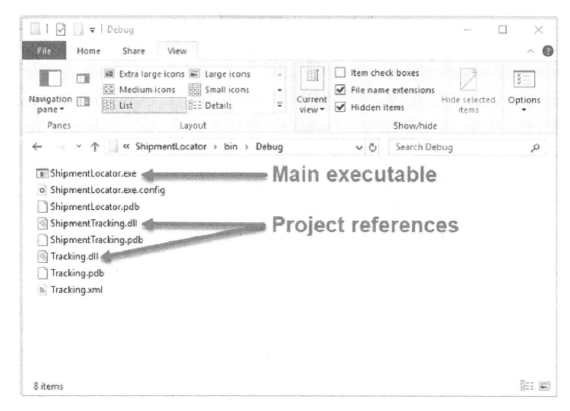

***Figure 1-13.***  *The contents of the Debug folder*

These files will be updated each time you build or run your project. If this folder is blank, perform a build of your solution by pressing F6 or by right-clicking the solution and clicking Build Solution from the context menu as seen in Figure 1-14.

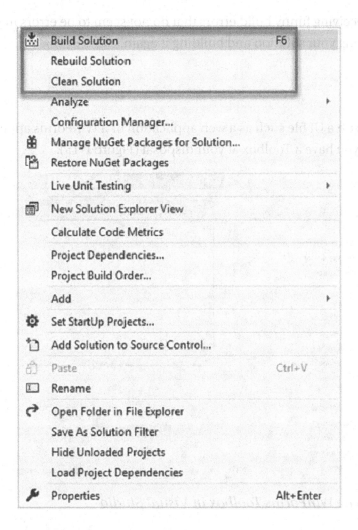

**Figure 1-14.** *Right-click solution options*

You might be wondering what the difference between Build Solution, Rebuild Solution, and Clean Solution is. The differences are as follows:

- Build Solution will do an incremental build of the solution of anything that has changed since the last build.

- Rebuild Solution will clean the solution and then rebuild the solution from scratch.

- Clean Solution will only clean the solution by removing any build artifacts left over by the previous builds.

If you are receiving funny build errors that do not seem to be errors in your code editor, try cleaning your solution and building it again.

## Toolbox

When dealing with a UI file such as a web application or a WinForms application, you will notice that you have a Toolbox at your disposal (Figure 1-15).

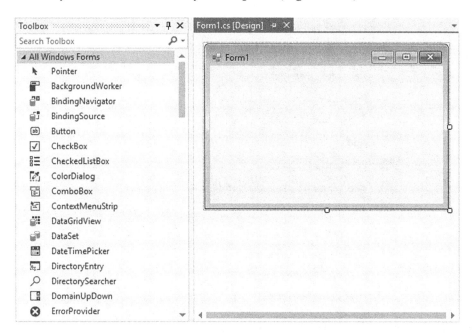

***Figure 1-15.*** *The WinForms Toolbox in Visual Studio*

The Toolbox allows you to add controls to your application such as text boxes, buttons, drop-down lists, and so on. This allows developers to design the UI of the application by dragging and dropping the relevant controls on the design surface.

You can also open the Toolbox by clicking the View menu and selecting the Toolbox menu item. It is worth noting that for some project types, you will not see any items in the Toolbox.

If you do not like the default layout of the Toolbox, you can right-click the tab or an individual item in the Toolbox and perform one of several actions from the context menu as seen in Figure 1-16.

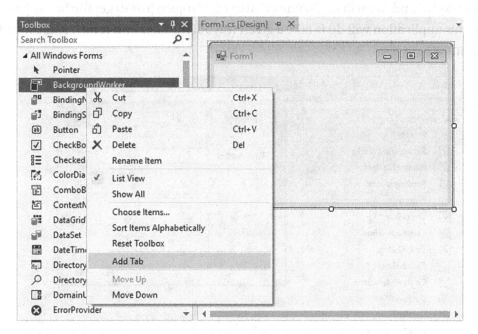

***Figure 1-16.*** *Toolbox context menu*

The context menu allows you to do the following:

- Rename an item

- Choose additional items

- Remove items

- Move items up and down

- Sort items

- Add a new tab

If you have third-party controls installed such as DevExpress or Telerik, you will find the controls specific to the installed components under their own tab in the Toolbox.

# The Code Editor

Let's add some basic UI components to our WinForms application as seen in Figure 1-17. To this code-behind, we will add some code to our project, just to get the ball rolling. All that this application will do is take a given waybill number and return some location data for it.

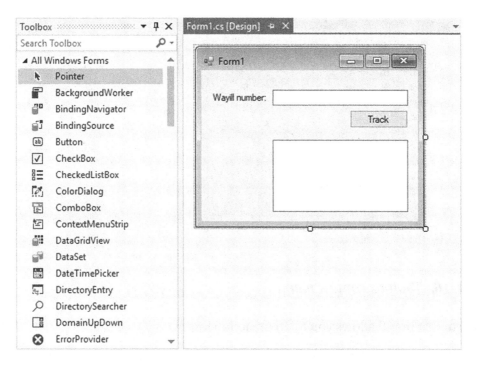

***Figure 1-17.*** *The application design*

The location data will be hard-coded in a Location class that was added to the project.

After adding the UI elements to the designer, swing over to the code window for the main WinForms application called Form1.cs. Add the code in Listing 1-1 to the code-behind.

You will notice after adding the code that Visual Studio starts to underline some of the added code as seen in Figure 1-18. This is because Visual Studio is making suggestions to improve the quality of your code.

*Listing 1-1.*  The Code-Behind Form1.cs

```csharp
private void BtnTrack_Click(object sender, EventArgs e)
{
    if (!(string.IsNullOrWhiteSpace(txtWaybill.Text)))
    {
        string waybillNum = txtWaybill.Text;
        if (WaybillValid())
        {
            Package package = new Package(waybillNum);
            Location packLoc = package.TrackPackage();
            if (packLoc != null)
            {
                txtLocationDetails.Text = $"Package location: " +
                    $"{packLoc.LocationName} with coordinates " +
                    $"Long: {packLoc.Long} and " +
                    $"Lat: {packLoc.Lat}";
            }
        }
        else
            MessageBox.Show("You have entered an invalid Waybill number");
    }
}
private bool WaybillValid()
{
    return txtWaybill.Text.ToLower().Contains("acme-");
}
```

The underlined code is code that Visual Studio is making suggestions for improvement on.

***Figure 1-18.***  *Visual Studio code improvement suggestions*

To view the details of the suggestion, hover your mouse over one of the underlined lines of code. Visual Studio will now display the details of the suggested change as seen in Figure 1-19.

```
string waybillNum = txtWaybill.Text;
if (WaybillValid())
{
    Package package = new Package(waybillNum);
    ╔═══════════════════════════════════════════╗
    ║ ♀ ▾ S│  ⁺ɪ class ShipmentTracking.Package  │ge();
    1ᴛ  │                                          │
    {   │  use 'var' instead of explicit type      │
        │                                          │ge location: " +
        │  Name can be simplified.                 │coordinates " +
        │                                          │
        │  Show potential fixes (Alt+Enter or Ctrl+.)│
    }   ╚═══════════════════════════════════════════╝
}
else
    MessageBox.Show("You have entered an invalid Waybill number");
```

***Figure 1-19.*** *Code change suggestion*

Here, we can see that Visual Studio is suggesting the use of the *var* keyword. At the bottom of the code editor, you will also see that Visual Studio displays the count of errors and warnings as seen in Figure 1-20.

***Figure 1-20.*** *Errors and warnings*

You are able to navigate between the warnings and errors by clicking the left and right arrows. You can also perform a code cleanup by clicking the little brush icon or by holding down Ctrl+K, Ctrl+E.

After cleaning up the code and adding the code suggestions that Visual Studio suggested, the code looks somewhat different as can be seen in Figure 1-21.

**Figure 1-21.** *Code suggestions applied*

With all the code suggestions applied, Visual Studio displays a clean bill of health in the status indicator at the bottom of the code editor.

# New Razor Editor

Visual Studio 2022 now allows developers to use the new Razor editor for local ASP.NET Core development with MVC, Razor Pages, and Blazor. This new Razor editor is based on a Language Server Protocol (LSP). The LSP defines the protocol used between the Visual Studio editor and a language server. Microsoft has therefore been able to add new functionality (more C# editing features) such as new code fixes and refactorings to Razor.

## What's Available?

As mentioned, new code fixes and refactorings are available such as

- Add missing usings

- Extract block to code-behind

- Add usings for component

- Fully qualify component

- Create component

Navigation support such as Go to Definition on components allows developers to quickly navigate throughout files. This means that when a developer presses F12 on a component tag, they can navigate to the component code. The new Razor editor also supports smarter syntax completions. Visual Studio Live Share is now also supported in Razor.

# Hot Reload

A welcome new feature in Visual Studio 2022 is the addition of Hot Reload. This works for both managed .NET and native C++ apps. Hot Reload saves a developer from having to stop the debug process between edits. This means less rebuilding, restarting, and renavigating to the specific location in the application you were debugging.

For a list of supported .NET app frameworks and scenarios, view the document at the following link: `https://docs.microsoft.com/en-us/visualstudio/debugger/hot-reload?view=vs-2022#supported-net-app-frameworks-and-scenarios`.

# Navigating Code

Visual Studio provides several features allowing developers to navigate code throughout the solution. Knowing how to use these navigation features will save you a lot of time.

# Navigate Forward and Backward Commands

If you look at the toolbar in Visual Studio, you will see the Navigate Forward (Ctrl+Shift+-) and Navigate Backward (Ctrl+-) buttons. These allow developers to return to the last 20 locations that the developer was at as seen in Figure 1-22.

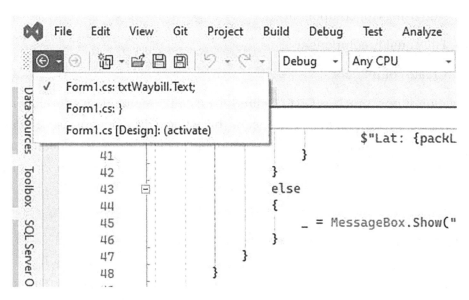

***Figure 1-22.***   *Navigate forward and backward*

You can also find these commands from the View menu under Navigate Backward and Navigate Forward.

# Navigation Bar

The navigation bar in Visual Studio as seen in Figure 1-23 provides drop-down boxes that allow you to navigate the code in the code base. You can choose a type or member to jump directly to it in the code editor.

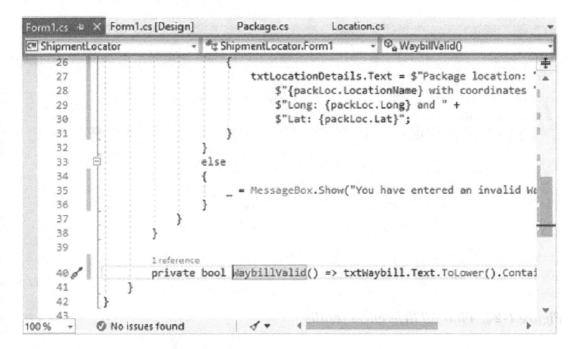

*Figure 1-23.* *Visual Studio navigation bar*

It is useful to take note that members defined outside the current code file will be displayed but will be disabled and appear gray. You can cycle through the drop-down boxes in the navigation bar by pressing the tab key.

Each drop-down also has its own individual function. The left drop-down will allow you to navigate to another project that the current file belongs to. To change the focus to another class or type, use the middle drop-down to select it. To navigate to a specific procedure or another member in a particular class, select it from the right drop-down.

# Find All References

Visual Studio allows you to find all the references for a particular element in your code editor. You can do this by selecting the code element and pressing *Shift+F12* or by right-clicking and selecting *Find All References* from the context menu.

| | Code | File | Line | Col | Project | Kind |
|---|------|------|------|-----|---------|------|
| ▲ ShipmentLocator (4) | | | | | | |
| ▲ 🗹 Location **packLoc** (4) | | | | | | |
| | if (packLoc != nu... | Form1.cs | 25 | 25 | ShipmentLocator | Read |
| | $"{packLoc.Loca... | Form1.cs | 28 | 32 | ShipmentLocator | Read |
| | $"Long: {packLo... | Form1.cs | 29 | 38 | ShipmentLocator | Read |
| | $"Lat: {packLoc.... | Form1.cs | 30 | 37 | ShipmentLocator | Read |

*'packLoc' references*  /  Entire Solution  /  Group by: Project then Definition  /  Search Find All References

***Figure 1-24.*** *Find All References results*

The find results are displayed in a tool window as seen in Figure 1-24. The toolbar for the find results tool window as seen in Figure 1-25 is also really helpful.

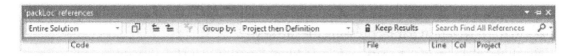

***Figure 1-25.*** *References window toolbar*

From here, you can do the following:

- Change the search scope
- Copy the selected referenced item
- Navigate forward or backward in the list

- Clear any applicable search filters (filters are added by hovering over a column in the results window and clicking the filter icon that is displayed)

- Change the grouping of the returned results

- Keep the search results (new searches are opened in a new tool window)

- Search the returned results by entering text in the Search Find All References text box

Hovering your mouse on a returned search result will pop up a preview screen of the code. To navigate to a search result, press the Enter key on a reference or double-click it.

## Find Files Faster

When compared to Visual Studio 2019, the Find in Files feature in Visual Studio 2022 is more than 2x faster for 95% of searches. Starting in Visual Studio 2022 17.1 Preview 3, Microsoft introduced indexed Find in Files. This means that according to benchmarks provided by Microsoft, all matches to a search query are returned in just over one second, making the search experience feel instantaneous.

## Reference Highlighting

Visual Studio makes it easy to see selected items in the code editor. If you click a variable, for example, you will see all the occurrences of that variable highlighted in the code editor as seen in Figure 1-26.

```
Form1.cs  ⊕ ✕  Form1.cs [Design]       Package.cs        Location.cs                              ▼
C# ShipmentLocator                    ▼ ⁕╪ ShipmentLocator.Form1        ▼ ⚙ BtnTrack_Click(object sender, E ▼
  15                                                                                                 ╬
                         1 reference
  16      ⊟               private void BtnTrack_Click(object sender, EventArgs e)                    ▲
  17                      {
  18      ⊟                   if (!(string.IsNullOrWhiteSpace(txtWaybill.Text)))
  19                          {
  20                              var waybillNum = txtWaybill.Text;
  21      ⊟                       if (WaybillValid())
  22                              {
  23                                  var package = new Package(waybillNum);
  24  🖉                             var packLoc = package.TrackPackage();
  25      ⊟                           if (packLoc != null)
  26                                  {
  27                                      txtLocationDetails.Text = $"Package location: '
  28                                          $"{packLoc.LocationName} with coordinates '
  29                                          $"Long: {packLoc.Long} and " +
  30                                          $"Lat: {packLoc.Lat}";
  31                                  }
  32                              }                                                                   ▼
100 %   ▼     ⚙ No issues found          │  ⚡ ▼   ◀ ▓▓▓▓▓▓▓▓▓▓▓▓▓▓▓▓▓▓▓▓▓          ▶
```

**Figure 1-26.**  *Default reference highlighting*

But did you know that you can change the color of the highlight from the Options in Visual Studio? Go to *Tools* ➤ *Options* ➤ *Environment* ➤ *Fonts and Colors* ➤ *Highlighted Reference* as seen in Figure 1-27.

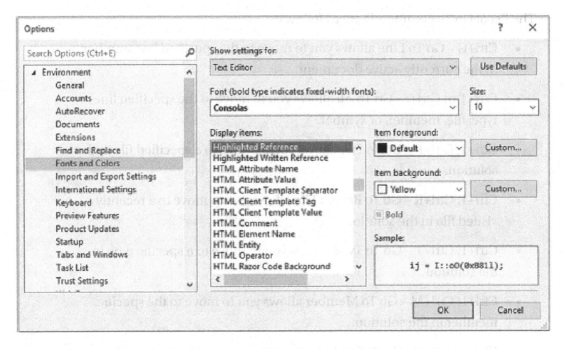

***Figure 1-27.*** *Change the Highlighted Reference color*

Change the color to yellow and click OK. All the references to the variable you just selected will now be highlighted in yellow.

# Go To Commands

I'll admit that these are probably the commands that I use the least in Visual Studio. All with the exception of Ctrl+G. Go ahead and open Visual Studio, and press Ctrl+G.

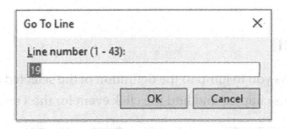

***Figure 1-28.*** *Go To Line*

As can be seen in Figure 1-28, a window pops up that allows you to jump to a specific line of code. This is incredibly useful when trying to explain something to another developer not sitting in the same room as you.

The list of Go To commands are as follows:

- Ctrl+G – Go To Line allows you to move to the specified line number in the currently active document.

- Ctrl+T or Ctrl+, – Go To All allows you to move to the specified line, type, file, member, or symbol.

- Ctrl+1, Ctrl+F – Go To File allows you to move to a specified file in the solution.

- Ctrl+1, Ctrl+R – Go To Recent File allows you to move to a recently visited file in the solution.

- Ctrl+1, Ctrl+T – Go To Type allows you to move to a specific type in the solution.

- Ctrl+1, Ctrl+M – Go To Member allows you to move to the specific member in the solution.

- Ctrl+1, Ctrl+S – Go To Symbol allows you to move to the specific symbol in the solution.

- Alt+PgDn – Go To Next Issue in File.

- Alt+PgUp – Go To Previous Issue in File.

- Ctrl+Shift+Backspace – Go To Last Edit Location.

While pressing Ctrl+1 might seem slightly finicky, you soon get used to it, and the commands start to feel more natural. Ctrl+Shift+Backspace is another command that I find very useful. This is especially true when editing large code files.

# Go To Definition

Go To Definition allows you to jump to the definition of the selected element. Go to the example project for this chapter, and find the click event for the Track button.

---

Just a reminder that the code for this book can be downloaded from GitHub at the following URL: `github.com/apress/getting-started-vs2022`.

---

In there, you will see that we are working with a class called `Package` that creates a new package we would like to track.

Place your cursor on `Package`, and hit F12 to jump to the class definition as seen in Figure 1-29. You can also hold down the Ctrl button and hover over the class name. You will notice that `Package` becomes a link you can click. Lastly, if you have your feet up and you only have your mouse to navigate with (the other hand is holding a cup of coffee), you can right-click and select *Go To Definition* from the context menu.

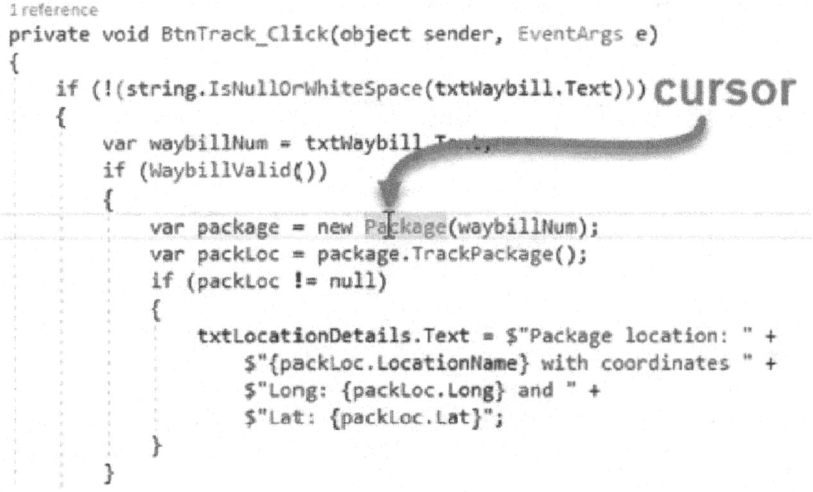

```
1 reference
private void BtnTrack_Click(object sender, EventArgs e)
{
    if (!(string.IsNullOrWhiteSpace(txtWaybill.Text))) cursor
    {
        var waybillNum = txtWaybill.Text;
        if (WaybillValid())
        {
            var package = new Package(waybillNum);
            var packLoc = package.TrackPackage();
            if (packLoc != null)
            {
                txtLocationDetails.Text = $"Package location: " +
                    $"{packLoc.LocationName} with coordinates " +
                    $"Long: {packLoc.Long} and " +
                    $"Lat: {packLoc.Lat}";
            }
        }
    }
```

*Figure 1-29.  Go To Definition*

# Peek Definition

Where Go To Definition navigates to the particular definition in question, Peek Definition simply displays the definition of the selected element in a pop-up. Place your cursor on `Package` and right-click. From the context menu, select Peek Definition.

```
16    private void BtnTrack_Click(object sender, EventArgs e)
17    {
18        if (!(string.IsNullOrWhiteSpace(txtWaybill.Text)))
19        {
20            var waybillNum = txtWaybill.Text;
21            if (WaybillValid())
22            {
23                var package = new Package(waybillNum);
```
```
                                            Package.cs   X
12
13    public Package(string waybillNumber)
14    {
15        WaybillNumber = waybillNumber;
16    }
17
18    public Location TrackPackage()
19    {
20        // Perform some funky tracking logic
21        //Return package location
22        var location = new Location();
23
24        return location;
25    }
26  }
27 }
```
```
24            var packLoc = package.TrackPackage();
25            if (packLoc != null)
26            {
```

*Figure 1-30.* *Peek Definition pop-up*

As can be seen in Figure 1-30, the pop-up window displays the code for the Package class. You can navigate through the code displayed in this pop-up as you would any other code window. You can even use Peek Definition or Go To Definition inside this pop-up.

In the pop-up window, right-click Location, and select Peek Definition from the context menu. The second Peek Definition will start a breadcrumb path as seen in Figure 1-31.

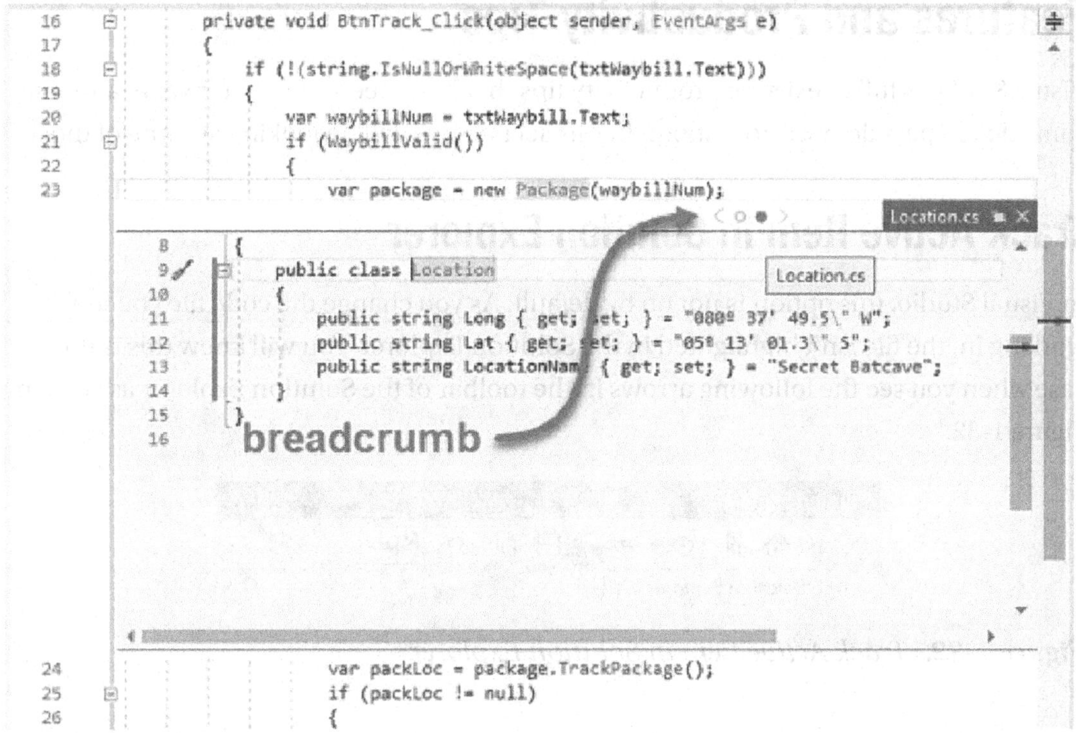

```
16         private void BtnTrack_Click(object sender, EventArgs e)
17         {
18             if (!(string.IsNullOrWhiteSpace(txtWaybill.Text)))
19             {
20                 var waybillNum = txtWaybill.Text;
21                 if (WaybillValid())
22                 {
23                     var package = new Package(waybillNum);
```

```
                                                      < o ● >              Location.cs  ■ X
 8        {
 9        public class Location                          Location.cs
10        {
11            public string Long { get; set; } = "080° 37' 49.5\" W";
12            public string Lat { get; set; } = "05° 13' 01.3\" S";
13            public string LocationNam { get; set; } = "Secret Batcave";
14        }
15    }
16        breadcrumb
```

```
24                 var packLoc = package.TrackPackage();
25                 if (packLoc != null)
26                 {
```

*Figure 1-31.*  *Breadcrumb path*

You can now navigate using the circles and arrows that appear above the Peek Definition pop-up window. The arrows only appear when you hover your mouse over the circles, but this makes it much easier to move between the code windows.

## Subword Navigation

Subword navigation is a very nice feature in Visual Studio 2022. Suppose you have a method name called DetermineValueOfFoo that consists of four subwords, namely, Determine, Value, Of, and Foo. Subword navigation allows you to move the caret to the next or previous subword in the string by holding down Ctrl+Alt+Left or Ctrl+Alt+Right. To select the previous or next subword, hold down Ctrl+Alt+Shift+Left or Ctrl+Alt+Shift+Right. This will select the next subword in the string. You can also turn on Select subword on double click by going to Tools ➤ Options ➤ Text Editor ➤ General and check the Select subword on double click option. Now, when you double-click a string, it will select the current subword you clicked instead of the entire string.

# Features and Productivity Tips

Visual Studio is full of existing productivity tips that have been around for years and that some developers do not know about. In this section, we will be looking at some of those.

## Track Active Item in Solution Explorer

In Visual Studio, this option is not on by default. As you change the code file you are working in, the file isn't highlighted in the Solution Explorer. You will know this is the case when you see the following arrows in the toolbar of the Solution Explorer as seen in Figure 1-32.

***Figure 1-32.*** *Track Active Item in Solution Explorer*

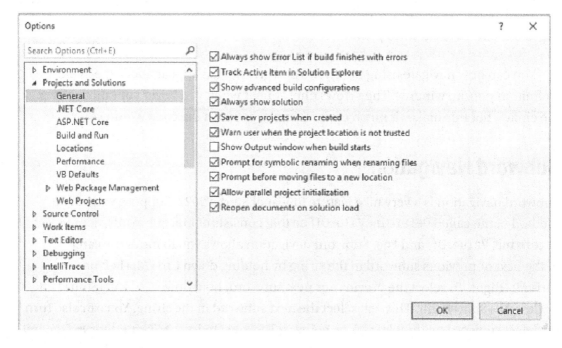

***Figure 1-33.*** *Track Active Item setting*

Clicking these arrows will highlight the file that you are currently editing in the Solution Explorer. I find this extremely useful, so I let Visual Studio permanently track the current file. To set this, click Tools ➤ Options ➤ Projects and Solutions ➤ General, and check Track Active Item in Solution Explorer as seen in Figure 1-33.

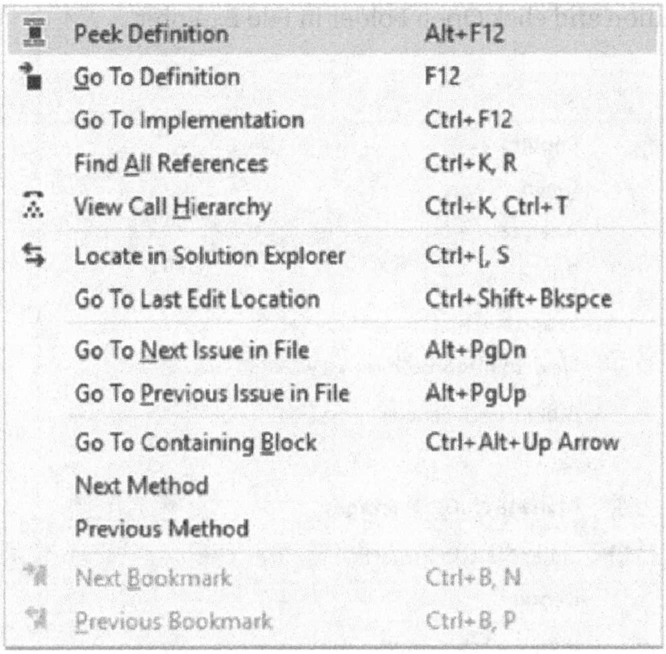

| | | |
|---|---|---|
| ▲ | Peek Definition | Alt+F12 |
| ▲ | Go To Definition | F12 |
| | Go To Implementation | Ctrl+F12 |
| | Find All References | Ctrl+K, R |
| ⚲ | View Call Hierarchy | Ctrl+K, Ctrl+T |
| ⇆ | Locate in Solution Explorer | Ctrl+[, S |
| | Go To Last Edit Location | Ctrl+Shift+Bkspce |
| | Go To Next Issue in File | Alt+PgDn |
| | Go To Previous Issue in File | Alt+PgUp |
| | Go To Containing Block | Ctrl+Alt+Up Arrow |
| | Next Method | |
| | Previous Method | |
| | Next Bookmark | Ctrl+B, N |
| | Previous Bookmark | Ctrl+B, P |

*Figure 1-34.* *Special context menu*

With this setting enabled, the arrows are not displayed in the toolbar of the Solution Explorer.

# Hidden Editor Context Menu

When you are in a code file, you can access a variety of menu items by right-clicking and selecting the menu items in the context menu. But did you know that you can hold down Alt+` to bring up a special context menu (that is different from right-click)? It has more editor commands in it as seen in Figure 1-34.

This gives you a little more control over navigating through errors, methods, etc., in your current code file.

# Open in File Explorer

Sometimes, you need to quickly get to the actual Visual Studio files of your solution. This might be to go and copy a file from the bin folder or to open a file in another text editor. To do this, you don't even need to leave Visual Studio. As seen in Figure 1-35, you can right-click the solution and click Open Folder in File Explorer.

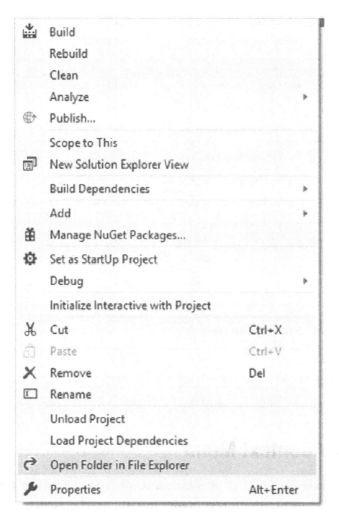

***Figure 1-35.***  *Open Folder in File Explorer*

This will open a new File Explorer window where your Visual Studio solution is located.

# Finding Keyboard Shortcut Mappings

Sometimes, when you use a keyboard shortcut, and nothing happens, you might be using it in the wrong context. To see what keyboard shortcuts are mapped to, head on over to Tools ➤ Options ➤ Environment ➤ Keyboard as seen in Figure 1-36.

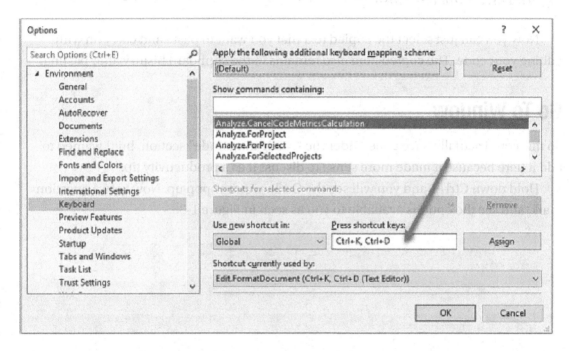

***Figure 1-36.***  *Find keyboard shortcut mappings*

Press the shortcut keys, and Visual Studio will show you what the shortcut is currently used for. This is also very useful for assigning new keyboard shortcuts to check that the keyboard shortcut you have in mind is not already bound to another command.

# Clipboard History

Visual Studio allows you to access your clipboard history. This is very useful if you have to copy and paste several items repeatedly.

Instead of going back and forth between copy and paste, simply hold down Ctrl+Shift+V to bring up the clipboard history as seen in Figure 1-37.

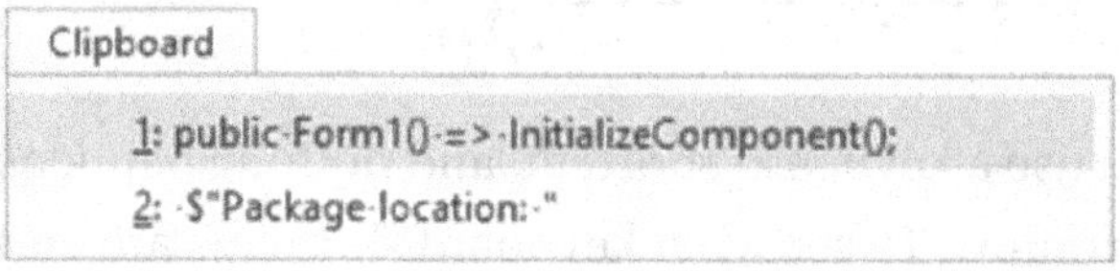

Clipboard

1: public·Form1()·=>·InitializeComponent();
2: ·$"Package·location:·"

*Figure 1-37.  Clipboard history*

Now you can just select the copied text that you want to paste and carry on with editing your code. The copied item also remains in the clipboard history after pasting.

## Go To Window

So this could actually have gone under the "Navigating Code" section, but I wanted to add it here because it made more sense to discuss it as a productivity tip.

Hold down Ctrl+T and you will see the Go To window pop up. Now type a question mark, and see the options available to you as seen in Figure 1-38.

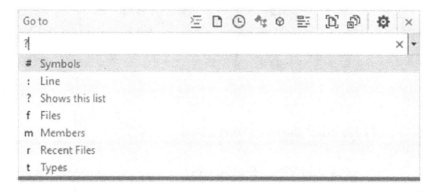

*Figure 1-38.  Go To window*

You can view the recent files by typing in an *r* instead of a question mark. Also nice to note is the ability to jump to a specific line of code. You will remember earlier in the chapter that we discussed the Go To commands and Ctrl+G in particular. Here, you can do the same thing by typing in : followed by the line number.

## Navigate to Last Edit Location

Earlier on in this chapter, we discussed the Navigate Backward and Navigate Forward commands. This is great, but if you want to navigate to the last place you made an edit in the code file, hold down Ctrl+Shift+Backspace. This will jump to the last place that you made an edit in one of your code files.

## Multi-caret Editing

This is a feature that I love using. Consider the SQL create table statement in Listing 1-2.

***Listing 1-2.*** Create SQL Table Statement

```
CREATE TABLE [dbo].[menu](
       [itemName] [varchar](50) NOT NULL,
       [category] [varchar](50) NOT NULL,
       [description] [varchar](50) NOT NULL,
 CONSTRAINT [PK_menu] PRIMARY KEY CLUSTERED
```

This is a rather small table, but sometimes we have very large tables that we need to work with. I want to create a simple C# class for this table and need to create some C# properties. Why type out everything when you can copy, paste, and edit all at once?

Paste the column names into a C# class file, then hold down Ctrl+Alt, and click in front of the first square bracket of each column as can be seen in Figure 1-39.

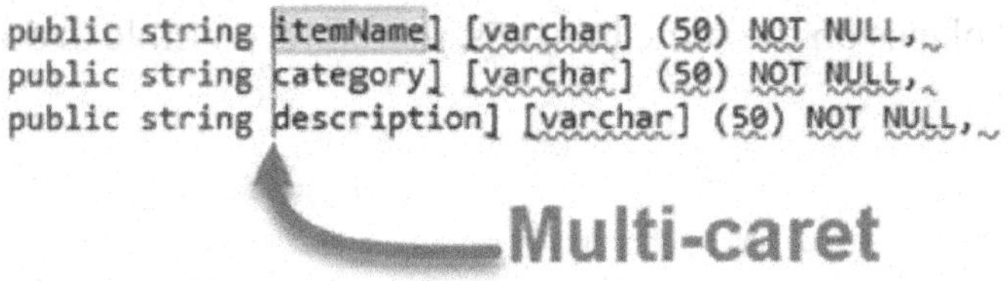

***Figure 1-39.*** *Multi-caret selection*

The cursor is placed at each line at the position you placed it. Now start typing the property definition. All the lines are edited. After typing `public string`, hit delete to remove the first square bracket.

I now want to add the `{ get; set; }` portion of my property. I can either do the same multi-caret selection or I can also select one or more characters and hold down Shift+Alt+. to select matching selections as seen in Figure 1-40.

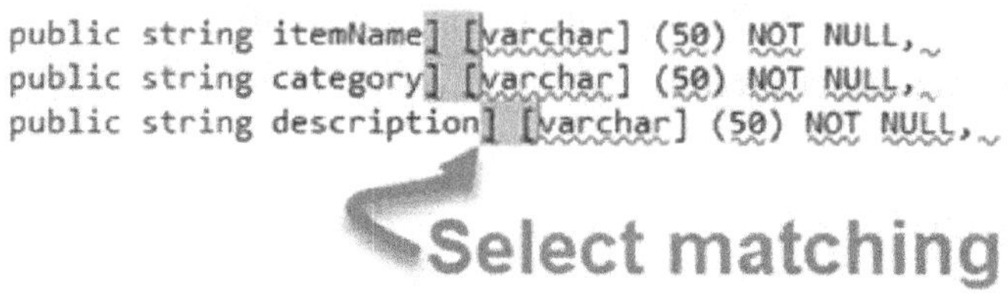

```
public string itemName] [varchar] (50) NOT NULL,
public string category] [varchar] (50) NOT NULL,
public string description] [varchar] (50) NOT NULL,
```

Select matching

***Figure 1-40.*** *Selecting matching selections*

This now allows me to easily select exactly all the lines I want to edit at the same time and allows me to paste the { get; set; } needed for my properties. I now end up with the completed code as seen in Figure 1-41.

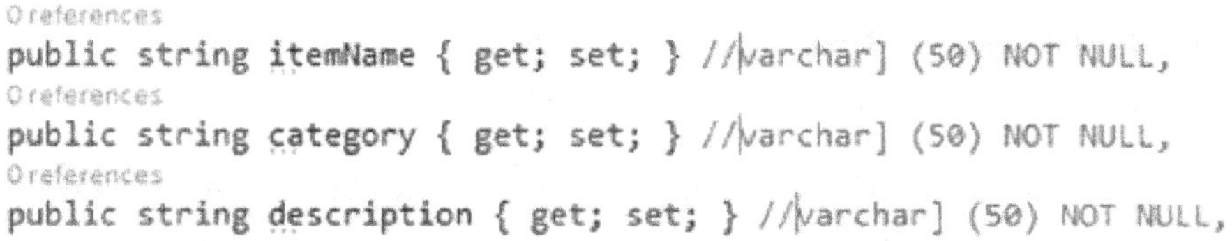

```
0 references
public string itemName { get; set; } //varchar] (50) NOT NULL,
0 references
public string category { get; set; } //varchar] (50) NOT NULL,
0 references
public string description { get; set; } //varchar] (50) NOT NULL,
```

***Figure 1-41.*** *Completed code properties*

Being able to easily select code or place a caret in several places on the same line or across lines allows developers to be flexible when editing code. Speaking about placing the caret in several places on the same line, it is, therefore, possible to do the one shown in Figure 1-42.

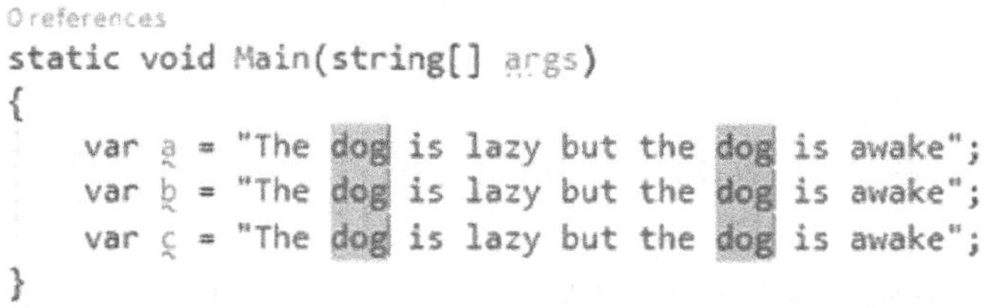

```
0 references
static void Main(string[] args)
{
    var a = "The dog is lazy but the dog is awake";
    var b = "The dog is lazy but the dog is awake";
    var c = "The dog is lazy but the dog is awake";
}
```

***Figure 1-42.*** *Multi-caret selection on the same line*

We can now edit everything at once (even if we have selected multiple places on the same line) as seen in Figure 1-43.

```
0 references
static void Main(string[] args)
{
    var a = "The cat is lazy but the cat is awake";
    var b = "The cat is lazy but the cat is awake";
    var c = "The cat is lazy but the cat is awake";
}
```

***Figure 1-43.*** *Multi-caret editing on the same line*

Holding down Ctrl+Z will also work to undo everything at once. If you want to insert carets at all matching selections, you can select some text and hold down Shift+Alt+; to select everything that matches your current selection as seen in Figure 1-44.

```
0 references
public string itemName { get; set; } //varchar] (50) NOT NULL,
0 references
public string category { get; set; } //varchar] (50) NOT NULL,
0 references
public string description { get; set; } //varchar] (50) NOT NULL,

0 references
static void Main(string[] args)
{
    var a = "The cat is lazy but the cat is awake";
    var b = "The cat is lazy but the cat is awake";
    var c = "The cat is lazy but the cat is awake";
}
```

***Figure 1-44.*** *Insert carets at all matching selections*

I selected the text "cat" and held down Shift+Alt+; and Visual Studio selected everything that matches. As you can see, it also selected the category property, which I don't want to be selected. In this instance, Shift+Alt+. will allow me to be more specific in my selection.

If you find yourself forgetting the keyboard shortcuts, you can find them under the Edit menu. Click Edit ➤ Multiple Carets to see the keyboard shortcuts.

# Sync Namespaces to Match Your Folder Structure

Another great feature is the ability to keep your namespaces in sync with your folder structure. This is useful when you need to restructure your solution by moving files around to new folders. What you want to do is ensure that the namespace in the file stays in sync with the new folder structure. To do this, place your cursor on the namespace name and hold down Ctrl+. to bring up the Quick Actions and Refactoring menu. Select the option to change the namespace to your folder name.

## Paste JSON As Classes

If you work with JSON often, the following feature is another gem. If you have copied some JSON and need an object to serialize and deserialize the JSON into (using Newtonsoft, for example), you can select Edit from the Visual Studio menu, and select the Paste Special option. From there, you will see an option to Paste JSON as Classes. You can do the same for XML. This will quickly generate the correct class structure to represent the JSON copied by yourself. This is a fantastic time saver.

## Enable Code Cleanup on Save

Another great feature in Visual Studio 2022 is the ability to perform a code cleanup on save. From the Tools menu, select Options ➤ Text Editor ➤ Code Cleanup as seen in Figure 1-45.

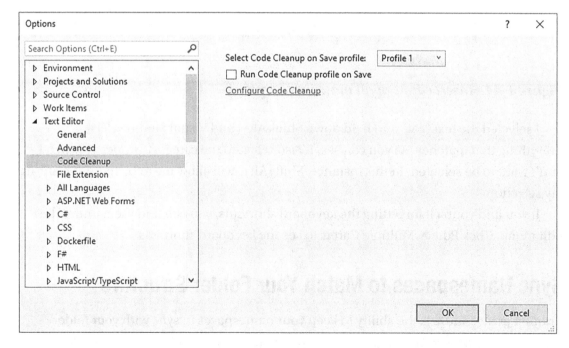

***Figure 1-45.*** *Code cleanup on save*

Here, you will see that you can configure the code cleanup options by clicking the link and selecting the available fixes to apply. Once you have configured a code cleanup profile, you can check the option to run the code cleanup profile when saving a file.

## Add Missing Using on Paste

Developers often copy and paste code found in another section of the project or from another online resource. Doing this usually requires developers to add the missing using statements. Now you can enable this feature to automatically add the missing using statements when pasting copied code. Go to Tools ➤ Options ➤ Text Editor ➤ C# ➤ Advanced, and scroll down a bit, and you will see an option to Add missing using directives on paste.

# Features in Visual Studio 2022

Visual Studio 2022 comes packed with a few very nice productivity features. A lot of thought has been put into making Visual Studio easy to navigate and to find things in Visual Studio 2022. The first feature I want to have a look at is Visual Studio Search.

## Visual Studio Search

I think that we can all agree that more speed equals improved productivity. The faster I can access a menu item, and the less time I have to spend looking for something, the more my productivity increases. This is where Visual Studio Search comes in.

If you hold down Ctrl+Q, you will jump to the search bar where you can immediately start typing as seen in Figure 1-46.

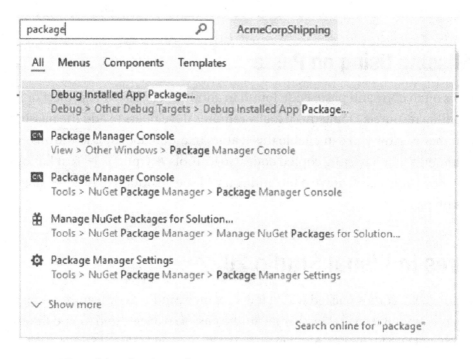

***Figure 1-46.*** *Visual Studio Search*

Visual Studio will perform the required search and display the results to you that you can further filter by clicking the Menus, Components, or Templates tabs. Visual Studio performs a fuzzy search, which means that even if you misspell a word, chances are that Visual Studio will know what you intended to type and return the correct results for you.

# Solution Filters

Sometimes, we have to work on Solutions that contain a lot of projects. More often than not, you as a developer will not be working on every project in that specific solution. This is where Solution Filters come in. They allow you to only load the projects that you care about or are actively working on. Consider the currently loaded solution as seen in Figure 1-47.

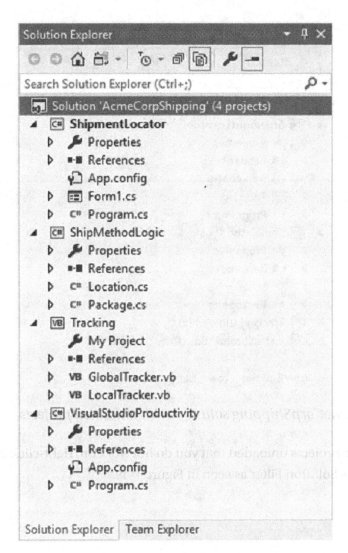

***Figure 1-47.*** *AcmeCorpShipping solution unfiltered*

You can see that all the projects are loaded in this solution. If we only work on the ShipmentLocator and ShipMethodLogic projects, we can create a Solution Filter to only load those projects. Right-click the projects that you don't work on, and click Unload Project from the context menu. Your solution will now look as in Figure 1-48.

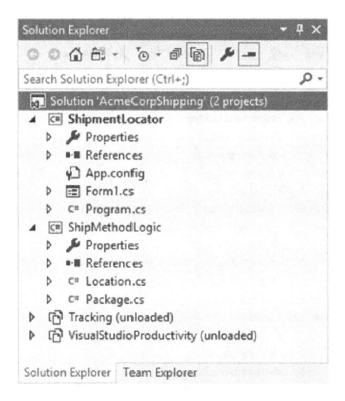

**Figure 1-48.**  *AcmeCorpShipping solution with unloaded projects*

Now, with the projects unloaded that you do not work on, right-click the solution and select Save As Solution Filter as seen in Figure 1-49.

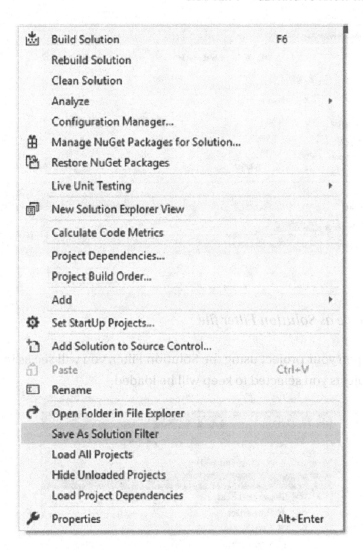

*Figure 1-49.* *Save As Solution Filter*

Visual Studio will now create a new type of solution file with an .slnf file extension as seen in Figure 1-50.

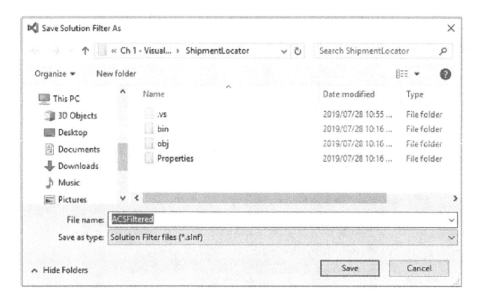

**Figure 1-50.** *Save as Solution Filter file*

When you open your project using the Solution Filter, you will see as in Figure 1-51 that only the projects you selected to keep will be loaded.

**Figure 1-51.** *Filtered solution*

Now with the filtered solution, if you click the solution, you will see that you can Load App Projects, Show Unloaded Projects, or Load Project Dependencies from the context menu as seen in Figure 1-52.

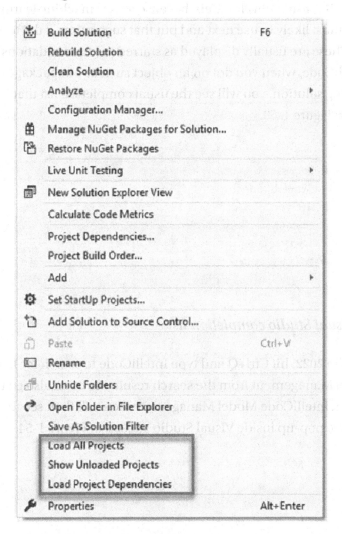

*Figure 1-52.  Filtered solution context menu*

You still have full control of the filtered solution from the context menu and can easily load the full solution as needed.

# Visual Studio IntelliCode

Visual Studio IntelliCode is a really nice feature that has been added to Visual Studio. Microsoft calls it AI-assisted development because it uses machine learning to figure out what you are most likely to use next and put that suggestion at the top of your completion list. These are usually displayed as starred recommendations.

Without IntelliCode, when you dot on an object such as our package object in the AcmeCorpShipping solution, you will see the usual completion list that Visual Studio pops up as seen in Figure 1-53.

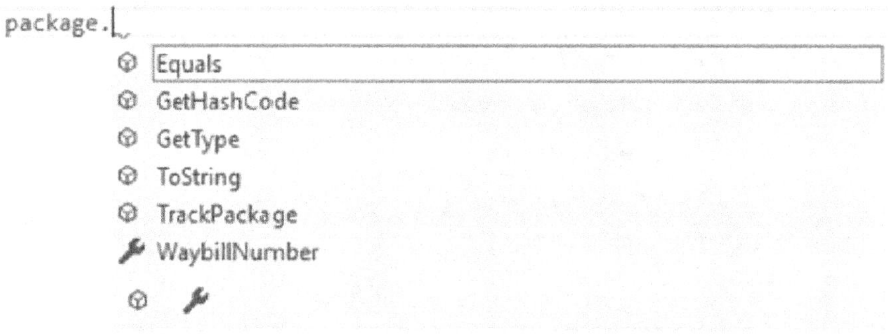

***Figure 1-53.*** *Visual Studio completion list*

In Visual Studio 2022, hit Ctrl+Q and type IntelliCode to search for IntelliCode. Select IntelliCode Model Management from the search results. You can also go to View ➤ Other Windows and click IntelliCode Model Management. You will then see the Visual Studio IntelliCode window pop-up inside Visual Studio as seen in Figure 1-54.

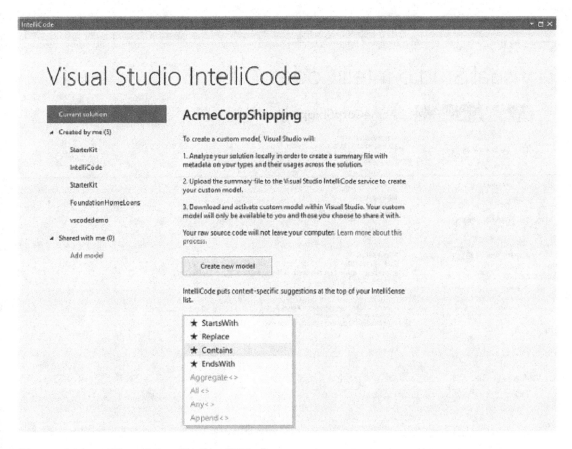

**Figure 1-54.**  *Visual Studio IntelliCode*

Click Create new model to allow Visual Studio IntelliCode to analyze your code and create the model. When Visual Studio has completed the analysis and created the model, you will be able to share the model with other developers (which is great for teams), delete the model, or retrain the model as seen in Figure 1-55.

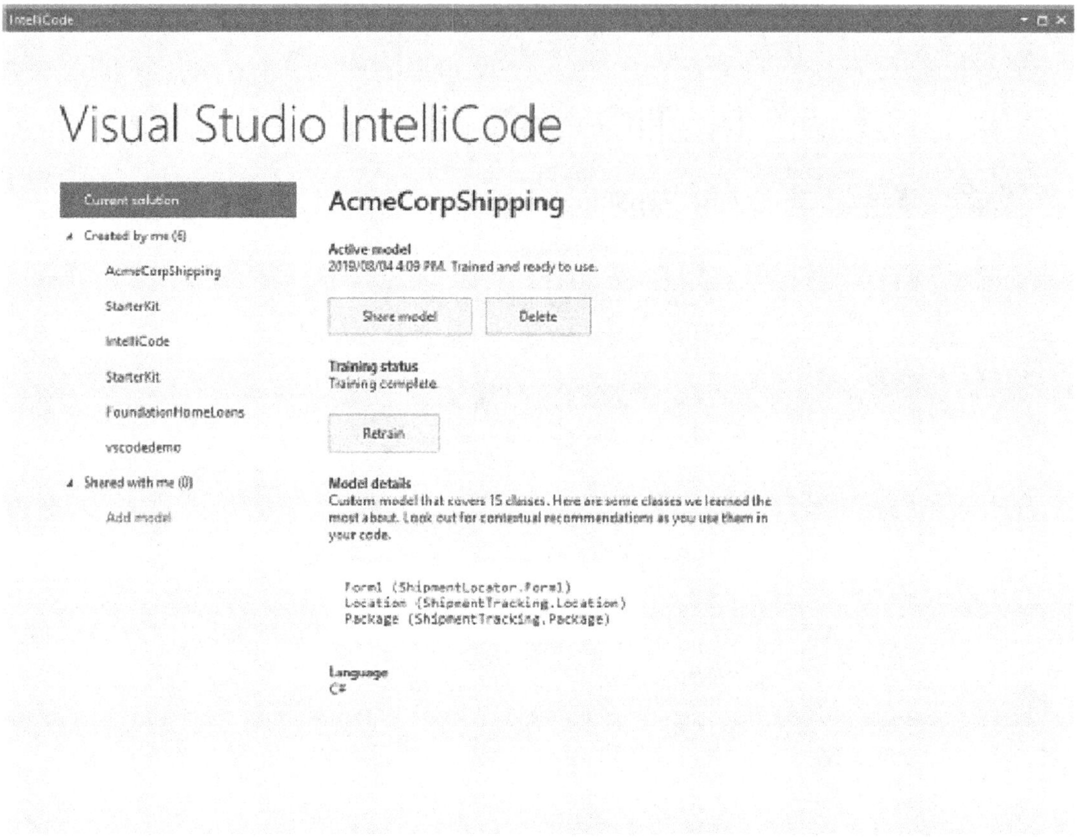

**Figure 1-55.**  *Visual Studio IntelliCode model completed*

This time around, if you dot on the package in the AcmeCorpShipping solution, you will see the starred recommendations from IntelliCode as seen in Figure 1-56.

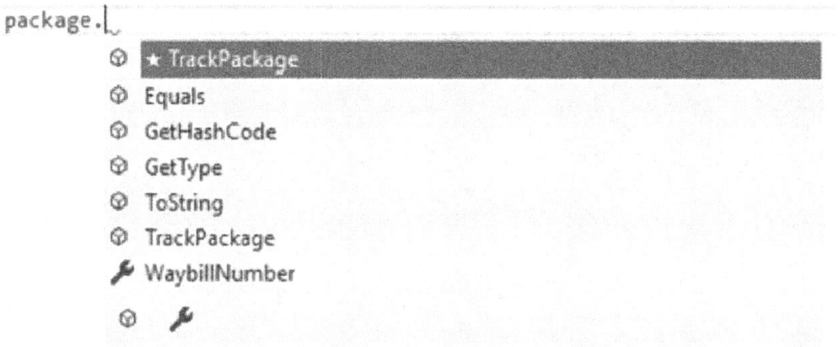

**Figure 1-56.**  *IntelliCode starred recommendations*

Compare this to the Visual Studio completion list in Figure 1-53. You can see that IntelliCode has identified the TrackPackage method as the most likely method that you will want to use.

IntelliCode uses open source GitHub projects with 100 stars or more to distill the wisdom of the community to generate recommendations for your code. To demonstrate how clever Visual Studio IntelliCode is, have a look at Figure 1-57.

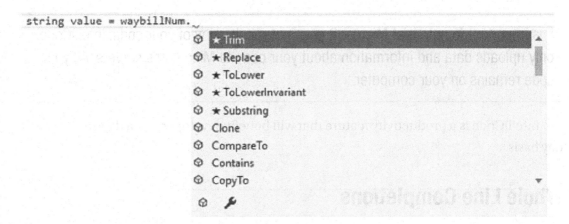

*Figure 1-57.* *IntelliCode acting on a string*

IntelliCode knows the most likely things I would want to do with a string variable and places those methods at the top of the suggestion list. The suggestions look quite a bit different when I am working with a string array as seen in Figure 1-58.

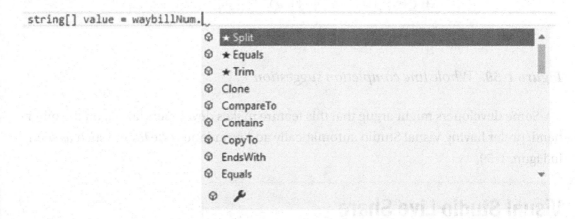

*Figure 1-58.* *IntelliCode acting on a string array*

This means that IntelliCode takes the current context into account when suggesting methods in the completion list. If you would like to view the model generated by IntelliCode, you can head on over to %TEMP%\Visual Studio IntelliCode. In one of the created folders, you will find a subfolder called "UsageOutput." Look for a JSON file in the "UsageOutput" folder. This is where the contents of the extracted data are stored for your model.

---

It is important to note that Microsoft does not receive any of your code. IntelliCode only uploads data and information about your code to Microsoft's servers. All your code remains on your computer.

---

IntelliCode is a productivity feature that will benefit developers on a day-to-day basis.

## Whole Line Completions

Visual Studio 2022 will automatically suggest code completions for you for the whole line it thinks that you are typing. As seen in Figure 1-59, you see that Visual Studio is suggesting adding a null check on the waybillNumber parameter.

```
1 reference
public Package(string waybillNumber)
{
    if (waybillNumber == null)        Tab  to accept  ⚙

    WaybillNumber = waybillNumber;
}
```

*Figure 1-59.* *Whole line completion suggestion*

Some developers might argue that this feature makes developers lazy. I, on the other hand, prefer having Visual Studio automatically add mundane code for me such as seen in Figure 1-59.

## Visual Studio Live Share

During my years of writing code, I have often needed to explain some portion of logic or feature of the code I am working with to another developer. This usually involves them having to get a copy of the code base from source control and us having to direct each other over a Skype call and quote line numbers to collaborate properly.

---

To find out more about Visual Studio Live Share, go to `https://visualstudio.microsoft.com/services/live-share/`.

---

Visual Studio Live Share is included by default in Visual Studio 2022. Visual Studio Live Share does not require developers to be all "set up" to assist each other or to collaborate on projects. This means that a developer running Visual Studio Code on a Linux machine can collaborate with another developer running Visual Studio 2022 on a Windows 10 machine.

To start a Visual Studio Live Share session, you need to click the Live Share icon in the top-right corner of Visual Studio 2022 as can be seen in Figure 1-60.

***Figure 1-60.***  *Visual Studio Live Share icon*

When you click the icon, Visual Studio starts up Live Share, and the progress is indicated as can be seen in Figure 1-61.

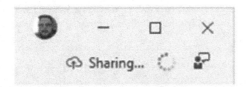

***Figure 1-61.***  *Visual Studio Live Share in progress*

When the sharing link has been generated, Visual Studio will display a notification as seen in Figure 1-62.

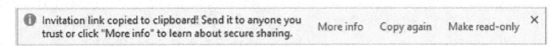

***Figure 1-62.***  *Visual Studio Live Share link generated*

It is copied to the clipboard by default, but you can copy it again, make it read-only, or learn more about secure sharing. When you share the link with a fellow developer, they simply have to paste the link into a browser to start the collaboration. Figure 1-63 shows the browser after pasting the link.

**Figure 1-63.** *Starting Visual Studio Live Share session*

In this example, I am sharing the link with a developer that is running Visual Studio Code on Linux Mint. Linux then pops up a Launch Application notification as seen in Figure 1-64.

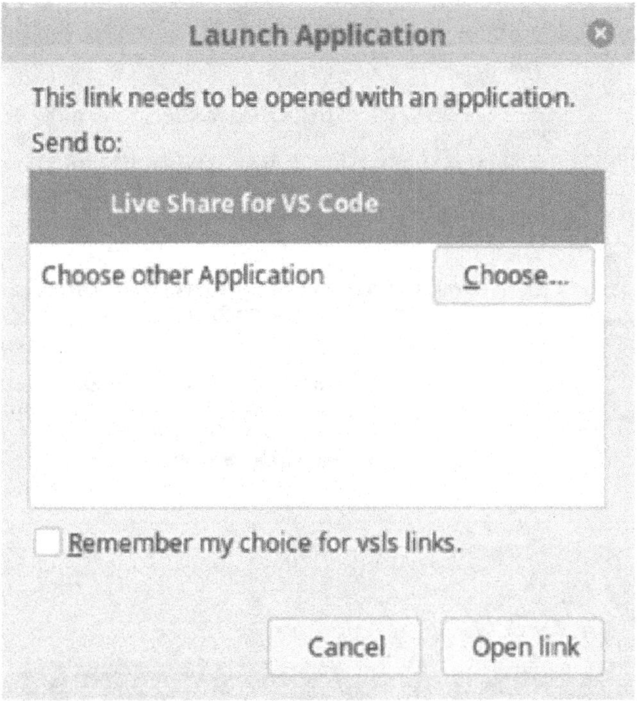

**Figure 1-64.** *Launch Application notification on Linux*

Visual Studio Code is already installed on the Linux machine; therefore, the Launch Application notification offers that as the default choice for opening vsls links. When you click the Open Link button, Visual Studio Code launches, and your Live Share session is initiated as seen in Figure 1-65. Visual Studio Code then has a copy of the code that I am sharing on my machine.

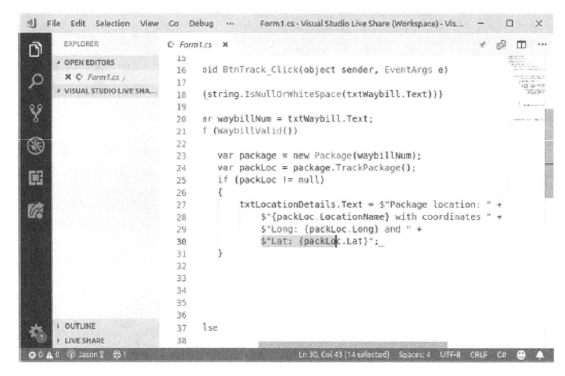

**Figure 1-65.**  *Visual Studio Live Share session*

As Jason navigates his way around the code, I can see this in my code via a marker that pops up momentarily displaying his name as seen in Figure 1-66.

```
var waybillNum = txtWaybill.Text;
if (WaybillValid())
{
    var package = new Package(waybillNum);
    var packLoc = package.TrackPackage();
    if (packLoc != null)
    {
        txtLocationDetails.Text = $"Package location: " +
            $"{packLoc.LocationName} with coordinates " +
            $"Long: {packLoc.Long} and " +
            $"Lat: {packLoc.Lat}";
                            Jason Williams
    }
```

**Figure 1-66.**  *I can see Jason's current position in the code*

Over in Visual Studio Code, Jason can see where I am via a similar marker that momentarily pops up my name as seen in Figure 1-67.

```
var package = new Package(waybillNum);
var packLoc = package.TrackPackage();
if (packLoc != null)
{
Dirk Strauss ationDetails.Text = $"Package location: " +
        $"{packLoc.LocationName} with coordinates " +
        $"Long: {packLoc.Long} and " +
        $"Lat: {packLoc.Lat}";
}
```

***Figure 1-67.*** *Jason can see my current position in the code*

This allows us to know what the other is doing and where we are working at any given time. In Visual Studio 2022, I now also have a new Live Share tab displayed as seen in Figure 1-68.

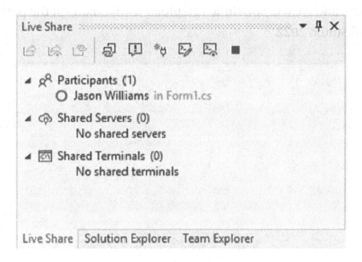

***Figure 1-68.*** *Live Share tab in Visual Studio 2022*

From there, I can end the Live Share session, share the terminal, manage shared servers, focus participants, or copy the sharing link again. At any time, I am in total control of what I share. It is also important to note that my code lives on my machine. It is not saved on the participant's machine.

# Summary

This chapter gave us a brief look around Visual Studio 2022. We explored the IDE and saw how to navigate code. Productivity features were discussed along with the requirements for installing Visual Studio 2022. Lastly, we had a look at some of the other features included in Visual Studio such as its powerful search capabilities, Solution Filters, IntelliCode, whole line completions, and Live Share.

In the next chapter, we will be getting our hands dirty and start working with Visual Studio by looking at the various project templates included in Visual Studio 2022. We will briefly discuss MAUI, as well as how to create a MAUI project. We will also discuss NuGet and how to use this in Visual Studio as well as managing nmp packages. A particular favorite feature of mine is Visual Studio's Code Snippets feature. We will see how to create and use code snippets to speed up your development. Visual Studio is also very customizable, and we will conclude Chapter 2 with looking at the personalization features in Visual Studio 2022.

# Working with Visual Studio 2022

If you have worked with previous versions of Visual Studio, you may find that Visual Studio 2022 does not break the mold. Visual Studio 2022 feels much the same as previous versions, and that's a good thing.

While there are new features and enhancements in Visual Studio 2022, developers find it easy to work with from the start. If you are new to Visual Studio, a few topics deserve a closer look. In this chapter, we are going to look at the following:

- Visual Studio project types and when to use them

- MAUI

- Managing NuGet packages

- Creating project templates

- Creating and using code snippets

- Using bookmarks and code shortcuts

- The Server Explorer window

- Visual Studio Windows

This chapter is an extension of Chapter 1 in many respects. Things that didn't make it into Chapter 1 are discussed in this chapter. I do believe, however, that these are essential to working with Visual Studio and benefit developers in their day-to-day coding.

© Dirk Strauss 2023
D. Strauss, *Getting Started with Visual Studio 2022*, https://doi.org/10.1007/978-1-4842-8922-8_2

# Visual Studio Project Types

Visual Studio 2022 allows developers to create a new project in several ways. The most obvious is when you start Visual Studio 2022. You are presented with the Start screen, as seen in Figure 2-1.

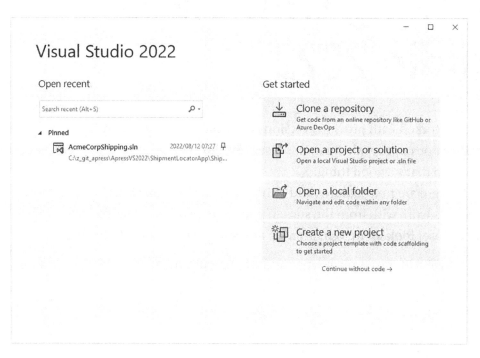

***Figure 2-1.*** *Visual Studio 2022 Start screen*

Here, you can see recent projects that you can pin to the Start screen and always keep available. If you right-click any recent projects, you can see a context menu pop up, as shown in Figure 2-2.

## Visual Studio 2019

Open recent

```
csharpdemo.sln                          2019/07/28 10:11 AM
C:\z_g   ⊯  Remove From List
              Unpin this item from the Recent Projects list
solid        Copy Path                          04/08 8:25 AM
C:\z_g
```

***Figure 2-2.*** *Context menu options on recent projects*

You can remove the project from the list, pin or unpin it, or copy the path to the project. Visual Studio 2022 has also made it relatively easy to get where you need to when working on projects. As seen in Figure 2-3, developers have a few options available when they are ready to start working with code.

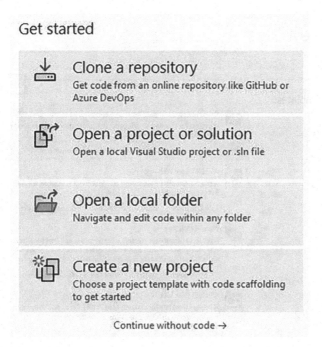

Figure 2-3.  *Get started section*

You can start by grabbing code from GitHub or Azure DevOps, opening a local Visual Studio project, opening a local folder to edit code files, creating a new project, or continuing without code.

If Visual Studio is already open, you can create a new project from the menu bar by clicking the New Project button, as seen in Figure 2-4. You can also hold down Ctrl+Shift+N.

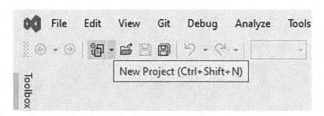

Figure 2-4.  *New Project toolbar button*

The Create a new project screen is displayed, as seen in Figure 2-5, and you have a whole new experience here, too, when it comes to finding the project type you want to create.

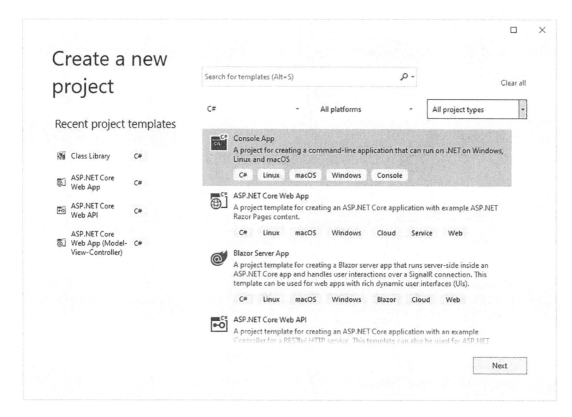

***Figure 2-5.*** *Create a new project*

You can see recent project templates displayed, which is excellent, should you need to get up and running with similar projects as what you have created before. You can also search for and filter project templates by language, platform, or project type, as seen in Figure 2-6.

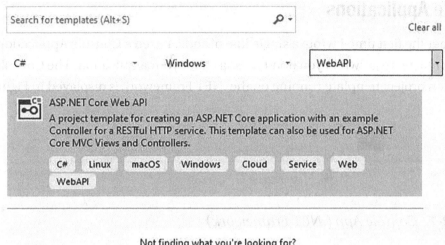

*Figure 2-6.* *Filter project templates*

You are, therefore, able to quickly find the most suitable project template.

---

Take note, though, that you may need to install a workload if you do not find the project template you want. To do this, click Install more tools and features. Refer to Chapter 1 to see how to use workloads in Visual Studio.

---

Of the several project templates available, let's see which ones there are and what project is suitable for specific situations.

# Various Project Templates

You can choose from a host of project templates in Visual Studio 2022. I would even go as far as to say that it's now even easier to find the template you need to use due to the filters in the Create a new project window. Let's have a look at a few of these project templates next.

## Console Applications

I remember the first time I wrote a single line of code. I used a Console Application, a great template to use when you don't need a UI for your application. The Console Application project template running on the .NET Framework is displayed in Figure 2-7.

***Figure 2-7.***  *Console App (.NET Framework)*

You shall notice that this application is suited for running on Windows machines. But what if you need to run the Console Application across platforms such as Windows, Linux, and macOS? Here is where .NET 6 comes into play.

The Console Application project template running on .NET 6 is displayed in Figure 2-8.

***Figure 2-8.***  *A .NET 6 Console App*

A few years ago (long before .NET 6 was ever a thing), I needed to create an application that could be triggered on a schedule. The application's executable would then be passed one of several parameters to determine which database to connect to.

The application had to run without any user intervention to perform some sort of maintenance task. Because no user intervention was needed, a Console Application best suited the use case. Be aware that a Console Application can accept user input, but for my purposes with this application, it was not necessary.

# Windows Forms Application

In contrast to the Console Application, the Windows Forms application template is used when you need to create an app that has a UI. The project template (like the Console Application) can run on the .NET Framework or .NET 6, as seen in Figure 2-9.

**Figure 2-9.**  *Windows Forms App (.NET 6 and .NET Framework)*

It is important to note that before .NET 6, there were two separate products: the .NET Framework and .NET Core. If you're part of the Old Guard, you will have worked extensively with the .NET Framework. With .NET Core, however, a process was set in motion that would change the face of .NET development forever. Being open source, .NET Core was rewritten from scratch and is designed to work across all platforms, such as Windows, Linux, and Mac.

Now, with .NET 6.0 going forward, developers will have just a single version of .NET (and it's just called .NET). Think of .NET 6 as a unified development platform that allows developers to create desktop, cloud, web, mobile, gaming, IoT, and AI applications.

# Windows Service

If you ever need to create a Windows application that continually runs in the background, performing some specific task, your best choice would be to use a Windows Service template as seen in Figure 2-10.

**Figure 2-10.**  *Windows Service (.NET Framework)*

Imagine that the application needs to monitor specific activity (be that in a database or file system) and then write messages to an event log. A Windows Service is ideally suited for this purpose.

Windows Services have an OnStart method that allows you to define what needs to happen when the service starts. By definition, Windows Services are long-running applications that need to poll or monitor the system it runs on. You will need to use a Timer component to enable the polling functionality.

---

A common mistake is to use a Windows Forms Timer for a Windows Service. You must ensure that you use the timer in the System.Timers.Timer namespace instead.

---

The System.Timers timer (Figure 2-11) that you add to the Windows Service will raise an Elapsed event at specific intervals.

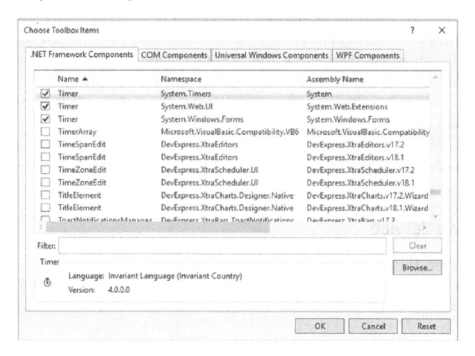

***Figure 2-11.*** *Various timer namespaces*

In this Elapsed event, you can write the code your service needs to run to do what it needs to do.

# Web Applications

If you need to create web-based applications, you will create an ASP.NET Web
Application. If you look at the project templates, you will notice that you can create an
ASP.NET Web Application that runs on .NET 6 using Razor Pages, as seen in Figure 2-12.

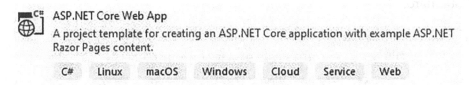

*Figure 2-12.* *ASP.NET Core Web Application template*

But wait a minute, didn't we just mention that it's now called .NET and no longer
.NET Core? With all the mentioning of .NET 6, we can easily confuse the fact that when
referring to ASP.NET Core 6.0, Microsoft still uses "Core" in the name. While the overall
platform does not use "Core" in the naming, the specific application model names still
do when referring to ASP.NET Core 6.0 and Entity Framework Core 6.0.

If you want to use a Model-View-Controller approach to create your web application,
you can select the ASP.NET Core Web App (Model-View-Controller) template, as seen in
Figure 2-13.

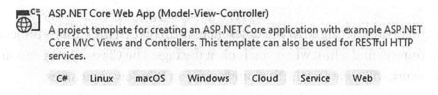

*Figure 2-13.* *ASP.NET Core MVC Web App template*

As seen in the template description, this template allows you to create a web
application using Views and Controllers.

# Class Library

The following project template we will look at is the Class Library. It is worth noting
that the Class Library creates a DLL that you can reuse in your applications. This is the
purpose of a Class Library project.

Many more project templates are available in Visual Studio and depend on the workloads you have installed.

As you see in Figure 2-14, the Class Library can be based on .NET, .NET Framework, or .NET Standard.

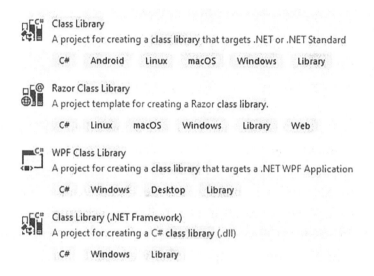

***Figure 2-14.*** *Class Library projects*

You might be wondering what the differences are between the various project templates. You will find a hint when you look at the tags. The Class Library running the .NET Framework will create a DLL that only works on Windows machines.

The Class Library running .NET or .NET Standard will create a library that will run on Windows, Linux, and macOS (it's, therefore, cross-platform).

.NET Standard's motivation was to establish more uniformity in the .NET ecosystem. With .NET 6 going forward, this introduces a different approach for uniformity and negates the need for .NET Standard in many cases.

The Class Library running on .NET Standard will allow you to share code between the .NET Framework and other .NET implementations, such as .NET Core. It is worth noting, however, that no new versions of .NET Standard will be released but that .NET 6 and future versions of .NET will still support .NET Standard 2.1 and earlier.

For more information regarding .NET Standard, have a look at the following article on Microsoft Docs: `https://docs.microsoft.com/en-us/dotnet/standard/net-standard`.

There are many more project templates to choose from, and the project templates you see will depend on your installed workloads. Explore some of the different workloads available to you, and see what project templates are available after installing a particular workload.

# MAUI

The last project template we will look at is probably the most exciting, and we will see how to create a .NET MAUI application in the next section. MAUI stands for Multiplatform App UI or simply .NET MAUI. .NET MAUI enables developers to build natively compiled iOS, Android, macOS, and Windows apps using C# and XAML in one codebase. It automatically changes the UI of your application to adapt to the native platform it's running on without having to use any additional code.

---

.NET MAUI applications for iOS do require a Mac build host. The following example will run the MAUI application we create using the Android Emulator.

---

To create a .NET MAUI application, you will need the latest Visual Studio 2022 17.3. You also need to ensure that you have installed the .NET Multiplatform App UI development workload, as seen in Figure 2-15.

*Figure 2-15.  The .NET MAUI workload*

It's a significant workload. When writing this book, it clocked in at just under 10 GB, so make sure you have enough hard drive space.

# Creating a MAUI Application

To get started with our first MAUI application, create a new project in Visual Studio and filter the project templates to display the MAUI project type, as seen in Figure 2-16.

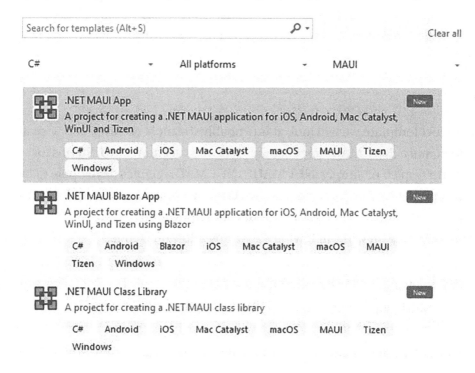

***Figure 2-16.*** *The .NET MAUI App project template*

Select the .NET MAUI App template and click the Next button. Give your solution a suitable name, select a location to create your application, and click the Next button. On the next screen, as of the writing of this book, only .NET 6.0 is available for the Framework selection. Clicking the Create button will create the project and restore the required NuGet package references. Once complete, you will see the project structure as illustrated in Figure 2-17.

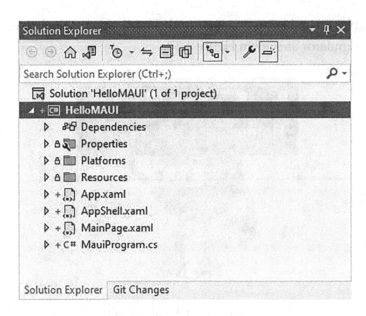

***Figure 2-17.*** *The HelloMAUI project structure*

From the Visual Studio toolbar, change the Debug Target drop-down to select the Android Emulator, as seen in Figure 2-18.

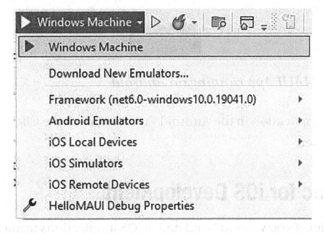

***Figure 2-18.*** *Choosing Android as the Debug Target*

Clicking the Android Emulator button will install the default Android SDK and Emulator. The Android SDK might also ask you to accept the required license agreements to continue. After this, the Android Emulator will start, and the application will be deployed to the Emulator. This might take some time, so be patient while the application is deployed to the Emulator. Once the application is deployed, it will be displayed in the Emulator as seen in Figure 2-19.

*Figure 2-19.* *The MAUI App running on Android*

In the running application in the Android Emulator, click the Click me button to increment the counter.

## Pairing to Mac for iOS Development

As mentioned earlier, if you want to build native iOS applications using .NET MAUI, you require access to Apple's build tools which can only be run on a Mac. You will therefore need to connect Visual Studio 2022 to a network-accessible Mac to build .NET MAUI applications for iOS. Visual Studio makes this process easy with the Pair to Mac feature. This will discover, connect, and authenticate with suitable Mac build hosts. The Pair to Mac allows developers to

- Write .NET MAUI iOS code in Visual Studio 2022.

- Use the Mac build host to compile and sign the iOS app using the build tools.

- Invoke the Mac builds securely via SSH.

- If an iOS device is plugged into the Mac, Visual Studio 2022 is notified of this, and the iOS toolbar will update accordingly.

For more information on enabling the Mac build host in Visual Studio using a network-connected Mac, see the following link on the Microsoft documentation site: `https://docs.microsoft.com/en-us/dotnet/maui/ios/pair-to-mac`.

As of the writing of this book, Visual Studio 2022 for Mac was still in preview. For more information on Visual Studio 2022 for Mac, see the following link: `https://visualstudio.microsoft.com/vs/mac/preview/`.

Visual Studio 2022 for Mac will bring fully native macOS UI applications built on .NET 6, including native support for the Apple M1 chip to Mac developers.

# Consuming REST Services in MAUI

Modern applications often use REST Web Services to provide some functionality to users. This can be anything from accessing data to providing cloud storage. When implementing this on a mobile device, you would need to determine if the device is connected to the Internet. If it is, then only can you consume the REST Web Service.

When writing any application, consuming a Web Service is quite straightforward. If this is your first time working with MAUI, you might be wondering how to accomplish this. MAUI will feel familiar if you're used to working with ASP.NET Core Web Applications and dependency injection.

In this section, I will show you how to consume a Web Service to get the current weather and ten-day forecast for Los Angeles using the Weather API at `www.weatherapi.com`. You need to create an account to get an API Key to use in your REST calls. I will not go through exactly how to do this. If you do not want to use the Weather API, you can choose another suitable service to consume. The focus here is consuming a Web Service, not the type of service being consumed. The logic detailed here remains the same. Let's have a look at the complete application first.

# The Complete Weather App

When running the application for the first time, you will see an empty screen, as illustrated in Figure 2-20.

*Figure 2-20.*  *Starting the Weather Forecast App*

The reason for this is so that I can show you how to add a command to click the Refresh button.

After you click the Refresh button, the application will call the weather service API and return the data to the UI for display, as seen in Figure 2-21.

***Figure 2-21.*** *The Refreshed Weather App*

As seen in Figure 2-22, the layout of the MAUI solution is straightforward. When creating the solution, it will be created with the Resources and Platforms folders. The Resources folder, as the name suggests, will contain any assets required for the application, such as images, icons, fonts, and so on. The Platforms folder contains the platform-specific code for Android, iOS, Mac Catalyst, Tizen, and Windows.

***Figure 2-22.*** *The Weather App solution*

# The Target Platforms

It is also worth noting that you do not need to carry any dead weight in your project. If you are creating an application that only runs on Android, iOS, and Mac Catalyst, you can remove unnecessary platforms. Edit your csproj file by right-clicking the project in the Solution Explorer and selecting Edit Project File from the context menu. There you can remove the targets for the platforms you don't need. Optionally, you can also remove the supported version information for the platforms you removed. Lastly, you can delete the removed platforms' directories under the Platforms folder.

## The Required NuGet Package

Figure 2-22 shows that the project contains a folder for models, services, and view models. We will be using an MVVM (Model View ViewModel) approach, and for this, be sure to include the CommunityToolkit.Mvvm NuGet package by Microsoft, as seen in Figure 2-23.

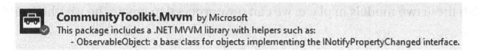

**CommunityToolkit.Mvvm** by Microsoft
This package includes a .NET MVVM library with helpers such as:
 - ObservableObject: a base class for objects implementing the INotifyPropertyChanged interface.

*Figure 2-23.* *The CommunityToolkit.Mvvm NuGet package*

## The Weather Models

The application uses two classes to model the weather data. You will need to create a folder called Model in your project to add these classes. The WeatherResults class contains the deserialized JSON data from the Weather Service API, and the CurrentWeather class takes what it needs from the WeatherResults class to display the forecast information. The code for the CurrentWeather class can be seen in Listing 2-1.

*Listing 2-1.* The CurrentWeather Class

```
namespace HelloMAUI.Model
{
    public class ForecastDay
    {
        public string DayOfWeek { get; set; }
        public string ImageUrl { get; set; }
        public int MinTemp { get; set; }
        public int MaxTemp { get; set; }
    }
}
```

The WeatherResults class was generated by copying the returned JSON data from the Weather Service API and using Paste JSON as Classes option, as discussed in Chapter 1, to create an object to deserialize the returned JSON.

---

I won't list the code for the WeatherResults class here because the code is generated from the JSON data returned from the Weather API and is relatively large. Your class will most likely differ from mine if you use a different API. Remember, the complete code is available on GitHub at the following link: github.com/apress/getting-started-vs2022.

---

With these two models in place, we can now proceed to create the weather service.

# The WeatherService

To consume the weather data from the Weather API, we need to create a Weather Service class under the Services folder. Create a folder called Services in your project, and add an Interface called IWeatherService and its implementation in a class called WeatherService.

*Listing 2-2.* The IWeatherService Interface

```
using HelloMAUI.Model;

namespace HelloMAUI.Services
{
    public interface IWeatherService
    {
        bool CanConnectToInternet();

        Task<WeatherResults> GetCurrentWeather();
    }
}
```

The Interface can be seen in Listing 2-2 and allows us to avoid tight coupling to the WeatherService class. This way, we can provide a contract for consuming entities to adhere to. The benefits of the Interface become apparent when we use dependency injection in our ViewModel. The Interface here specifies that any implementing class must provide an implementation for checking the Internet connection and getting the current weather. The Interface does not care about the actual implementation (the code you write to check for Internet connection and get the weather). The WeatherService class can be seen in Listing 2-3.

***Listing 2-3.*** The WeatherService Class

```
using System.Net.Http.Json;
using HelloMAUI.Model;

namespace HelloMAUI.Services
{
    public class WeatherService : IWeatherService
    {
        IConnectivity _connectivity;
        WeatherResults weather = new();
        HttpClient httpClient;

        public WeatherService(IConnectivity connectivity)
        {
            _connectivity = connectivity;
            httpClient = new HttpClient();
        }

        public bool CanConnectToInternet()
        {
            return _connectivity?.NetworkAccess == NetworkAccess.Internet;
        }

        public async Task<WeatherResults> GetCurrentWeather()
        {
            var baseUrl = "https://api.weatherapi.com/v1";
            var endP = "forecast.json";
            var key = "91e3647d6ece446d969130840220309";
            var city = "Los Angeles";

            var url = $"{baseUrl}/{endP}?key={key}&q={city}&days=10&aqi=no&
            alerts=no";
```

```
        var response = await httpClient.GetAsync(url);

        if (response.IsSuccessStatusCode)
        {
            weather = await response.Content.ReadFromJsonAsync<Weather
            Results>();
        }

        return weather;
    }
  }
}
```

The WeatherService class implements the IWeatherService Interface as seen in the class declaration `public class WeatherService : IWeatherService`. Because we do this, we now must satisfy the implementations for checking to see if we can connect to the Internet and get the current weather in our WeatherService class. The constructor for the class uses the `IConnectivity` Interface passed to it via dependency injection. It then uses this to allow the WeatherService to provide an implementation in the CanConnectToInternet method for checking to see if the application is currently connected to the Internet. The GetCurrentWeather method then provides the implementation for calling the API to get the current weather data.

---

It is important to note that if you use a different API, your GetCurrentWeather method will be different.

---

The first thing we need to do is provide the service with a URL to get the data. In this case, the Weather API service URL is defined along with the end point, auth key, and other data that I have just hard-coded here. In reality, you would want to keep things such as auth keys and other secrets in Azure Key Vault or similar to secure your secrets and keep those out of source control. My API call is for Los Angeles, but you would probably want to be more dynamic and get the users' current location to pass to the Weather API service. For simplicity's sake, I have just hard-coded the data and used that to construct the URL to call the correct end point for the API.

Next, we need to use the HTTP Client to asynchronously get a response from our API call using the GetAsync method of the HTTP Client. This means the data is fetched on a background task so that it doesn't lock up our UI in any way.

---

Because we are fetching data, we are using GetAsync, but the HTTP Client also allows us to call PUT, POST, and PATCH, by using the appropriate async method calls if we want to change data.

---

We will then use the new JSON Deserializer that is part of .NET. This will be surfaced as a helper method on our response. Our response will contain the content returned from the API call and a status code. The status code allows us to check to see if our GET request was successful. We do this using if (response.IsSuccessStatusCode) before deserializing the data.

***Listing 2-4.*** Reading the Weather Data

```
weather = await response.Content.ReadFromJsonAsync<WeatherResults>();
```

The code we are referring to is seen in Listing 2-4. Earlier in the WeatherService class, we newed up a WeatherResults object called weather to contain the data from our API call. We then call the Content method on the response. The content will contain the JSON data from the GetAsync API call. Because we added a using statement to System.Net.Http.Json, we can call the ReadFromJsonAsync to give me a WeatherResults object containing the JSON data from the API call. The ReadFromJsonAsync will then deserialize the JSON data and return it as a WeatherResults object.

This is all the code you need to consume the API to return the weather results for Los Angeles. Excluding the URL construction, this logic amounts to five lines of code to do the actual API call. Next, we need to consume our weather service in the view model.

# The MainViewModel

We are using an MVVM approach in our weather forecast application. MVVM stands for Model View ViewModel. Start by creating a folder called ViewModel and create a partial class called MainViewModel, as seen in Listing 2-5.

*Listing 2-5.* The MainViewModel Class

```
using System.Collections.ObjectModel;
using System.Diagnostics;
using CommunityToolkit.Mvvm.ComponentModel;
using CommunityToolkit.Mvvm.Input;
using HelloMAUI.Model;
using HelloMAUI.Services;

namespace HelloMAUI.ViewModel
{
    public partial class MainViewModel : ObservableObject
    {
        readonly IWeatherService _weatherService;
        public ObservableCollection<ForecastDay> TenDayForecast { get; }
        = new();

        [ObservableProperty]
        string currentCity;
        [ObservableProperty]
        int currentTemp;
        [ObservableProperty]
        string currentCondition;
        [ObservableProperty]
        int feelsLike;
        [ObservableProperty]
        string currentIcon;

        public MainViewModel(IWeatherService weatherService)
        {
            _weatherService = weatherService;
        }

        [RelayCommand]
        async Task GetWeatherAsync()
        {
            try
            {
```

```
if (!_weatherService.CanConnectToInternet())
{
    await Shell.Current.DisplayAlert("Error!", "You are not
    connected to the Internet", "OK");
}
else
{
    var weatherResults = await _weatherService.
    GetCurrentWeather();

    CurrentCity = weatherResults.location.name;
    CurrentTemp = (int)weatherResults.current.feelslike_f;
    CurrentCondition = weatherResults.current.
    condition.text;
    FeelsLike = (int)weatherResults.current.feelslike_f;
    CurrentIcon = $"https:{weatherResults.current.
    condition.icon}";

    foreach (var forecast in weatherResults.forecast.
    forecastday)
    {
        var dow = "Today";
        if (DateTime.Parse(forecast.date) !=
        DateTime.Today)
        {
            dow = DateTime.Parse(forecast.date).
            ToString("ddd");
        }

        var forecastDay = new ForecastDay()
        {
            DayOfWeek = dow,
            MinTemp = (int)forecast.day.mintemp_f,
            MaxTemp = (int)forecast.day.maxtemp_f,
        ImageUrl = $"https:{forecast.day.condition.icon}"
        };

        TenDayForecast.Add(forecastDay);
```

```
                    }
                }
            }
            catch (Exception ex)
            {
                Debug.WriteLine(ex);
                await Shell.Current.DisplayAlert("Error!", "Weather Service
                Call Failed", "OK");
            }
        }
    }
}
```

There is a lot going on here, so let's break it down a bit. We want to give our view the ability to display the forecast data. We do this by creating an observable collection of ForecastDay. This can be seen in the line of code `public ObservableCollection<Fore castDay> TenDayForecast { get; } = new();`. An observable collection has built-in notifications when things are added or removed. This means that I do not need to add any observable properties because I will not be raising a property change notification on the observable collection. I will just add and remove items into the observable collection, which will take care of raising the notifications to .NET MAUI.

The next thing we want to do is use our weather service. After adding the appropriate using statement, we need to provide access to that service by injecting it into the view model via the constructor, as seen in Listing 2-6.

***Listing 2-6.*** The MainViewModel Constructor

```
public MainViewModel(IWeatherService weatherService)
{
    _weatherService = weatherService;
}
```

This is dependency injection in action.

---

You would also have noticed it being used in the WeatherService constructor earlier in Listing 2-3 for IConnectivity.

---

This means that when we create the view model, we can tell it what it needs to be aware of. Essentially, we are telling it what its dependencies are in order for it to be able to fulfill its role as a view model in our application. We now need to create a method to call our weather service. This is the GetWeatherAsync method. Here, we can utilize the CanConnectToInternet method to check if our application is connected to the Internet before attempting to call the weather service. If we are connected to the Internet, we can call our weather service to get the current weather using the code `var weatherResults = await _weatherService.GetCurrentWeather();`. We then just add to our observable collection using a foreach loop.

---

The forecast data is small, so I am adding this data to the observable collection using a foreach loop. If you are dealing with thousands of items, you might want to use another, more performant method of adding to your observable collection. James Montemagno has a fantastic MVVM Helpers library that adds essential methods such as AddRange, RemoveRange, Replace, and ReplaceRange to the ObservableCollection. The link to this library on GitHub is `https://github.com/jamesmontemagno/mvvm-helpers`.

---

We now need to provide a way to call this method to get the weather data from our UI. To do this, we will turn our GetWeatherAsync method into a command by decorating it with the `[RelayCommand]` attribute. This is made possible by all the goodness contained in the Community Toolkit. The relay command attribute automatically generates ICommand properties from declared methods.

You can see the generated code contained in the project Dependencies for the GetWeatherAsync method, as seen in Figure 2-24.

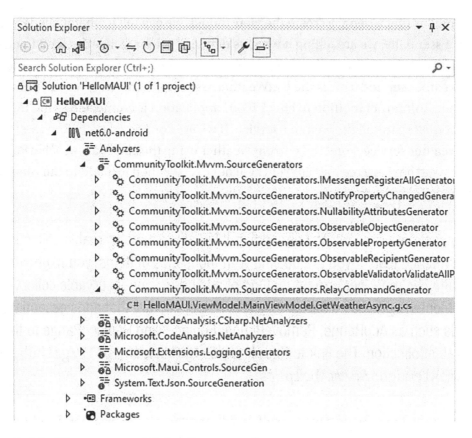

*Figure 2-24.*  *The generated RelayCommand*

Lastly, before we step off from the topic of our view model, I want to discuss the ObservableObject class and ObservableProperty attributes seen in the view model. Our view model inherits from the ObservableObject base class which is provided to us by the Community Toolkit. The ObservableObject base class allows other classes to inherit it to make their properties observable. This means that we can decorate our fields with the [ObservableProperty] attribute, and the magic of code generation does the rest for us.

To see these properties, again, under Dependencies, open up the generated file for the MainViewModel, as seen in Figure 2-25. A lot of code was generated for us without worrying about how it's done. The Community Toolkit is an excellent resource. Our view model is now ready for prime time. Before we can build our UI, we need to link the view model, our weather service, and the view itself. We, therefore, need to register those dependencies in the MauiProgram class. Let's look at this next.

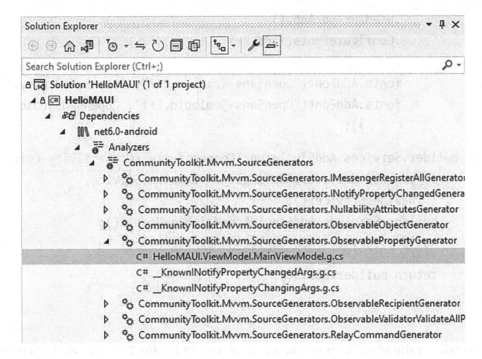

*Figure 2-25.* *The generated MainViewModel observable properties*

# Registering Dependencies

To use our dependencies in our application, we need to register those dependencies with the built-in IServiceCollection .

*Listing 2-7.* The MauiProgram Class

```
using HelloMAUI.Services;
using HelloMAUI.ViewModel;

namespace HelloMAUI;

public static class MauiProgram
{
        public static MauiApp CreateMauiApp()
        {
        var builder = MauiApp.CreateBuilder();
        builder
```

```
.UseMauiApp<App>()
.ConfigureFonts(fonts =>
{
fonts.AddFont("OpenSans-Regular.ttf", "OpenSansRegular");
fonts.AddFont("OpenSans-Semibold.ttf", "OpenSansSemibold");
        });

builder.Services.AddSingleton<IConnectivity>(Connectivity.Current);
    builder.Services.AddSingleton<IWeatherService,
    WeatherService>();
  builder.Services.AddSingleton<MainViewModel>();
  builder.Services.AddSingleton<MainPage>();

  return builder.Build();
}
}
```

The code for the MauiProgram class can be seen in Listing 2-7. You will notice that I have simply registered the dependencies by calling the AddSingleton method. This tells my code to create this service once and keep it around, returning the same instance to me whenever required. Because we only have one main page, using AddSingleton is fine for this demo. There are two other methods, too, called AddTransient and AddScoped. The differences between these are

- AddTransient creates a new service each time it is requested.

- AddScoped creates a new service once for each request.

- AddSingleton will be created the first time they are requested, and any subsequent request will be served the same instance.

Your mileage will vary here, and you need to decide on the appropriate use case for your application. Please take notice of the line that registers our weather service with the IServiceCollection as seen in the following line of code: `builder.Services. AddSingleton<IWeatherService, WeatherService>();`. This is the reason we use Interfaces. We are telling our application that whenever something requests IWeatherService, give it the WeatherService class that contains the implementation for our IWeatherService Interface. This loose coupling allows us to easily swap out the implementation contained in the WeatherService class and replace it with some other implementation. We have now registered our page (MainPage), our view model (MainViewModel), and our weather service (IWeatherService) with the IServiceCollection. We can now go ahead and start building the UI for our application.

# Building the MainPage View

The XAML for the view is contained in the MainPage.xaml file, as seen in Figure 2-22. I won't post the entire XAML code here. You can get all this code from the GitHub repo at github.com/apress/getting-started-vs2022. I will, however, highlight some of the parts in the XAML that we use to bind to our MainViewModel class.

*Listing 2-8.* Exposing Namespaces and Models

```
<?xml version="1.0" encoding="utf-8" ?>
<ContentPage xmlns="http://schemas.microsoft.com/dotnet/2021/maui"
             xmlns:x="http://schemas.microsoft.com/winfx/2009/xaml"
             xmlns:model="clr-namespace:HelloMAUI.Model"
             xmlns:viewmodel="clr-namespace:HelloMAUI.ViewModel"
             x:Class="HelloMAUI.MainPage"
             x:DataType="viewmodel:MainViewModel">
```

As seen in Listing 2-8, we can tell our XAML page that it needs to be aware of the MainViewModel to which it needs to bind. To bind the values of current city, current temperature, current condition, feels like, and current icon (these are the fields in the MainViewModel with the [ObservableProperty] attribute), we can bind to XAML elements as seen in Listing 2-9.

*Listing 2-9.* The CurrentCity Binding to a Label

```
<Label
            Text="{Binding CurrentCity}"
            SemanticProperties.HeadingLevel="Level2"
            FontSize="15"
            HorizontalOptions="Center" />
```

To bind to the forecast data contained in our ObservableCollection object on the view model, we can create a CollectionView XAML element.

As seen in Figure 2-26, we can set its ItemsSource to the TenDayForecast object and tell it to use the ForecastDay model to bind its elements. When the refresh button is clicked, the CollectionView will be populated with the forecast data. The code for the refresh button simply references the command on our MainViewModel, which is our GetWeatherCommand generated for us, seen earlier in Figure 2-24. The code for the refresh button is seen in Listing 2-10.

***Listing 2-10.*** The Refresh Button

```
<Button Text="Refresh"
            Command="{Binding GetWeatherCommand}"
            Grid.Row="1"
            Margin="5" />
```

```
<CollectionView ItemsSource="{Binding TenDayForecast}"
                Header="{Binding TenDayForecast}">
    <CollectionView.HeaderTemplate[...]>
    <CollectionView.ItemTemplate>
        <DataTemplate x:DataType="model:ForecastDay">
            <Grid Padding="10">
                <Grid.RowDefinitions[...]>
                <Grid.ColumnDefinitions[...]>

                <Label Grid.Column="0"
                    Text="{Binding DayOfWeek}"
                    FontSize="12"
                    FontAttributes="Bold"
                    HorizontalOptions="StartAndExpand" />

                <Image Grid.Column="1"...]/>

                <Label Grid.Column="2"...]/>

                <Label Grid.Column="4"...]/>

            </Grid>
        </DataTemplate>
    </CollectionView.ItemTemplate>
</CollectionView>
```

***Figure 2-26.*** *The forecast CollectionView*

All the moving parts should now be hooked up for our weather application to pull data from the API and return the weather information for Los Angeles, including the ten-day forecast. The next topic that I want to touch on is using SQLite in your MAUI application.

# Using SQLite in a MAUI Application

In the previous section, we looked at how to consume an API in a MAUI application. For that reason, I will not step through all the details of this application. I reused the existing weather service application and ripped out everything not applicable to the SQLite functionality we wanted to implement. The SQLite app is a simple to-do application, and the solution is seen in Figure 2-27.

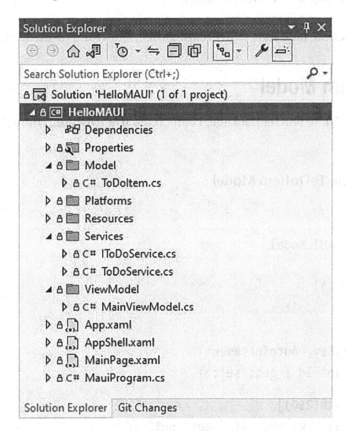

*Figure 2-27.* *The SQLite project structure*

As before, I have a Services folder containing the ToDoService and its IToDoService Interface. I have a Model folder containing the ToDoItem class. Lastly, I have the ViewModel folder with the MainViewModel class. You can see that the project structure follows the same pattern as before. The only difference here is that in addition to the Community Toolkit, I have added additional NuGet packages for SQLite, as seen in Figure 2-28.

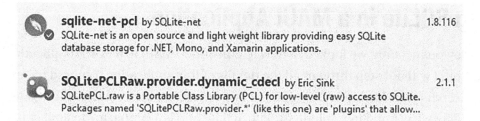

*Figure 2-28.* *The SQLite NuGet packages*

In the next section, let's start with creating the model for a to-do item.

## The ToDoItem Model

After adding the SQLite NuGet package, I can create the ToDoItem model as seen in Listing 2-11.

*Listing 2-11.* The ToDoItem Model

```
using SQLite;

namespace HelloMAUI.Model
{
    [Table("todo")]
    public class ToDoItem
    {
        [PrimaryKey, AutoIncrement]
        public int Id { get; set; }

        [MaxLength(250)]
        public string ToDoText { get; set; }

    }
}
```

I can now bring in the SQLite namespace, which allows me to add SQLite-specific attributes to my model. This model maps to a table in SQLite called todo because I have added the [Table("todo")] attribute to my class. I can now define additional attributes on my model properties, in this case, specifying that my Id property is an auto-incrementing primary key and that the text that contains the to-do item cannot be longer than 250 characters.

# The ToDoService

As with the weather application's service, we are creating an Interface called IToDoService. The code is in Listing 2-12.

*Listing 2-12.* The IToDoService Interface

```
using HelloMAUI.Model;

namespace HelloMAUI.Services
{
    public interface IToDoService
    {
        Task Init();
        Task AddToDo(string todoItem);
        Task<IEnumerable<ToDoItem>> GetToDoItems();
    }
}
```

This defines a contract for each implementing class to provide an implementation for initializing the database, adding to-do items, and reading all the to-do items.

*Listing 2-13.* The ToDoService

```
using HelloMAUI.Model;
using SQLite;

namespace HelloMAUI.Services
{
    public class ToDoService : IToDoService
```

```csharp
    {

        private SQLiteAsyncConnection _db;
        readonly string _dbPath;

        public ToDoService()
        {
            _dbPath = Path.Combine(Environment.GetFolderPath(Environment.
            SpecialFolder.MyDocuments), "mydb.db");
        }

        public async Task Init()
        {
            if (_db != null)
                return;

            _db = new SQLiteAsyncConnection(_dbPath);
            _ = await _db.CreateTableAsync<ToDoItem>();
        }

        public async Task AddToDo(string todoText)
        {
            await Init();

            var todoItem = new ToDoItem
            {
                ToDoText = todoText
            };

            var result = await _db.InsertAsync(todoItem);
        }

        public async Task<IEnumerable<ToDoItem>> GetToDoItems()
        {
            await Init();
            return await _db.Table<ToDoItem>().ToListAsync();
        }
    }
}
```

As seen in Listing 2-13, the service is really straightforward. By adding the SQLite namespace via the using statement, we can create a SQLiteAsyncConnection object that accepts a path to the database file called mydb.db. The Init method checks to see if the database exists and, if not, creates the database with the todo table from the ToDoItem. Because the SQLite connection is asynchronous, we can call the InsertAsync and ToListAsync methods to insert and get to-do items.

# The MainViewModel

The MainViewModel provides an ObservableCollection of ToDoItem and creates an ObservableProperty for the isRefreshing field, as seen in Listing 2-14. This way, if the collection of to-do items is busy being refreshed, we can control that if the user clicks the refresh button multiple times.

*Listing 2-14.* The MainViewModel Class

```
using System.Collections.ObjectModel;
using CommunityToolkit.Mvvm.ComponentModel;
using CommunityToolkit.Mvvm.Input;
using HelloMAUI.Model;
using HelloMAUI.Services;

namespace HelloMAUI.ViewModel
{
    public partial class MainViewModel : ObservableObject
    {
        readonly IToDoService _service;
        public ObservableCollection<ToDoItem> ToDoItems { get; set; }
        = new();

        [ObservableProperty]
        bool isRefreshing;

        public MainViewModel(IToDoService service)
        {
            _service = service;
        }
```

```csharp
[RelayCommand]
async Task AddTodo()
{
    var item = await Application.Current.MainPage.Display
    PromptAsync("To Do Item", "Enter To-Do Item.", "Add", "Cancel");
    if (item != null)
    {
        await _service.AddToDo(item);
        await Refresh();
    }
}

[RelayCommand]
async Task GetAllTodoItems()
{
    if (IsRefreshing)
        return;

    var todoItems = await _service.GetToDoItems();

    if (todoItems.Count() > 0)
        ToDoItems.Clear();

    foreach (var item in todoItems)
    {
        var todo = new ToDoItem()
        {
            ToDoText = item.ToDoText,
            Id = item.Id
        };

        ToDoItems.Add(todo);
    }
}

[RelayCommand]
async Task Refresh()
{
```

```
        if (!IsRefreshing)
        {
            IsRefreshing = true;
            ToDoItems.Clear();

            var todoItems = await _service.GetToDoItems();

            foreach (var item in todoItems)
            {
                var todo = new ToDoItem()
                {
                    ToDoText = item.ToDoText,
                    Id = item.Id
                };

                ToDoItems.Add(todo);
            }

            IsRefreshing = false;
        }
    }
  }
}
```

Again, the code in the view model is relatively straightforward. We use dependency injection to inject our ToDo Service via the constructor. We then set up the methods to add to-do items, read to-do items, and refresh the to-do items to act as commands by adding the [RelayCommand] attribute to each one. These allow us to use our ToDo Service to add and read items from SQLite. The last thing we need to do is register the service dependencies with the IServiceCollection.

# Registering Dependencies

The services are registered in the MauiProgram class by adding them as Singletons to the IServiceCollection, as seen in Listing 2-15.

***Listing 2-15.*** Registering the Services

```
using HelloMAUI.Services;
using HelloMAUI.ViewModel;

namespace HelloMAUI;

public static class MauiProgram
{
        public static MauiApp CreateMauiApp()
        {
        var builder = MauiApp.CreateBuilder();
        builder
                .UseMauiApp<App>()
                .ConfigureFonts(fonts =>
                {
                fonts.AddFont("OpenSans-Regular.ttf", "OpenSansRegular");
                fonts.AddFont("OpenSans-Semibold.ttf", "OpenSansSemibold");
            });

                builder.Services.AddSingleton<IToDoService, ToDoService>();
                builder.Services.AddSingleton<MainViewModel>();
                builder.Services.AddSingleton<MainPage>();

                return builder.Build();
        }
}
```

We are telling our application that whenever something requests IToDoService,
give it the ToDoService class that contains the implementation for our IToDoService
Interface. This loose coupling allows us to easily swap out the implementation contained
in the ToDoService class and replace it with another implementation. We have now
registered our page (MainPage), our view model (MainViewModel), and our to-do
service (IToDoService) with the IServiceCollection. We can now go ahead and start
building the UI for our application.

# Building the MainPage View

The XAML for the view is contained in the MainPage.xaml file, as seen in Figure 2-27. I won't post the entire XAML code here. You can get all this code from the GitHub repo at github.com/apress/getting-started-vs2022. I will, however, highlight some of the parts in the XAML that we use to bind to our MainViewModel class.

***Listing 2-16.*** Exposing Namespaces and Models

```
<?xml version="1.0" encoding="utf-8" ?>
<ContentPage xmlns="http://schemas.microsoft.com/dotnet/2021/maui"
             xmlns:x="http://schemas.microsoft.com/winfx/2009/xaml"
             xmlns:model="clr-namespace:HelloMAUI.Model"
             xmlns:viewmodel="clr-namespace:HelloMAUI.ViewModel"
             x:Class="HelloMAUI.MainPage"
             x:DataType="viewmodel:MainViewModel">
```

As seen in Listing 2-16, we can tell our XAML page that it needs to be aware of the MainViewModel to which it needs to bind. The isRefreshing field in the MainViewModel with the [`ObservableProperty`] attribute is bound to the RefreshView XAML element, as seen in Listing 2-17.

***Listing 2-17.*** The IsRefreshing Binding

```
<RefreshView Command="{Binding RefreshCommand}" IsRefreshing="{Binding
IsRefreshing}">
```

To bind to the to-do items data contained in our ObservableCollection object on the view model, we can create a ListView XAML element.

As seen in Figure 2-29, we can set its ItemsSource to the ToDoItems object and tell it to use the ToDoItem model to bind its elements. When the Get button is clicked, the ListView populates with to-do items, if any exist in the database. The code for the Get button references the command on our MainViewModel, which is the GetAllTodoItemsCommand that was generated for us. The code for the Get button is seen in Listing 2-18.

***Listing 2-18.*** The Get Button

```
<Button Text="Get"
            Command="{Binding GetAllTodoItemsCommand}"
            Grid.Row="1"
            Margin="5" />
```

```
<ListView ItemsSource="{Binding ToDoItems}"
          SeparatorVisibility="Default"
          SeparatorColor="LightGrey">
    <ListView.Header[...]>
    <ListView.ItemTemplate>
        <DataTemplate x:DataType="model:ToDoItem">
            <ViewCell>
                <Grid Padding="10">

                    <Grid.RowDefinitions[...]>
                    <Grid.ColumnDefinitions[...]>

                    <Label Grid.Column="0"
                           Text="{Binding Id}"
                           FontSize="10"
                           HorizontalOptions="StartAndExpand"
                           VerticalTextAlignment="Center"/>

                    <Label Grid.Column="1"
                           Text="{Binding ToDoText}"
                           FontSize="10"
                           HorizontalOptions="StartAndExpand"
                           VerticalTextAlignment="Center"/>

                </Grid>
            </ViewCell>
        </DataTemplate>
    </ListView.ItemTemplate>
</ListView>
```

***Figure 2-29.*** *The to-do ListView*

We also have another button on the view to create a new to-do item. This will call the AddTodoCommand that prompts the user for a to-do item to add. The code for the Add button is seen in Listing 2-19.

***Listing 2-19.*** The Add Button

```
<Button Text="Add"
                Command="{Binding AddTodoCommand}"
                Grid.Row="1"
                Margin="5" />
```

All the moving parts should now be hooked up for our to-do application to read and write data to the SQLite database.

Running the application for the first time will not display anything when we click the Get button as seen in Figure 2-30.

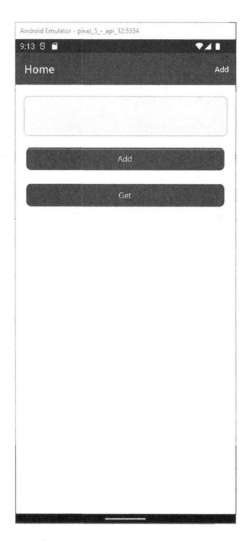

***Figure 2-30.*** *The empty to-do app*

Clicking the Add button prompts you for input, as seen in Figure 2-31.

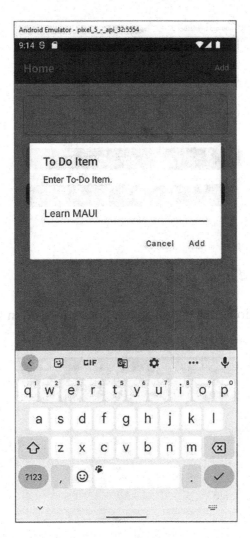

***Figure 2-31.***  *The add to-do item prompt*

After adding the to-do item, it is displayed in the list view on your UI, as seen in Figure 2-32.

***Figure 2-32.*** *The added to-do item*

As you add more to-do items, your list view grows, as seen in Figure 2-33.

***Figure 2-33.*** *Additional to-do items*

If you are seeing this page, you are debugging your application in an Emulator. Stop debugging and open the deployed application in the Emulator directly. The added to-do items will still be returned if you click the Get button. This is because the SQLite database still contains the items you added earlier. SQLite is an excellent solution for persisting data, especially when using mobile applications.

# Managing NuGet Packages

As a software developer, being able to reuse code is essential to any modern development effort. Being able to share code is the cornerstone of a healthy development community. Many developers create handy code libraries that can add functionality to your particular application.

This is where NuGet becomes an essential tool for developers to create, share, and consume helpful code. As a developer, you can package a DLL and other required content needed for the DLL to function correctly into a NuGet package.

NuGet is just a ZIP file with a .nupkg extension containing the DLLs you have created for distribution. Included inside this package is a manifest file that contains additional information, such as the version number of the NuGet package.

Packages uploaded to nuget.org are public and available to all developers that use NuGet in their projects. However, developers can create NuGet packages that are exclusive to a particular organization and not publicly available. We will have a look at hosting your NuGet feeds later on. For now, let's look at how to use NuGet in your Visual Studio project.

# Using NuGet in Visual Studio

Developers can access NuGet from within Visual Studio, but you can also browse `www.nuget.org` to find packages to use in your applications. In the following example, we will be using NuGet from within Visual Studio to add functionality to our ShipmentLocator application.

I have added a login form to the ShipmentLocator application, as seen in Figure 2-34. I want to encrypt the password typed in by the user and compare that to the encrypted password in the database.

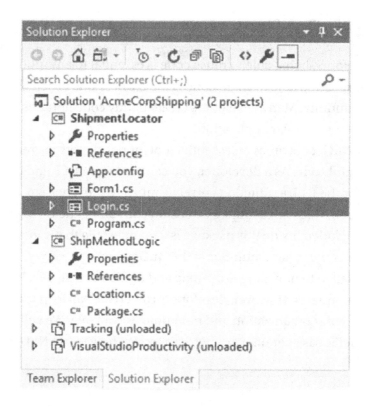

***Figure 2-34.*** *Login form added*

---

As a rule, you should never be able to decrypt a password. If you can decrypt a password, so can others with more malicious intentions. After user registration, the encrypted password is stored in a database. Login requests are then encrypted and compared with the encrypted password in the database. If it's a match, they are authenticated.

---

This is a very basic login screen but illustrates how to use NuGet in your projects.

You can roll your own solution when it comes to encryption. Another route to take is to check NuGet to see if there are any solutions available that you can use.

To add a NuGet package to your project, right-click the project in the Solution Explorer and click Manage NuGet Packages from the context menu, as seen in Figure 2-35.

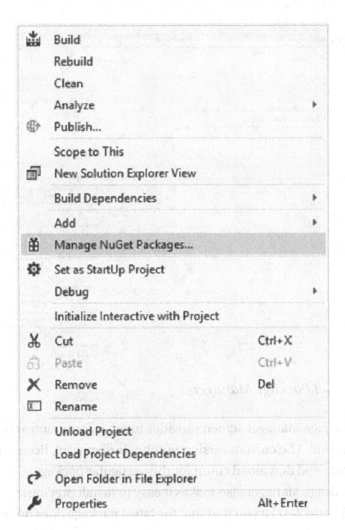

***Figure 2-35.*** *Manage NuGet Packages*

From the NuGet Package Manager screen displayed, you can search for a NuGet package based on the keywords you enter. As seen in Figure 2-36, I will use a NuGet package called EncryptValidate that provides encryption functionality.

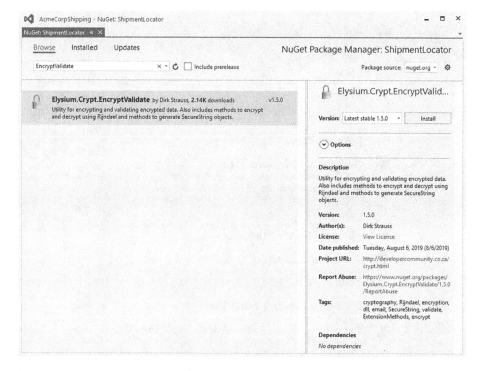

***Figure 2-36.*** *NuGet Package Manager*

The NuGet Package Manager screen provides much information about the package you are going to install. The current version number is displayed, license information, project URL, author, and download count for the particular package.

The NuGet Package Manager also makes it easy to install previous versions of the NuGet package (Figure 2-37) if you find that the latest package does not work correctly with your code.

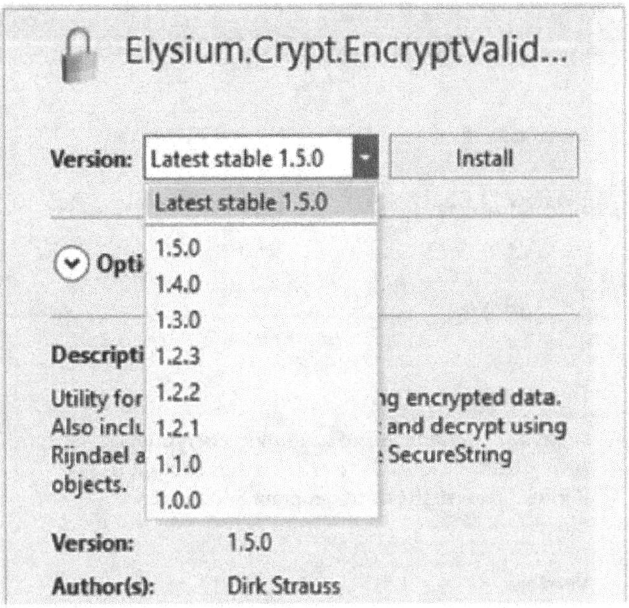

***Figure 2-37.*** *Installing previous versions*

This allows you to roll back to a previous version quickly should you need to. After installing the package, the NuGet Package Manager indicates that this package has been installed, as seen in Figure 2-38.

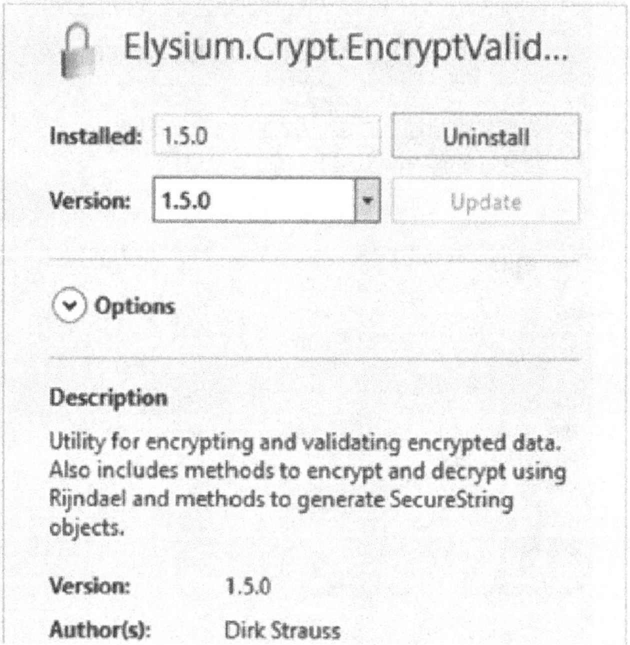

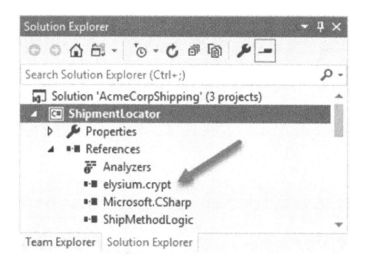

**Figure 2-38.** *NuGet package installed*

Figure 2-39 shows the NuGet package in the Visual Studio references.

**Figure 2-39.** *References*

With NuGet, everything you need to use the package is added to your project. Now that we have added the EncryptValidate package to our project, let's start adding some code as seen in Listing 2-20.

***Listing 2-20.*** ValidateLogin Method

```
private bool ValidateLogin()
{
    var blnLogin = false;
    try
    {
        var password = txtPassword.Text;
        // This encrypted password would be read from a database
        var storedEncrPassw = ReadEncryptedValueFromDatabase;
        if (ValidateEncryptedData(password, storedEncrPassw))
        {
            blnLogin = true;
        }
    }
    catch (Exception ex)
    {
        _ = MessageBox.Show(ex.Message);
    }
    return blnLogin;
}
```

The encrypted password is stored in the database. It is read in and stored in the storedEncrPassw variable. The clear-text password and the stored encrypted password are then validated. If validation succeeds, the user is logged in.

---

Remember, the code for this project is available on GitHub at github.com/apress/getting-started-vs2022.

---

By adding a single NuGet package, we have added functionality to encrypt passwords, validate encrypted passwords, and encrypt and decrypt text using Rijndael, converting text to a SecureString object, reading the value from the SecureString object, and more. All this functionality has been added without having to write the logic ourselves.

This is the power that NuGet provides. You, as a developer, need to consider using it if you do not already do so.

## Hosting Your Own NuGet Feeds

Sometimes, you might need to create and share packages only available to a limited audience. Think of the developers inside your organization. Perhaps the company you work with does not allow the sharing of code with a public audience. Perhaps the code you want to share is specific to your organization and unsuitable for a public audience. Whatever the situation, NuGet supports private feeds in the following ways:

- Local feed – On a network file share.

- NuGet.Server – On a local HTTP server.

- NuGet gallery – Hosted on an Internet server using the NuGet Gallery project, you can manage users and features to allow searching and exploring available packages similar to nuget.org.

Other NuGet hosting solutions support the creation of remote private feeds. Some of these are

- Azure Artifacts

- MyGet – `https://myget.org/`

- ProGet – `https://inedo.com/proget`

- TeamCity – `www.jetbrains.com/teamcity/`

For a complete list of NuGet hosting products and for more information on creating your NuGet feeds, have a look at the following link on Microsoft Docs: `https://docs.microsoft.com/en-us/nuget/hosting-packages/overview`.

## Managing nmp Packages

In a similar vein to NuGet, nmp allows you to install and manage packages that can be used in Node.js as well as ASP.NET Core apps. If you are unfamiliar with nmp, you can read more about it by looking at the nmp documentation at `https://docs.npmjs.com/`.

With Visual Studio 2022, the nmp package manager is available for CLI-based projects. This allows you to download nmp modules similar to the way you would download NuGet packages in an ASP.NET Core project.

The package manager can be opened by right-clicking the nmp node in the Solution Explorer as seen in Figure 2-40.

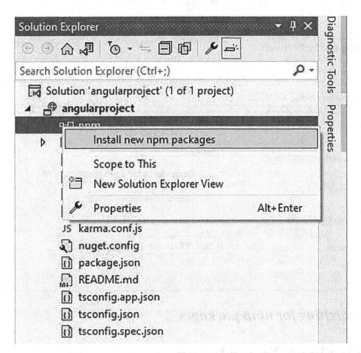

***Figure 2-40.*** *Installing new nmp packages*

You can now search for nmp packages and then select one to install as seen in Figure 2-41. Clicking the Install Package button installs the package.

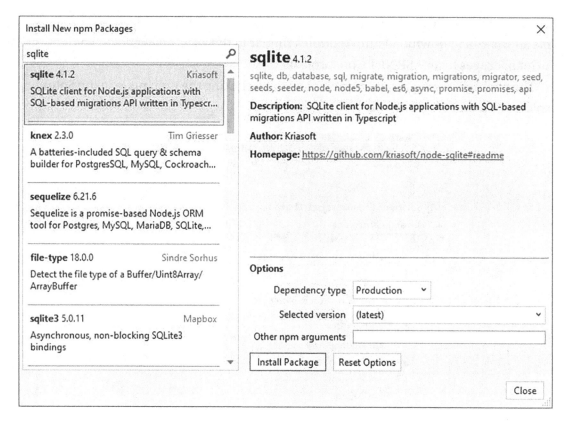

***Figure 2-41.*** *Searching for nmp packages*

# Creating Project Templates

Sometimes, developers create class libraries and code that they need to use repeatedly across various new projects. What developers end up doing is copying and pasting code into new class libraries. However, there is an easier way to create projects that reuse code you have previously written.

Enter Visual Studio project templates. These templates allow developers to speed up their development by including previously written code in new projects. Let's assume we have created a project called ProjectUtilities (as seen in Figure 2-42) that contains various helper methods.

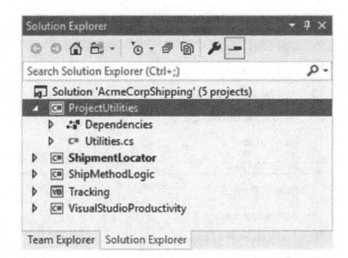

*Figure 2-42.* *ProjectUtilities project*

We will need to use this Class Library over and over in various projects. So I have decided to create a project template from it.

From the Project menu, click Export Template, as seen in Figure 2-43.

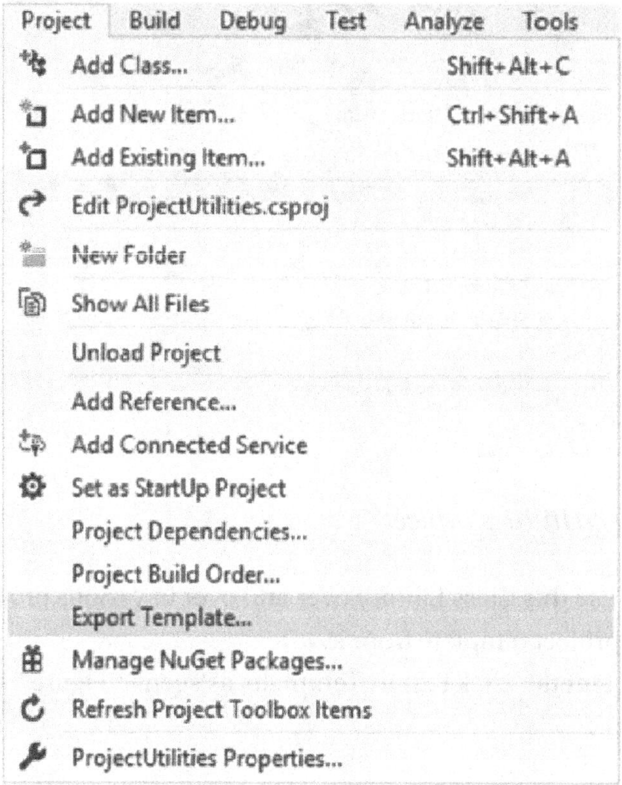

*Figure 2-43.* Export template

The Export Template Wizard is displayed as seen in Figure 2-44. This allows you to specify which template you need to create. The options are creating a Project template or an Item template. A Project template is what we are after in this example, but you can also create an Item template. This allows you to add the code via the Add New Item dialog box in Visual Studio.

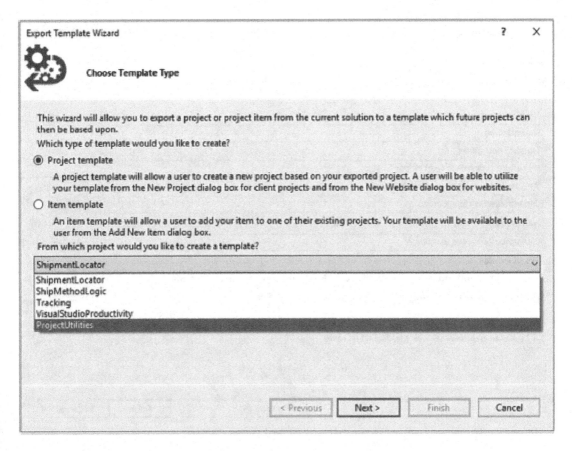

***Figure 2-44.*** *Export Template Wizard*

For this example, however, we keep the Project template option selected and select the project to export from the drop-down list. This drop-down lists all the projects in my Visual Studio solution. Select the ProjectUtilities project, and click the Next button.

The following window is where one can enter various template options (Figure 2-45). Here, I can give the template a proper name and description, specify the icon and preview images, and select to import the template into Visual Studio automatically. Click Finish to create the new project template.

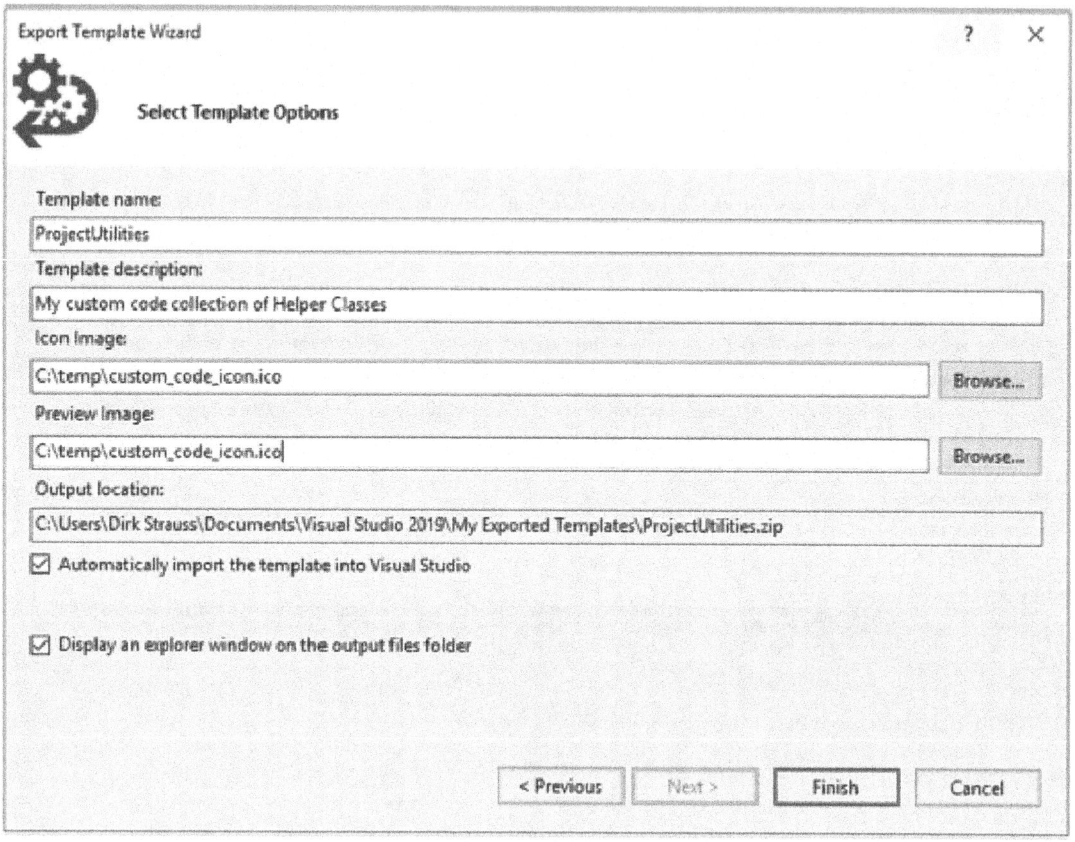

**Figure 2-45.** *Add template options*

The next time I create a new project in Visual Studio, I can search for my Custom project template (Figure 2-46) and have it available for me to select.

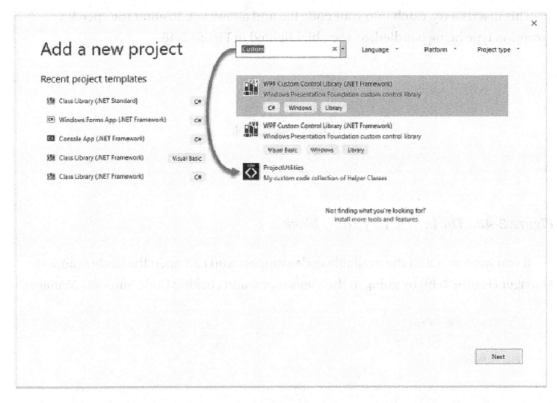

*Figure 2-46.* *Add a new project*

# Creating and Using Code Snippets

Code snippets in Visual Studio are small blocks of reusable code that you can insert into your code file by using a shortcut and tabbing twice or using the right-click menu.

As an example (Figure 2-47), open a C# code file in Visual Studio and type the word try and hit the tab key twice.

*Figure 2-47.* *Inserting a try code snippet*

This inserts a try-catch into your code file and allows you to enter the specific exception type being handled, as seen highlighted in Figure 2-48.

**Figure 2-48.** *The inserted try-catch block*

If you want to see all the available code snippets, you can open the Code Snippets Manager (Figure 2-49) by going to the Tools menu and clicking Code Snippets Manager.

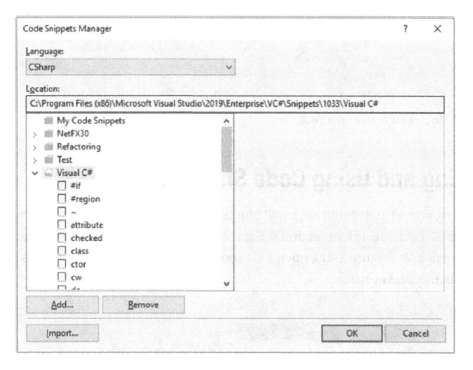

**Figure 2-49.** *Code Snippets Manager*

You can also hold down Ctrl+K, Ctrl+B to open the Code Snippets Manager window. Clicking each code snippet displays the description, shortcut, snippet type (expansion or surrounds with), and author. While some shortcuts are obvious (do, else, enum, for, and so on), others are not and might take some getting used to remembering to enter the shortcut and tabbing twice to insert the snippet.

If you can't remember the shortcut, you can invoke the snippets by hitting Ctrl+K, Ctrl+X (as seen in Figure 2-50) while inside the code file you are editing. This will display a menu in place that will allow you to search for and select the specific code snippet you want to use.

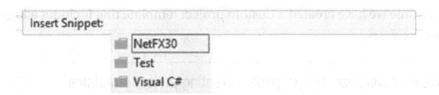

*Figure 2-50.  Ctrl+K, Ctrl+X to invoke a code snippet*

You can also right-click and select Snippets and Insert Snippet from the context menu. The last way to insert a code snippet is via the menu bar by going to Edit, IntelliSense, and clicking Insert Snippet. Visual Studio also allows developers to create their own code snippets. Let's have a look at that process next.

## Creating Code Snippets

If there is one thing I wish, it is that there was a friendly interface baked into Visual Studio for creating and adding code snippets. Perhaps one day, but we have to use what we have now.

This is through the use of an XML file. The basic snippet template XML looks as in Listing 2-21.

*Listing 2-21.  Basic Snippet Template*

```xml
<?xml version="1.0" encoding="utf-8"?>
<CodeSnippets xmlns="http://schemas.microsoft.com/VisualStudio/2005/
CodeSnippet">
    <CodeSnippet Format="1.0.0">
        <Header>
            <Title></Title>
        </Header>
        <Snippet>
```

```
        <Code Language="">
            <![CDATA[]]>
        </Code>
      </Snippet>
    </CodeSnippet>
</CodeSnippets>
```

Let's assume we have created a Custom project template that includes a logging class in our helper classes.

---

Refer to the previous section regarding creating project templates.

---

This logging class will always be added to all new projects going forward, and I have to include it in the catch block of every try. The code for the logging class is basically as in Listing 2-22.

***Listing 2-22.*** Basic Logging Class

```
public static class Logger
{
    public static void Log(string message)
    {
        // Perform some sort of logging
    }
}
```

Inside my code, I would like to be able to automatically add the code to log the error every time I insert a try-catch. The code snippet (Listing 2-23) file I create must import the namespace and expand or surround the required code. Replacement parameters have also been defined in the snippet file for the Exception type by surrounding the word to replace (namely, expression) with the $ characters.

***Listing 2-23.*** Custom Try-Catch Snippet

```
<?xml version="1.0" encoding="utf-8"?>
<CodeSnippets xmlns="http://schemas.microsoft.com/VisualStudio/2005/
CodeSnippet">
```

```xml
<CodeSnippet Format="1.0.0">
    <Header>
        <Title>Try Catch Log</Title>
        <Author>Dirk Strauss</Author>
        <Description>Creates a try catch that includes logging.
        </Description>
        <Shortcut>tryl</Shortcut>
        <SnippetTypes>
            <SnippetType>Expansion</SnippetType>
            <SnippetType>SurroundsWith</SnippetType>
        </SnippetTypes>
    </Header>
    <Snippet>
        <Declarations>
          <Literal>
            <ID>expression</ID>
            <ToolTip>Exception type</ToolTip>
            <Function>SimpleTypeName(global::System.Exception)
            </Function>
          </Literal>
        </Declarations>
         <Code Language="CSharp">
           <![CDATA[
           try
           {
               $selected$
           }
           catch ($expression$ ex)
           {
               Logger.Log(ex.Message);
               $end$
                   throw;
           }
           ]]>
         </Code>
```

```xml
            <Imports>
                <Import>
                    <Namespace>ProjectUtilities</Namespace>
                </Import>
            </Imports>
        </Snippet>
    </CodeSnippet>
</CodeSnippets>
```

It is also worth noting that the code snippet might be XML, but the file extension must be .snippet for Visual Studio to be able to import it. If you refer to Figure 2-49, you will notice an Import button on the Code Snippets Manager screen.

Click that button; browse for and import your newly created code snippet for the custom try-catch. You will notice that I have defined the shortcut as `try1` for try-catch log.

This time, if you type the `try1` shortcut into your code window, you will see that the description and title of the custom try-catch are displayed, as seen in Figure 2-51.

***Figure 2-51.*** *Custom try-catch to include logging*

When you hit the tab key twice, the custom code snippet is inserted, and the required namespace, ProjectUtilities, which we created earlier as a project template, is imported along with the code snippet. This can be seen in Figure 2-52.

```
1    using ProjectUtilities;
2    using System;
3
4    namespace ShipmentTracking
5    {
         2 references
6        public class Package
7        {
             1 reference
8            public string WaybillNumber { get; private set; }
9
             1 reference
10           public Package(string waybillNumber)...
14
             1 reference
15           public Location TrackPackage()
16           {
17               // Perform some funky tracking logic
18               //Return package location
19               var location = new Location();
20
21               try
22               {
23
24               }
25               catch (Exception ex)
26               {
27                   Logger.Log(ex.Message);
28
29                   throw;
30               }
31
```

***Figure 2-52.*** *Added try-catch including namespace*

This new code snippet is now available in all your future projects. Your C# code snippets live in the Documents folder in \Visual Studio 2022\Code Snippets\Visual C#\My Code Snippets.

---

The code snippet schema reference is available on Microsoft Docs at the following link: https://docs.microsoft.com/en-us/visualstudio/ide/code-snippets-schema-reference?view=vs-2019.

---

More often than not, you will create your own code snippets based on an existing code snippet. This allows you to reuse functionality you know is working in the existing snippet and include it in your own.

Code snippets are a very powerful productivity feature in Visual Studio.

# Using Bookmarks and Code Shortcuts

You will likely be working on an extensive code base at some point in your career. Do this for a while, and you will get bogged down with remembering where a specific bit of code is or where you need to go to get to a specific portion of logic.

Visual Studio can assist developers in bookmarking certain sections of code and add shortcuts to other areas of code. Let's have a look at what bookmarks and shortcuts are and when to use them.

## Bookmarks

Let's say that you are busy finishing up for the day, but just before you check in your code, you notice that some code doesn't look right. It is a method with a single return statement, and you know you can use an expression body for methods.

You don't have the time to play around further because you have already passed the point that you need to leave for home. So in order not to forget to have a closer look at this tomorrow, you decide to bookmark the method.

Place your cursor at the line of code you want to return to, and hold down Ctrl+K, Ctrl+K and Visual Studio will add a bookmark, as seen in Figure 2-53.

```
                              1 reference
  48    ⊟       private bool WaybillValid()
  49              {
🔖50                  return txtWaybill.Text.ToLower().Contains("acme-");
  51              }
  52
  53    ⌊ }
  54
```

*Figure 2-53.*  *Bookmark in Visual Studio*

The bookmark is added to the side of the code editor and is indicated by a single black bookmark icon.

To see all the bookmarks in your project, you can hold down Ctrl+K, Ctrl+W or go to the View menu item, select Other Windows, and then click Bookmark window.

The Bookmarks window is displayed as seen in Figure 2-54. From the toolbar in the Bookmarks window, you can group bookmarks in folders, navigate between bookmarks, navigate between bookmarks in the current folder, toggle a bookmark on the currently selected line in code, disable all bookmarks, and delete bookmarks.

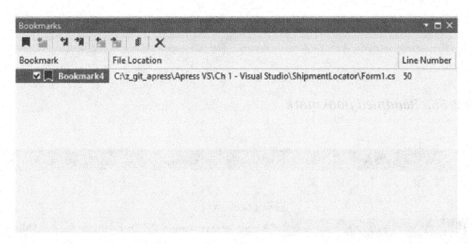

***Figure 2-54.*** *Bookmarks window*

However, another feature not so obvious by looking at this Bookmarks window is the ability to rename bookmarks. To rename a bookmark, click a selected bookmark, and you will see that the name (in this case, "Bookmark4") becomes editable.

Now you can rename your bookmark to something more relevant to what you need to remember, as seen in Figure 2-55. Go ahead and add some more bookmarks to other random areas of code. Your Bookmarks window will end up looking full as seen in Figure 2-56.

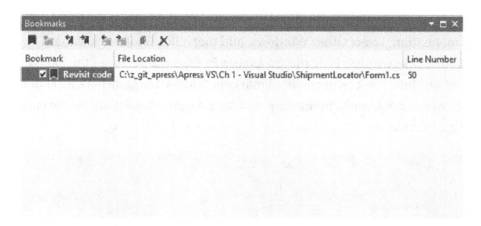

**Figure 2-55.** *Renamed bookmark*

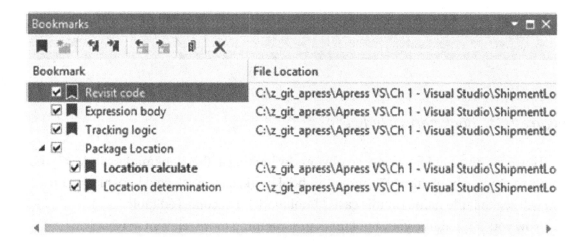

**Figure 2-56.** *Bookmarks collection*

Now click the delete button on the Bookmarks toolbar. The bookmark is deleted without any confirmation from the user.

This is something I can sort of understand. Imagine how irritating it would be having to confirm every delete, especially when you want to remove only a subsection of bookmarks from your collection.

For this reason, I use bookmarks only as a short-term solution to remind me to go and perform some action in code or refactor something I think needs refactoring.

For me, a bookmark is something I will come back to within the next day or so. Something I don't want to put off doing. It is, therefore, a temporary placeholder to something I need to revisit.

But what if I wanted to go and add a more permanent pointer to some logic in the code? This is where code shortcuts come in. Let's have a look at this next.

## Code Shortcuts

The ability to add code shortcuts in Visual Studio is more helpful when you need to jump to a certain section of code regularly. To add a shortcut to a specific section of code in Visual Studio, you need to place your cursor on the line of code you need to revisit and press Ctrl+K, Ctrl+H.

Visual Studio will then add the shortcut, as seen in Figure 2-57. To view all the shortcuts added to your project, hold down Ctrl+\, Ctrl+T or go to the View menu, and select Task List to open the Task List window, as seen in Figure 2-58.

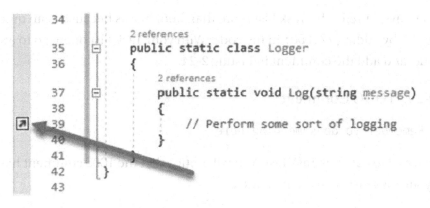

***Figure 2-57.***  *Code shortcut added indicator*

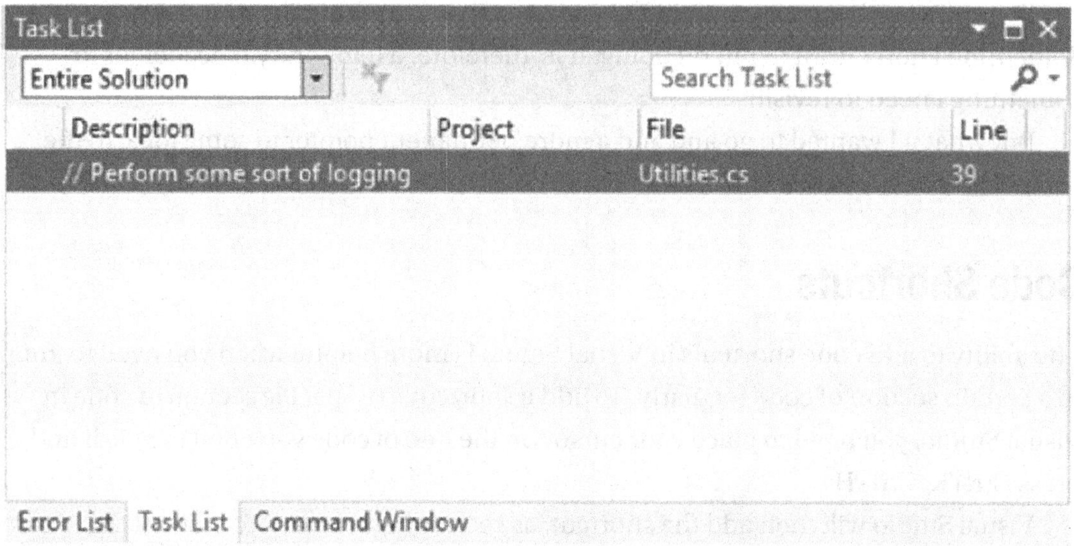

**Figure 2-58.** *The Task List*

In some ways, I prefer the Task List more than bookmarks because I can quickly add items to revisit by adding //TODO: in my code. With your Task List open, go to any place in your code, and add the comment in Listing 2-24.

**Listing 2-24.** TODO Comment

```
// TODO: Remember to do something here
```

Now have a look at your Task List. You will notice that the TODO comment has been added to your Task List, as seen in Figure 2-59.

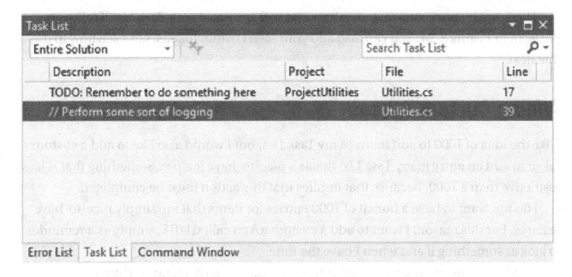

*Figure 2-59.* *TODO comments in the Task List*

This is a nice and quick method for adding reminders to your code so that you can easily refer to them and navigate to them by double-clicking the item in the Task List. You can, therefore, use the Task List to take you directly to the predefined location in the code.

In Visual Studio, TODO is what we call a predefined token. Therefore, a comment in your code that uses a predefined token will appear in your Task List. The tokenized comment is made up of the following:

- The comment marker, which is //

- The predefined token (TODO in our example)

- The rest of the comment

The code in Listing 2-24 is a valid comment using a token and will appear in the Task List. Visual Studio includes the following default tokens:

- HACK

- TODO

- UNDONE

- UnresolvedMergeConflict

137

These are by no means case sensitive and will appear in your Task List if following the form in Listing 2-24. You can also add your own custom tokens. Let's see how to do that next.

## Adding Custom Tokens

I like the idea of TODO to add items to my Task List, but I would also like to add a custom token to add an entry in my Task List that is a nice-to-have feature. Something that is less restrictive than a TODO, because that implies that this action must be completed.

I do not want to have a bunch of TODO entries for items that are simply nice-to-have features. For this reason, I want to add a custom token called NOTE, simply as a reminder to look at something if and when I have the time.

To add the custom token, go to the Tools menu, and click Options. Under Environment, select Task List as seen in Figure 2-60.

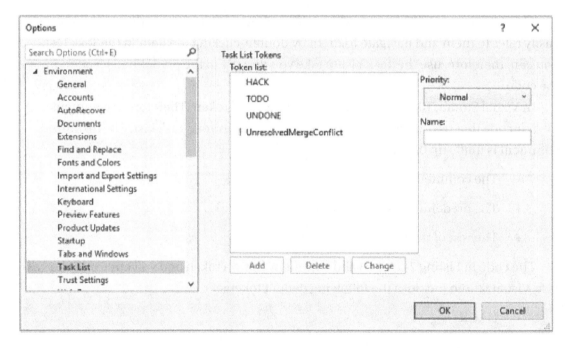

***Figure 2-60.*** *Add custom tokens*

In the Name text box, add the word NOTE and set the priority to Low. Then click the Add button. The custom token NOTE is added, as seen in Figure 2-61.

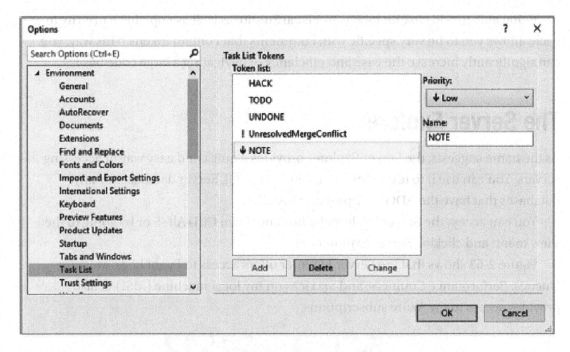

***Figure 2-61.*** *The custom token added*

Adding a NOTE to your code pops up in your Task List as a low-priority task, as seen in Figure 2-62.

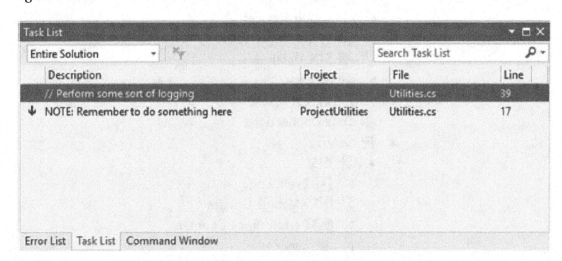

***Figure 2-62.*** *Adding a NOTE token comment*

Being able to add custom tokens in Visual Studio, as well as applying a priority to each, allows you to be very specific with comments that contain tokens. This way, you can significantly increase the ease and efficiency of navigating a large code base.

# The Server Explorer

As the name suggests, the Server Explorer provides a quick and easy way of accessing servers. You can use it to test connections and view SQL Server databases or any databases that have the ADO.NET provider installed.

You can access the Server Explorer by holding down Ctrl+Alt+S or by going to the View menu and clicking Server Explorer.

Figure 2-63 shows that the Server Explorer offers access to Event Logs, Message Queues, Performance Counters, and Services on my local machine (MSI). It also provides access to my Azure subscriptions.

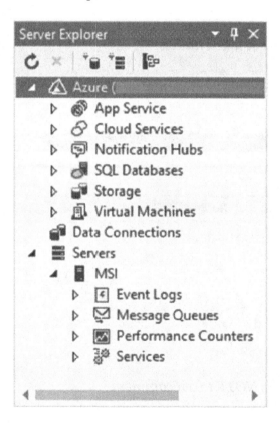

***Figure 2-63.*** *Server Explorer*

I have a local instance of SQL Server installed, so now I can connect to this instance right from within Visual Studio by clicking Connect to Database.

This displays a window allowing you to choose a data source, as seen in Figure 2-64. You can connect to various data sources, but we are only interested in Microsoft SQL Server for now. Select that from the list and click Continue.

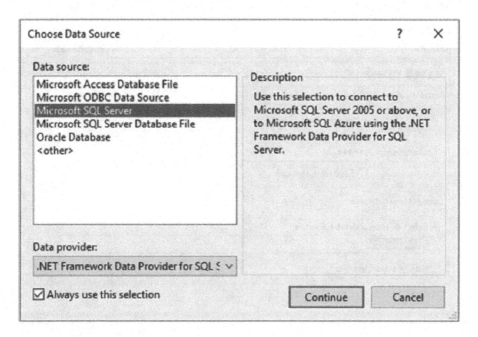

*Figure 2-64.* *Choose Data Source*

The following window (Figure 2-65) allows you to define your connection to the database. Here, you need to specify the server name and the authentication type, and if SQL Server Authentication is selected, provide the username and password.

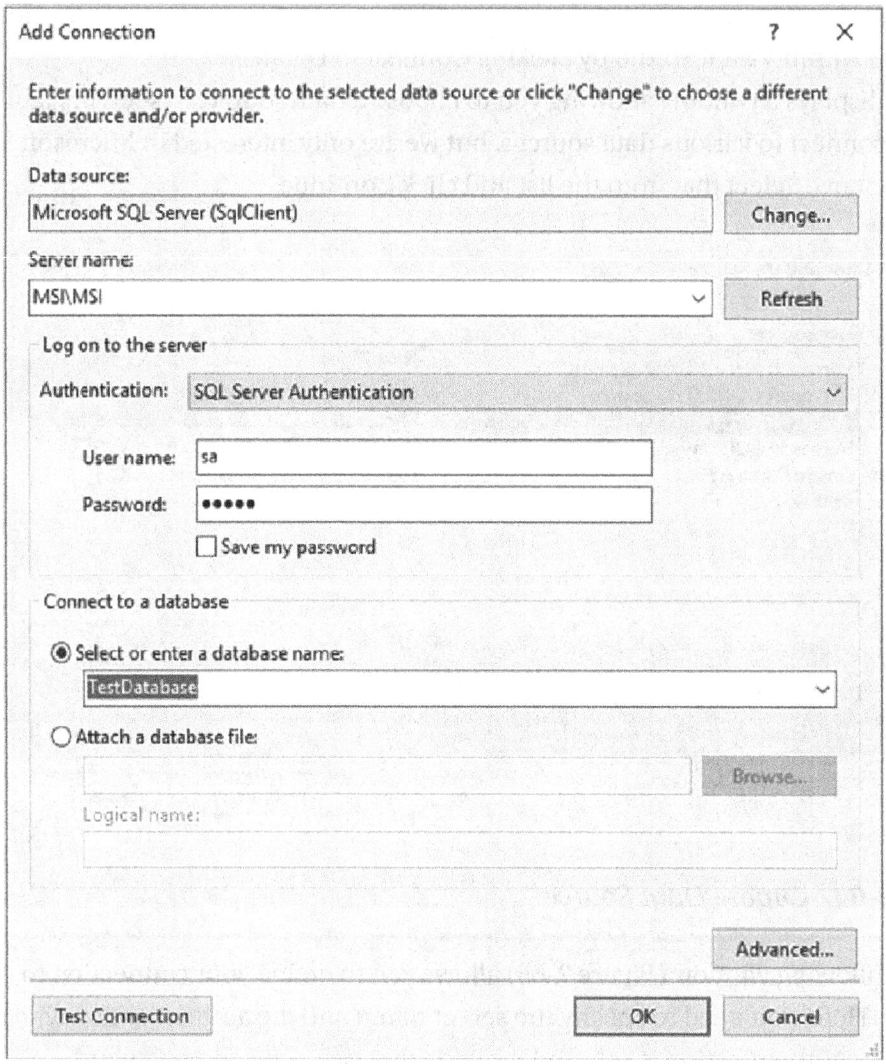

**Figure 2-65.** *Add Connection*

This allows you to select a database from the list to connect to. You can click the Test Connection button to check if the connection settings are correct.

After adding the database to your Server Explorer, you will see the instance added to your list from where you can expand the various nodes to view Tables, Views, and Stored Procedures, as seen in Figure 2-66.

**Figure 2-66.**  *Database added to Server Explorer*

By double-clicking a table, Visual Studio displays the table designer for you and a create table SQL statement, as seen in Figure 2-67.

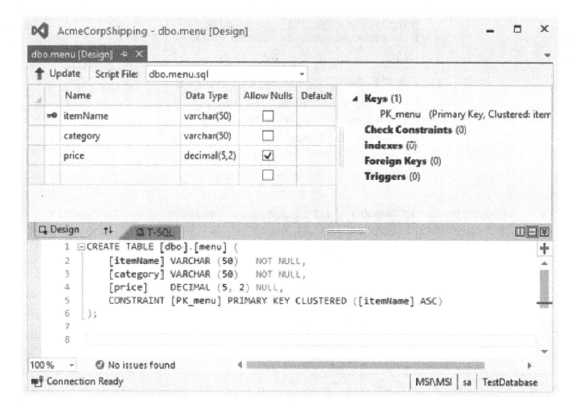

***Figure 2-67.*** *Table designer*

From this window, you can easily update the table. The create table statement in Figure 2-67 is listed in Listing 2-25.

***Listing 2-25.*** Create Table Statement

```
CREATE TABLE [dbo].[menu] (
    [itemName] VARCHAR (50)   NOT NULL,
    [category] VARCHAR (50)   NOT NULL,
    [price]    DECIMAL (5, 2) NULL,
    CONSTRAINT [PK_menu] PRIMARY KEY CLUSTERED ([itemName] ASC)
);
```

We can now modify the menu table by altering the SQL statement as shown in Listing 2-26.

**Listing 2-26.** Modified Create Table Statement

```
CREATE TABLE [dbo].[menu] (
    [itemName] VARCHAR (50)    NOT NULL,
    [category] VARCHAR (50)    NOT NULL,
    [price]    DECIMAL (5, 2) NULL,
    [priceCategory]    VARCHAR (5) NULL,
    CONSTRAINT [PK_menu] PRIMARY KEY CLUSTERED ([itemName] ASC)
);
```

I want to add a price category field to the table. When I modify the create table statement, I see the changes reflected in the table designer, as seen in Figure 2-68.

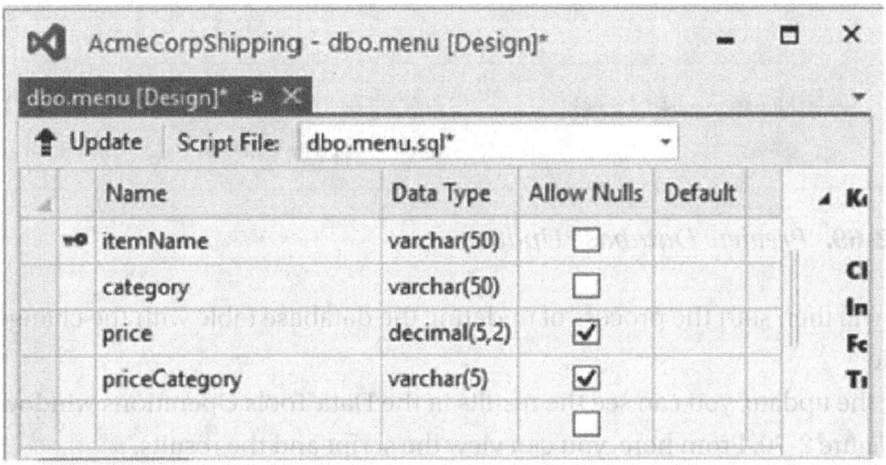

**Figure 2-68.** *Table design updated*

The changes have not been applied to my table yet. To update the table, I need to click the Update button.

This allows me to preview the database updates, as seen in Figure 2-69. If you do not want to let Visual Studio update the table, you can have it generate the script by clicking the Generate Script button. Alternatively, you can go ahead and click the Update Database button.

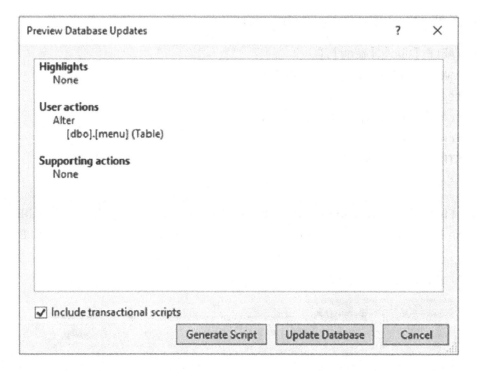

*Figure 2-69.* *Preview Database Updates*

This will then start the process of updating the database table with the changes you made.

After the update, you can see the results in the Data Tools Operations window, as seen in Figure 2-70. From here, you can view the script and the results.

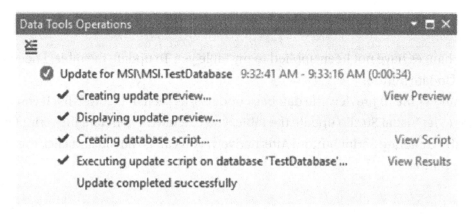

*Figure 2-70.* *Data Tools Operations*

# Running SQL Queries

The Server Explorer also allows developers to run SQL queries from within Visual Studio. Go ahead, right-click a table (Figure 2-71), and click New Query from the context menu.

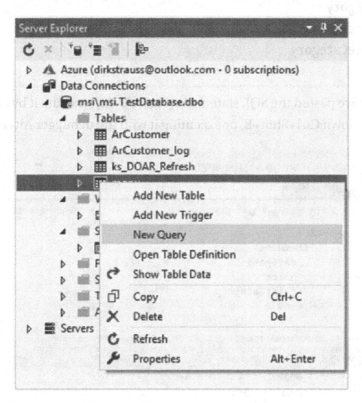

***Figure 2-71.*** *Run a SQL query*

---

Note that the context menu changes depending on what item you have right-clicked in the Server Explorer. When right-clicking a table, you see items related to a SQL table. When right-clicking a View, you see items specific to the View, such as Show Results and Open View Definition. The context menu will display the Execute command when right-clicking a Stored Procedure.

---

Copy the SQL query in Listing 2-27. You will have had to create the table using the CREATE statement in Listing 2-26.

***Listing 2-27.*** SQL Select Statement

```
SELECT
        itemName
        , category
        , price
        , priceCategory
FROM menu
```

When you have pasted the SQL statement (Figure 2-72), execute it by clicking the run button, holding down Ctrl+Shift+E, or executing it with the debugger Alt+F5.

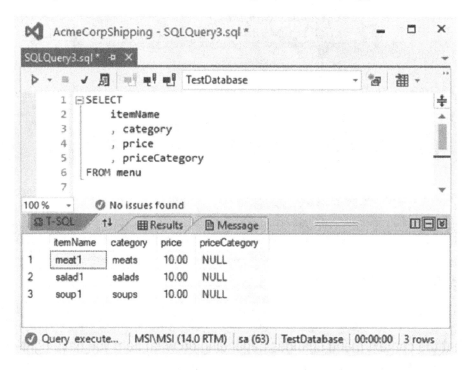

***Figure 2-72.*** *Running a select statement*

If you are used to pressing F5 in SQL Server Management Studio, you might find yourself starting the Visual Studio debugger instead of running the query. I find clicking the run button easier to avoid my muscle memory faux pas.

Adding additional items to the table is quickly done by running the INSERT statement in Listing 2-28.

***Listing 2-28.*** Insert Statement

```
INSERT INTO [dbo].[menu]
        ([itemName],[category],[price],[priceCategory])
        VALUES
        ('bread','breads',2.50,'baker')
```

If we rerun the SELECT statement, you will see that the entry has been added to the table, as seen in Figure 2-73.

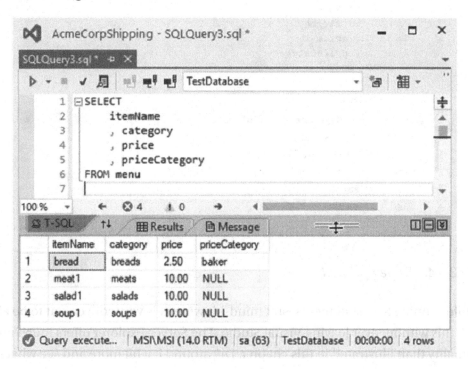

***Figure 2-73.*** *New item inserted*

From the results in Figure 2-73, we can see that by adding the priceCategory column, we have a few NULL fields in the menu table. Let's change that by running the SQL statement in Listing 2-29.

***Listing 2-29.*** SQL Update Statement

```
UPDATE menu
SET priceCategory = 'DELI'
WHERE category IN ('meats', 'salads', 'soups')
```

When we look at the table data after the UPDATE statement (Figure 2-74), you will see that the table has been updated to display the correct priceCategory values for the items in the table.

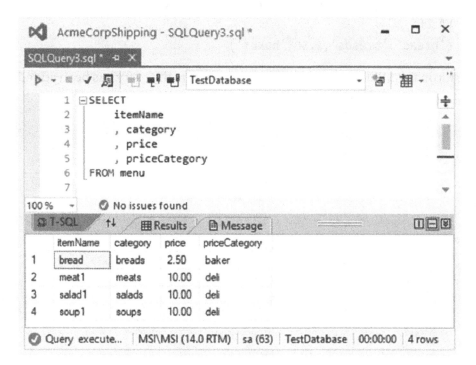

***Figure 2-74.*** *Table updated*

While running SQL statements isn't mind-blowing, it is very convenient to be able to do all this without ever leaving Visual Studio. The Server Explorer offers much more functionality than illustrated in this chapter. Dig around it a bit more and see what the Server Explorer can do for your productivity.

# Visual Studio Windows

I have often maintained that developers get stuck in a rut when working with Visual Studio. They tend to stick to what they know and keep doing things that way until the cows come home.

This isn't necessarily a bad thing, but developers might miss out on some of the excellent tools and features that Visual Studio provides. In this section, I want to briefly discuss two items found under the View ➤ Other Windows menu, as seen in Figure 2-75.

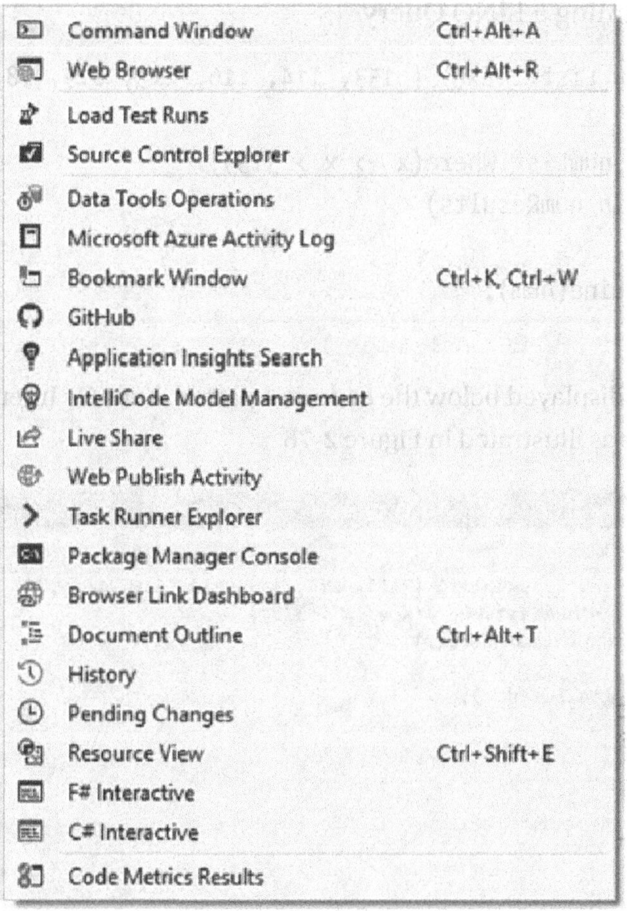

| | | |
|---|---|---|
| ⊡ | Command Window | Ctrl+Alt+A |
| ▧ | Web Browser | Ctrl+Alt+R |
| ⚡ | Load Test Runs | |
| ✓ | Source Control Explorer | |
| ⚙ | Data Tools Operations | |
| ▢ | Microsoft Azure Activity Log | |
| ⌐ | Bookmark Window | Ctrl+K, Ctrl+W |
| ◯ | GitHub | |
| ♀ | Application Insights Search | |
| ◉ | IntelliCode Model Management | |
| ↩ | Live Share | |
| ⊕ | Web Publish Activity | |
| ❯ | Task Runner Explorer | |
| ⊡ | Package Manager Console | |
| ⊕ | Browser Link Dashboard | |
| ▤ | Document Outline | Ctrl+Alt+T |
| ◔ | History | |
| ◕ | Pending Changes | |
| ▣ | Resource View | Ctrl+Shift+E |
| ▦ | F# Interactive | |
| ▦ | C# Interactive | |
| ☐ | Code Metrics Results | |

***Figure 2-75.*** *Other Windows in Visual Studio*

There are too many windows to discuss in this chapter, but I will touch on two that I find very useful.

# C# Interactive

How often have you wanted to test a tiny bit of code to see if it works correctly? Well, with C# Interactive, you can do just that without having to debug your entire solution. Found toward the bottom of the View ➤ Other Windows menu, C# Interactive is almost hidden. But gems usually are, and you'll love using it if you don't already.

Click C# Interactive and paste the following code in Listing 2-30. After pasting the code into C# Interactive, hit the Enter key to run the code.

***Listing 2-30.*** Running a LINQ Query

```
var numList = new List<int>() { 153, 114, 116, 213, 619, 18, 176, 317,
212, 510 };
var numResults = numList.Where(x => x > 315);
foreach(var num in numResults)
{
   Console.WriteLine(num);
}
```

The results are displayed below the code you pasted. Your C# Interactive window should now appear as illustrated in Figure 2-76.

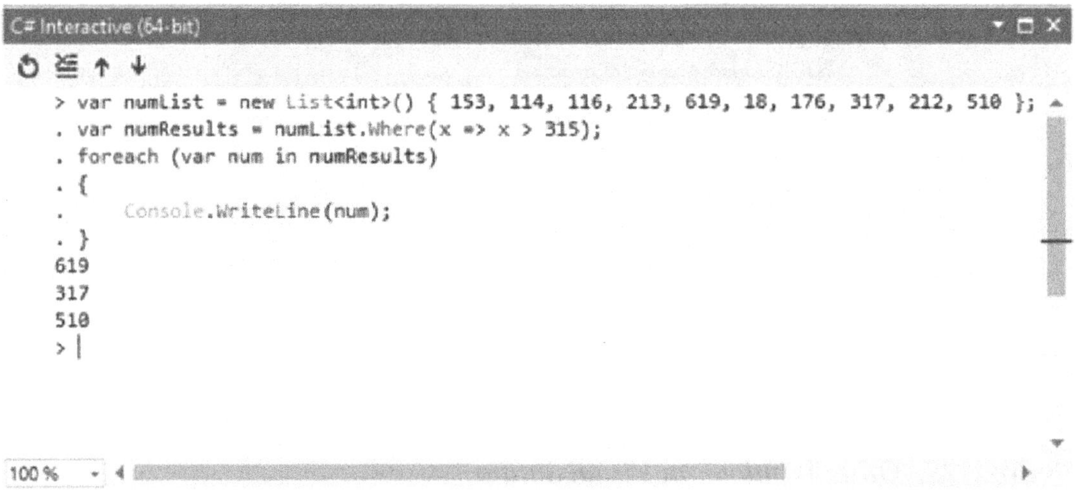

***Figure 2-76.*** *C# Interactive code results*

C# Interactive is what we refer to as a REPL (Read-Eval-Print Loop). Being able to input expressions that are evaluated and having the results returned makes on-the-spot debugging possible in Visual Studio.

C# Interactive supports IntelliSense, so you get the same kind of editor experience as in Visual Studio. For a list of available keyboard shortcuts, REPL commands, and Script directives that C# Interactive supports, just type in #help and press the Enter key.

# Code Metrics Results

The project we have been using in this chapter is really not complex. It is just to illustrate the concepts in this book. If you take a more complex project, one of the projects you have worked on at work, this next screen looks a lot different.

Code Metrics Results (Figure 2-77) is a set of measurements that allow developers to gain a better insight into the code they produce.

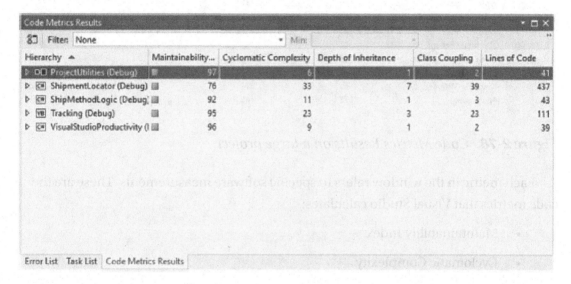

*Figure 2-77.* *Code Metrics Results*

The image in Figure 2-77 results from the ShipmentLocator application we have used throughout this chapter. It's not a complex application; therefore, the metrics might all seem fine.

---

Please note that it will be blank when you first open the Code Metrics Results screen. You need to click the Calculate Code Metrics for Solution button in the top-left corner of the window.

---

Looking at the same screen (Figure 2-78) for a more complex project (one of my old legacy projects), the metrics are pretty different.

| Hierarchy ▲ | Maintainability Index | Cyclomatic Complexity | Depth of Inheritance | Class Coupling | Lines of Code |
|---|---|---|---|---|---|
| ▷ Authentication (Debu | 76 | 723 | 4 | 147 | 5 150 |
| ▷ Common (Debug) | 86 | 933 | 4 | 158 | 7 033 |
| ▷ Comms (Debug) | 78 | 1 537 | 4 | 177 | 10 756 |
| ▷ Core (Debug) | 77 | 25 186 | 7 | 902 | 155 980 |
| ▷ Core.Data (Debug) | 77 | 19 932 | 4 | 692 | 142 517 |
| ▷ Crypto (Debug) | 80 | 31 | 1 | 18 | 320 |
| ▷ SysEnvironment (Deb | 100 | 1 | 1 | 0 | 13 |
| ▷ Service (Release) | 72 | 427 | 4 | 67 | 2 266 |
| ▷ Business (Debug) | 82 | 3 987 | 1 | 42 | 19 292 |
| ▷ Helpers (Debug) | 82 | 146 | 2 | 88 | 1 437 |
| ▷ Lib (Debug) | 76 | 892 | 1 | 207 | 7 148 |
| ▷ Security (Debug) | 85 | 77 | 1 | 18 | 486 |
| ▷ TestApp (Debug) | 78 | 1 645 | 4 | 173 | 11 653 |

***Figure 2-78.*** *Code Metrics Results on a large project*

Each metric in the window refers to specific software measurements. These are the code metrics that Visual Studio calculates:

- Maintainability Index

- Cyclomatic Complexity

- Depth of Inheritance

- Class Coupling

- Lines of Code

These metrics allow developers to understand what portions of code need to be refactored or more rigorously tested. It also allows developers to identify potential risks in their software. Ratings in this window are also color-coded so developers can quickly identify trouble spots.

## Maintainability Index

The maintainability index represents a value between 0 and 100, illustrating how easy it is to maintain the code. The higher the value, the more maintainable your code is.

## Cyclomatic Complexity

This metric measures the structure of your code and how complex it is. It uses the number of code paths it finds that flow through the program to calculate this score. A higher number indicates a complex control flow and is, therefore, harder to test and maintain. The numbers displayed in Figures 2-77 and 2-78 are totaled for each project in the solution. Here, it makes sense to expand the hierarchy and drill down to the individual methods to see where the problem areas lie.

## Depth of Inheritance

As the name suggests, this metric measures the number of classes inherited from each other. This goes all the way down to the base class. A high number indicates deep inheritance, which is bad. Any changes to a base class can break code further up in the derived classes. Here, you want to see a lower score.

## Class Coupling

Class Coupling measures how many classes a single class uses. A high number is bad, and a low number is good. Class Coupling has been shown to predict software failures accurately. With a high coupling score, the maintenance and reusability of the class become difficult because it depends on too many other types.

## Lines of Code

The lines of code here are based on the count of the IL code. So this isn't an accurate count of lines of code in the source file. Nevertheless, you will agree that a high count indicates that a lot is happening. Expanding the projects and viewing the code counts for individual methods allow you to see which methods are trying to do too much. A high line count indicates a method that is harder to maintain. Try to refactor these methods and simplify them.

# Send Feedback

The Visual Studio team takes feedback seriously. So much so that it drives much of what they do to improve Visual Studio.

If you are experiencing a problem in Visual Studio 2022, click the feedback button, as seen in Figure 2-79.

**Figure 2-79.**  *Send Feedback button*

You can now report a problem or suggest a feature right from inside Visual Studio 2022.

As developers, we should take the time to report issues we encounter. It can be anything from crashes to slow performance or something else unexpected.

# Personalizing Visual Studio

Visual Studio is one of the most popular IDEs available and does a fantastic job at increasing your productivity. It also allows developers to personalize their experience based on their individual workflow needs. The Visual Studio team is also planning to add additional features in the future that will accommodate developers who are neurodiverse or who might have learning challenges. Let's look at some of these improvements that help you personalize Visual Studio.

## Adjust Line Spacing

In Visual Studio 2022, developers can specify the line spacing for the text editor. To increase the line spacing, on the Tools menu, click Options and select Text Editor ➤ General and look under the Display group as seen in Figure 2-80.

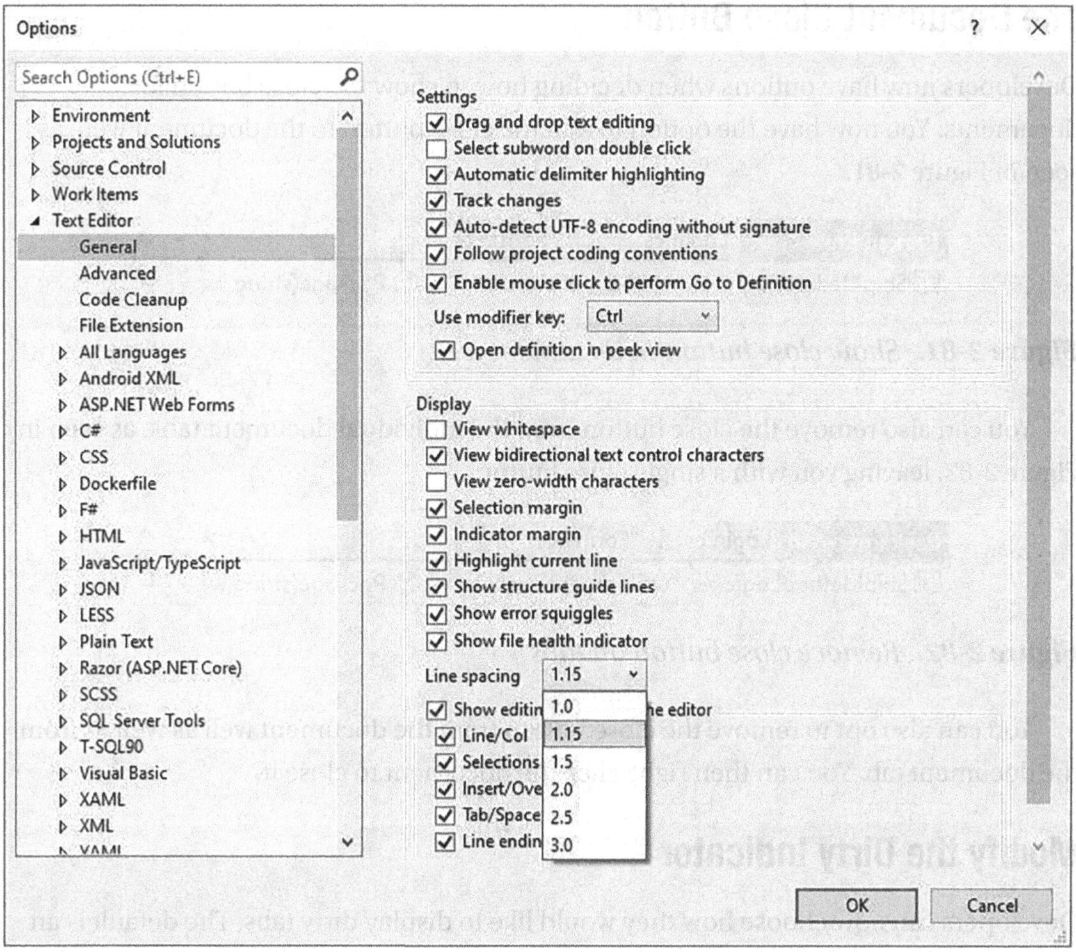

**Figure 2-80.** *Adjust line spacing*

Admittedly, the options might not suit everyone, and I hope that Visual Studio allows custom values to be entered here in a future release. Nevertheless, being able to space the lines of code vertically is a quality-of-life improvement for many developers that spend most of their working day in front of Visual Studio.

# Document Management Customizations

There are several small but welcome changes to how developers manage documents. The Document Tabs group under Tools, Options, Environment, Tabs, and Windows has had several new options added compared to previous versions of Visual Studio. Let's have a look at some of these.

## The Document Close Button

Developers now have options when deciding how to show the close button for documents. You now have the option to add the close button to the document well, as seen in Figure 2-81.

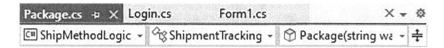

***Figure 2-81.*** *Show close button in document well*

You can also remove the close button from the individual document tabs, as seen in Figure 2-82, leaving you with a single close button.

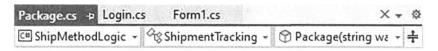

***Figure 2-82.*** *Remove close button on tabs*

You can also opt to remove the close button from the document well as well as from the document tab. You can then right-click the document to close it.

## Modify the Dirty Indicator

Developers can now choose how they would like to display dirty tabs. The default is an asterisk to the right of the file name, as seen in Figure 2-83.

***Figure 2-83.*** *The default dirty indicator*

You can also change this indicator to be a dot, as seen in Figure 2-84.

***Figure 2-84.*** *The dot dirty indicator*

The dot does make the tab slightly bigger, but it is a more explicit indicator that the document has unsaved changes. What is nice, however, is that if you have set the close button to be visible on document tabs, the dot will change into a close button when you hover over it.

## Show Invisible Tabs in Italics in the Tab Drop-Down

The ability to display hidden tabs in italics is something you might not know that you want until you see it in action. The tab drop-down displays all your open tabs, as seen in Figure 2-85.

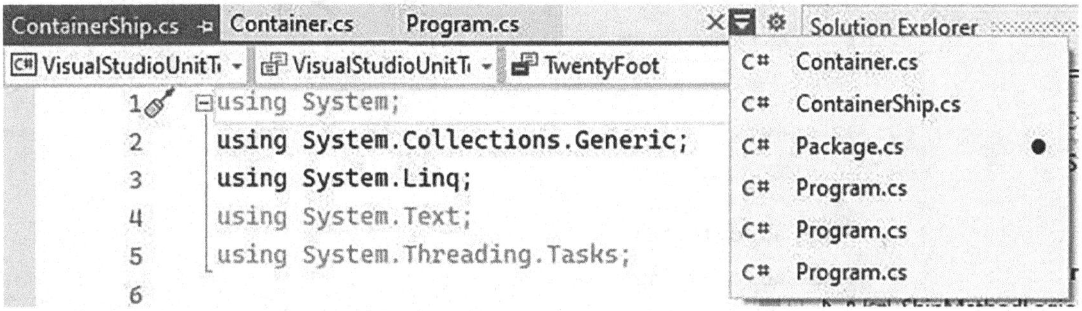

***Figure 2-85.*** *Invisible tabs not in italics*

The trick is knowing which documents are currently visible and which are not.

With this option set to show hidden documents in italics, the hidden tabs are immediately discernable, as seen in Figure 2-86. This is especially helpful when looking at that Program.cs file.

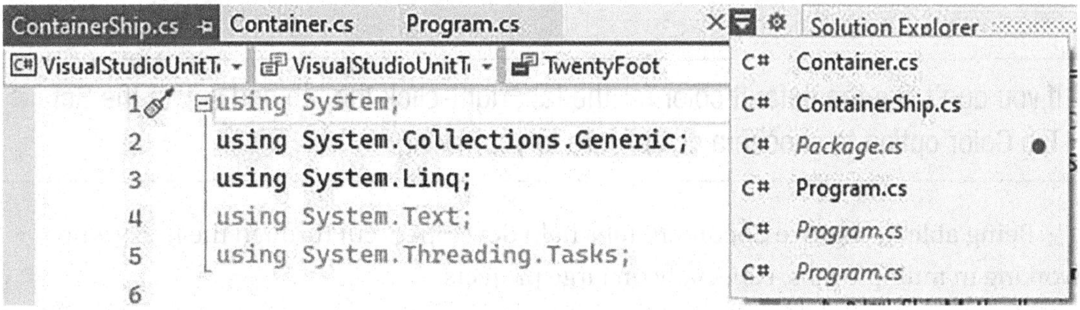

***Figure 2-86.*** *Invisible tabs displayed in italics*

159

## Colorize Document Tabs

I'm sure the images displayed here will not be in color if you read the print book. Showing the color changes on tabs will, therefore, not make sense. Instead, I will show you where you can change this option.

As seen in Figure 2-87, you can colorize document tabs by Project or File Extension (or choose no coloring, which is the default). Playing around with this option allows you to find a setting that is convenient for you.

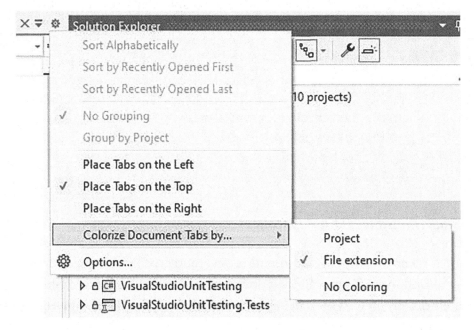

***Figure 2-87.*** *Colorizing document tabs*

---

If you don't like the default color for the tab, right-click the tab and select the Set Tab Color option to choose a color more to your liking.

---

Being able to colorize document tabs help developers cut through the noise when working in multiple tabs, especially on large projects.

## Tab Placement

The ability to choose the tab placement is something many of you might welcome.

As seen in Figure 2-88, the tabs can be displayed on the left or, as in Figure 2-89, on the right.

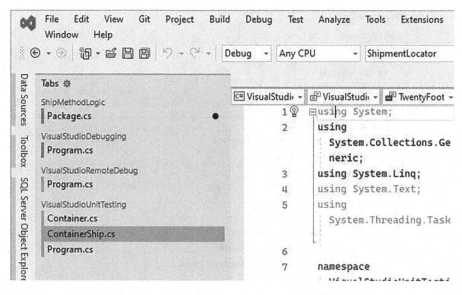

***Figure 2-88.***  *Document tabs on the left*

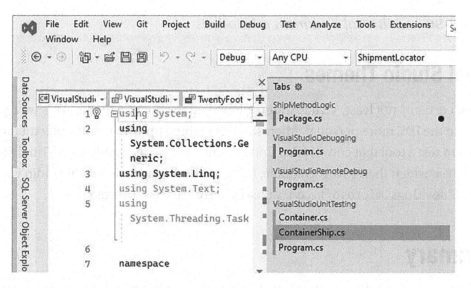

***Figure 2-89.***  *Document tabs on the right*

The left and right placement of tabs also highlights the color options better.

More flexibility is given to developers by allowing them to choose the minimum and maximum tab width as seen in Figure 2-90.

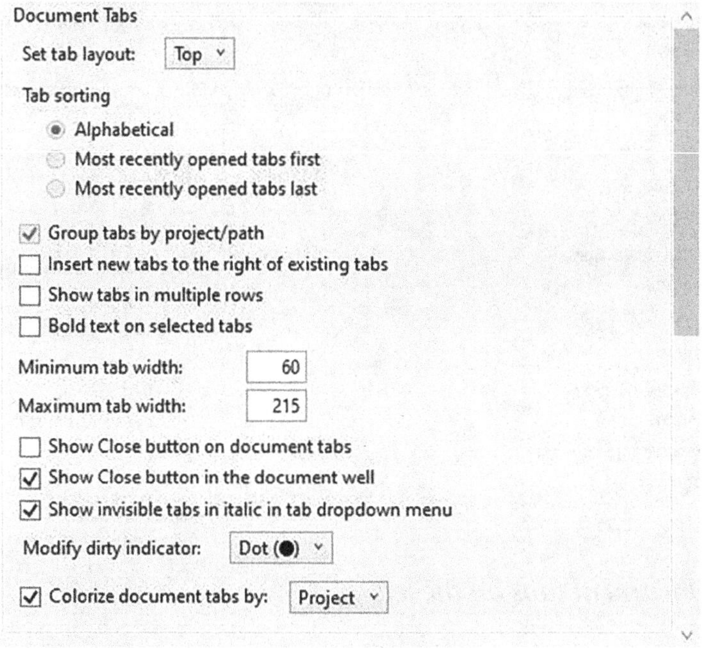

***Figure 2-90.***  *Additional document tab options*

## Visual Studio Themes

Last but certainly not least, Visual Studio allows you to choose a theme. This way, you can make the IDE more personal. Microsoft has teamed up with community theme authors to test a tool that converts VS Code themes to be compatible with Visual Studio 2022. To see which themes are available, follow this link and style Visual Studio your way: `https://devblogs.microsoft.com/visualstudio/custom-themes/`.

## Summary

Wow, this was a long chapter. We looked at many Visual Studio features and how to make working with Visual Studio better for you. We saw several project templates available to developers, including the new MAUI project template. We saw how to create a MAUI application that consumes a REST Service to display weather information and how to use SQLite to persist data. Visual Studio's personalization features also allow developers to make it their own. Visual Studio 2022 is a powerhouse in the world of IDEs. I hope this chapter has shed some light on what is possible when developing world-class applications using Visual Studio 2022.

# CHAPTER 3

# Debugging Your Code

Debugging code is probably one of the most essential tasks that a developer performs. Being able to run your application and pause the execution of code midway is a lifesaver. But there is a lot more to debugging than just setting breakpoints and viewing results.

In this chapter, we will be discussing the options available to you as a developer that needs to effectively debug their code. We will be looking at

- Using breakpoints, conditional breakpoints, breakpoint actions and labels, and exporting breakpoints

- Using data tips

- The DebuggerDisplay attribute

- Diagnostic Tools and Immediate Window

- Attaching to a running process

- Remote debugging

Visual Studio gives developers all the required tools in order to effectively debug the code you are experiencing problems with. Without being able to debug your code, it will be virtually impossible to resolve any issues you might be experiencing.

Not being able to effectively debug your application (not knowing how to effectively use the tools you have) is just as bad as not having the tools to debug with in the first place.

## Working with Breakpoints

If you are familiar with debugging in Visual Studio, this chapter might seem like old hat for you. Stick around, there might be sections discussed here that you didn't know about.

If you are new to Visual Studio, the concept of debugging in Visual Studio is when you run your application with the debugger attached. Debugging allows you to step

© Dirk Strauss 2023
D. Strauss, *Getting Started with Visual Studio 2022*, https://doi.org/10.1007/978-1-4842-8922-8_3

through the code and view the values stored in variables. More importantly, you can see how those values change.

## Setting a Breakpoint

The most basic task of debugging is setting a breakpoint. Breakpoints mark the lines of code that you want Visual Studio to pause at, allowing you to take a closer look at what the code is doing at that particular point in time. To place a breakpoint in code, click the margin to the left of the line of code you want to inspect as seen in Figure 3-1.

```
36  ⊟        try
37           {
38               var password = txtPassword.Text;
39
40               // This encrypted password would be read
41               // from a database based on the username
42               var storedEncrPassw = ReadEncryptedValueFromDatabase;
43
44  ⊟          if (ValidateEncryptedData(password, storedEncrPassw))
45               {
46                   blnLogin = true;
47               }
48           }
```

***Figure 3-1.*** *Setting a breakpoint*

This line of code is contained in the `ValidateLogin()` method. The method is called when the user clicks the login button. Press F5 or click Debug ➤ Start Debugging to run your application. You can also just click the Start button as shown in Figure 3-2.

***Figure 3-2.*** *The Start button*

After you start debugging, and a breakpoint is hit, the debug toolbar in Visual Studio changes as seen in Figure 3-3.

**Figure 3-3.** *Debug toolbar when breakpoint hit*

The Start button now changes to display Continue. Remember, at this point, your code execution is paused in Visual Studio at the breakpoint you set earlier.

In order to step through your code, you can click the step buttons as displayed in Figure 3-4.

**Figure 3-4.** *Step buttons*

From left to right, these buttons are as follows:

- Step Into (F11)

- Step Over (F10)

- Step Out (Shift+F11)

When you step into a method, you jump to the point in the editor where that method's code is. If you do not want to step into the method, you can click the Step Over button or press F10 to carry on with the next line of code. If you are inside a method and want to step out and continue debugging the calling code, click the Step Out button or press Shift+F11.

## Step into Specific

Imagine that we need a method that generates a waybill number based on specific business rules. Then, when the application starts, the text box field is auto populated with the generated waybill number.

The code used to generate the random waybill functionality is listed in Listing 3-1.

***Listing 3-1.*** Waybill Generation Code

```
private string GenerateWaybill(string partA, int rndNum) => $"{partA}-
{rndNum}-{DateTime.Now.Year}-{DateTime.Now.Month}";
private string WBPartA() => "acme-";
private int WBPartB(int min, int max)
{
    var rngCrypto = new RNGCryptoServiceProvider();
    var bf = new byte[4];
    rngCrypto.GetBytes(bf);
    var result = BitConverter.ToInt32(bf, 0);
    return new Random(result).Next(min, max);
}
```

In the form load of the tracking application, we then make a call to the GenerateWaybill() method and pass it the other two methods WBPartA() and WBPartB() as parameters as seen in Listing 3-2.

***Listing 3-2.*** Form Load

```
private void Form1_Load(object sender, EventArgs e)
{
    var frmLogin = new Login();
    _ = frmLogin.ShowDialog();
    txtWaybill.Text = GenerateWaybill(WBPartA(), WBPartB(100,2000));
}
```

If you had placed a breakpoint on the line of code that contains the GenerateWaybill() method and step into the methods by pressing F11, you would first step into method WBPartA(), then into method WBPartB(), and lastly into the GenerateWaybill() method.

Did you know that you can choose which method to step into? When the breakpoint is hit, hold down Alt+Shift+F11 and Visual Studio will pop up a menu for you to choose from as seen in Figure 3-5.

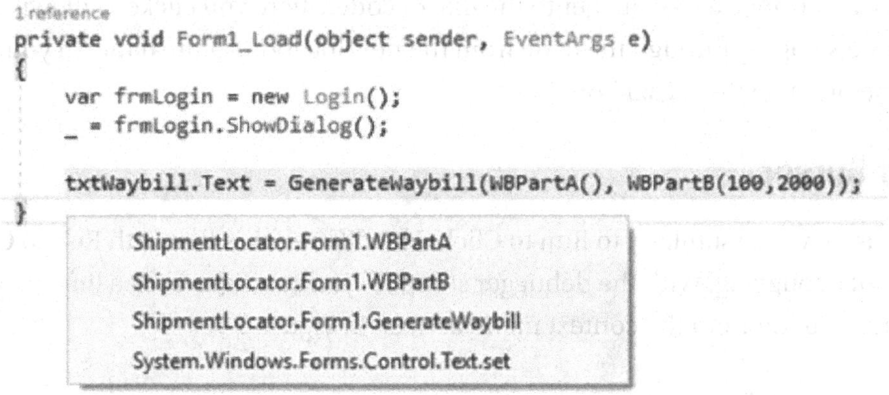

```
1 reference
private void Form1_Load(object sender, EventArgs e)
{
    var frmLogin = new Login();
    _ = frmLogin.ShowDialog();

    txtWaybill.Text = GenerateWaybill(WBPartA(), WBPartB(100,2000));
}
```

| ShipmentLocator.Form1.WBPartA |
| ShipmentLocator.Form1.WBPartB |
| ShipmentLocator.Form1.GenerateWaybill |
| System.Windows.Forms.Control.Text.set |

***Figure 3-5.*** *Step into specific*

Simply select the method you want to step into and off you go.

# Run to Click

When you start debugging and you hit a breakpoint, you can jump around quickly within the code by clicking the Run to Click button. While in the debugger, hover your mouse over a line of code as seen in Figure 3-6, and click the Run to Click button that pops up.

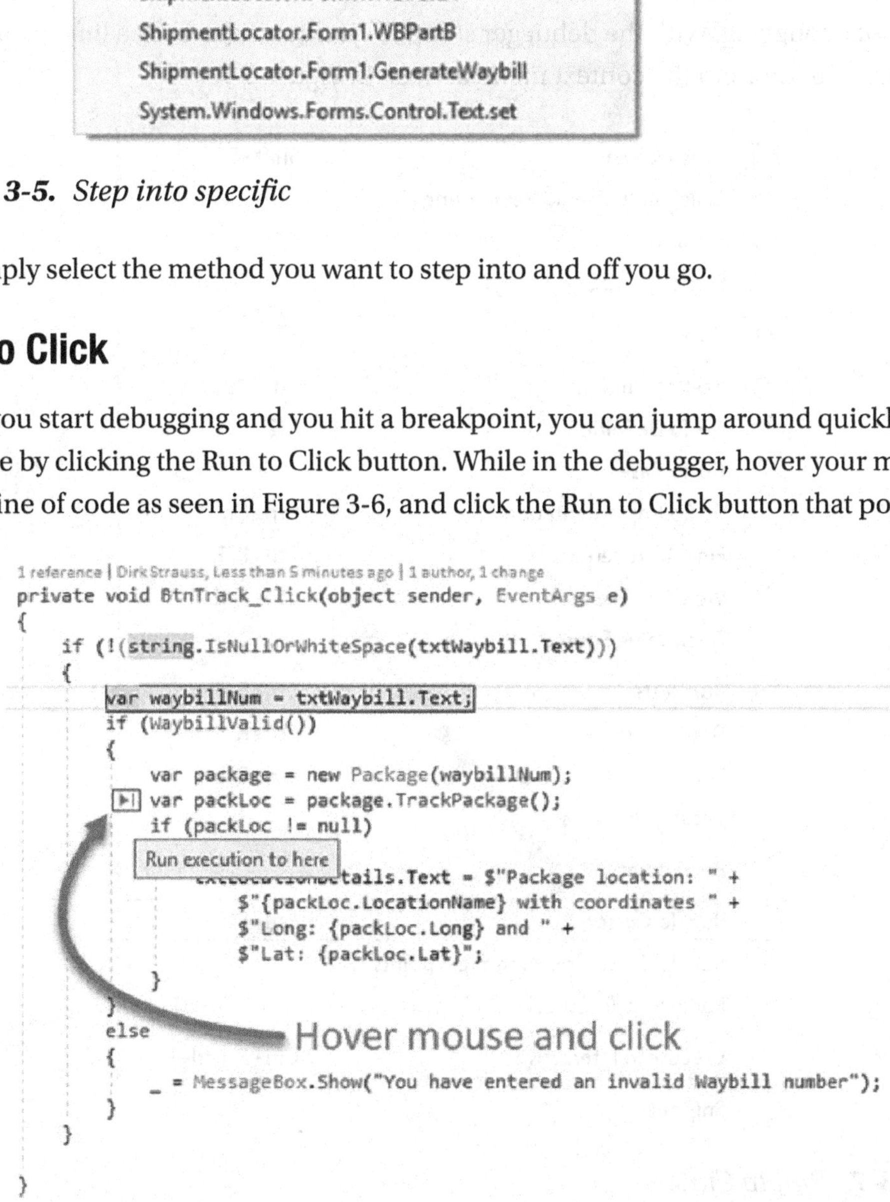

```
1 reference | Dirk Strauss, Less than 5 minutes ago | 1 author, 1 change
private void BtnTrack_Click(object sender, EventArgs e)
{
    if (!(string.IsNullOrWhiteSpace(txtWaybill.Text)))
    {
        var waybillNum = txtWaybill.Text;
        if (WaybillValid())
        {
            var package = new Package(waybillNum);
       ▶| var packLoc = package.TrackPackage();
            if (packLoc != null)
            Run execution to here
               ......tails.Text = $"Package location: " +
                        $"{packLoc.LocationName} with coordinates " +
                        $"Long: {packLoc.Long} and " +
                        $"Lat: {packLoc.Lat}";
            }
        }
        else          Hover mouse and click
        {
            _ = MessageBox.Show("You have entered an invalid Waybill number");
        }
    }
}
```

***Figure 3-6.*** *Run to Click*

This will advance the debugger to the line of code where you clicked, allowing you to continue stepping through the code from the new location. Quite handy if you do not want to be pressing F10 a gazillion times.

## Run to Cursor

Run to Cursor works similarly to Run to Click. The difference is that with Run to Cursor you are not debugging. With the debugger stopped, you can right-click a line of code and click Run to Cursor from the context menu as seen in Figure 3-7.

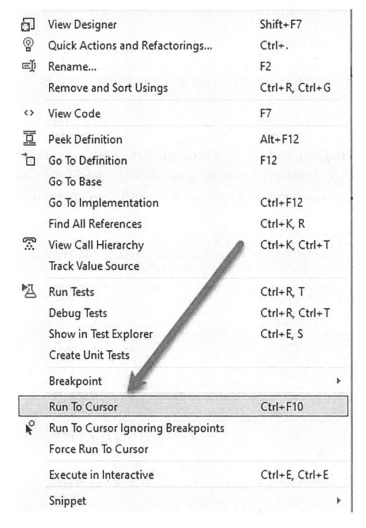

***Figure 3-7.*** *Run to Cursor*

Doing this will start the debugger and set a temporary breakpoint on the line you right-clicked. This is useful for quickly setting a breakpoint and starting the debugger at the same time. When you reach the breakpoint, you can continue debugging as normal.

Be aware though that you will be hitting any other breakpoints set before the temporary breakpoint first. So, you will need to keep on pressing F5 until you reach the line of code you set the temporary breakpoint on.

## Force Run to Cursor

Visual Studio 2022 will now allow you to skip any breakpoints between the line of code your breakpoint is on and the line of code that you want to debug. This is done with Force Run to Cursor on the context menu which can be seen in Figure 3-7. You can also easily access this while debugging as seen in Figure 3-8.

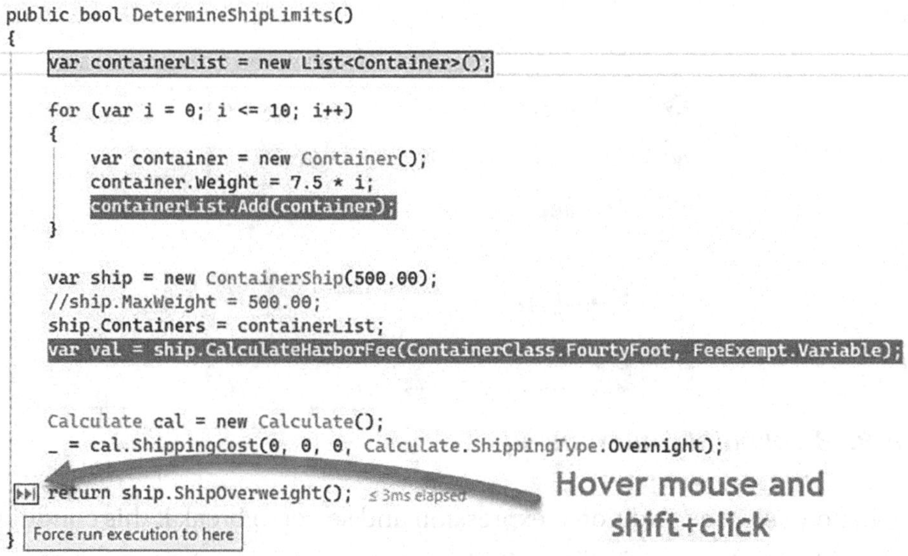

```csharp
public bool DetermineShipLimits()
{
    var containerList = new List<Container>();

    for (var i = 0; i <= 10; i++)
    {
        var container = new Container();
        container.Weight = 7.5 * i;
        containerList.Add(container);
    }

    var ship = new ContainerShip(500.00);
    //ship.MaxWeight = 500.00;
    ship.Containers = containerList;
    var val = ship.CalculateHarborFee(ContainerClass.FourtyFoot, FeeExempt.Variable);

    Calculate cal = new Calculate();
    _ = cal.ShippingCost(0, 0, 0, Calculate.ShippingType.Overnight);

    return ship.ShipOverweight();   ≤ 3ms elapsed
}
```

Hover mouse and shift+click

Force run execution to here

***Figure 3-8.** Force Run to Cursor*

Here, we have a breakpoint at the top of the method that is currently hit, and the debugger is paused. I want to run the cursor to the return statement, but there are two breakpoints between where my debugger is and where I want to be. To skip the breakpoints in the middle, hover the mouse over the line that you want to move to next, and hold down the Shift key. The Run to execution button with the single arrow (as seen in Figure 3-6) now changes to the Force run execution to here button with a double arrow as seen in Figure 3-8. This will now advance the debugger to the line of code you forced the debugger to, skipping all the breakpoints in between. This is especially convenient since I do not have to remove my breakpoints, nor do I have to keep on pressing F5 for each breakpoint hit.

## Conditional Breakpoints and Actions

Sometimes, you need to use a condition to catch a bug. Let's say that you are in a for loop, and the bug seems to be data related. The erroneous data only seems to enter the loop after several hundred iterations. If you set a regular breakpoint, you will be pressing F10 until your keyboard stops working.

This is a perfect use case for using conditional breakpoints. You can now tell the debugger to break when a specific condition is true. To set a conditional breakpoint, right-click the breakpoint, and click Conditions from the context menu as seen in Figure 3-9.

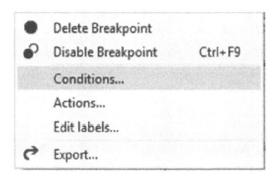

***Figure 3-9.***  *Breakpoint context menu*

You can now select a conditional expression and select to break if this condition is true or when changed as seen in Figure 3-10.

We will discuss Actions shortly.

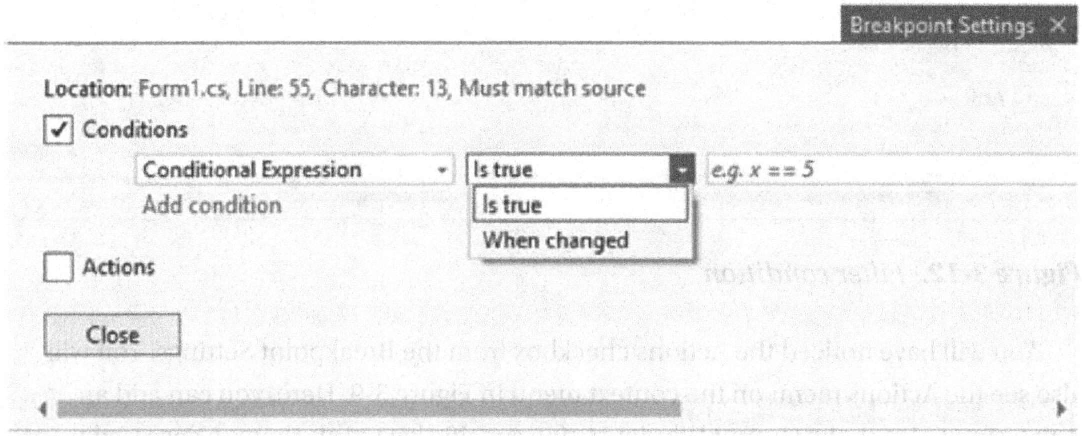

***Figure 3-10.*** *Conditional expression*

You can also select to break when the Hit Count is equal to, a multiple of, or greater or equal to a value you set as seen in Figure 3-11.

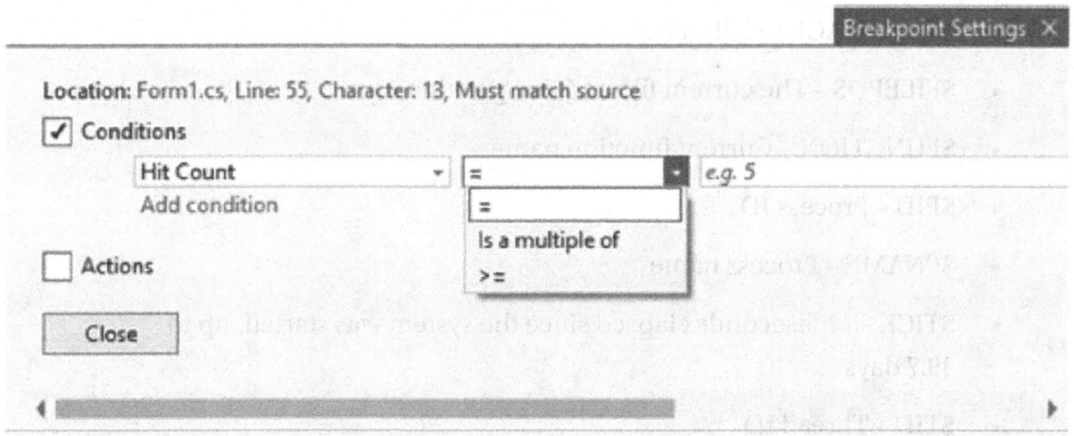

***Figure 3-11.*** *Hit Count condition*

The last condition you can set on a conditional breakpoint is a Filter as seen in Figure 3-12.

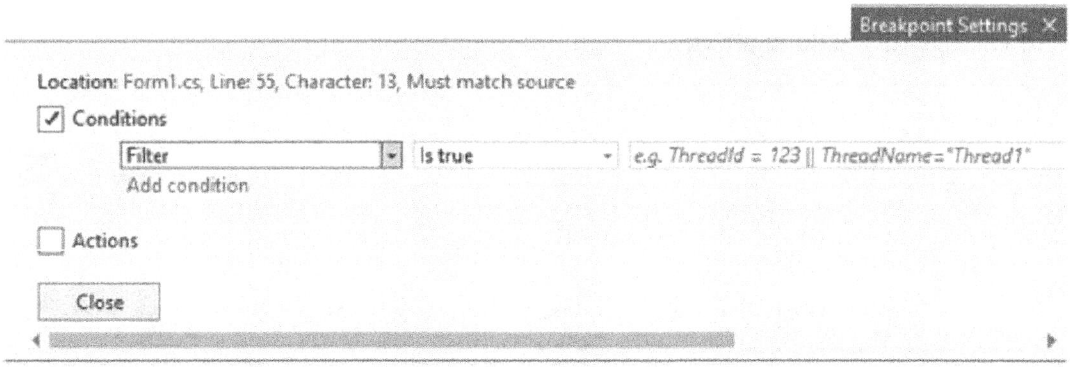

*Figure 3-12.*  *Filter condition*

You will have noticed the Actions checkbox from the Breakpoint Settings. You will also see the Actions menu on the context menu in Figure 3-9. Here, you can add an expression to log to the Output Window using specific keywords that are accessed using the $ symbol.

The special keywords are as follows:

- $ADDRESS – Current instruction

- $CALLER – Previous function name

- $CALLSTACK – Call stack

- $FILEPOS – The current file and line position

- $FUNCTION – Current function name

- $PID – Process ID

- $PNAME – Process name

- $TICK – Milliseconds elapsed since the system was started, up to 49.7 days

- $TID – Thread ID

- $TNAME – Thread name

You can now use these special keywords to write an entry to the Output Window. You can include the value of a variable by placing it between curly braces (think of interpolated strings). Listing 3-3 shows an example of an expression that uses the $FUNCTION keyword.

***Listing 3-3.*** Action Expression

```
The value of the counter = {iCount} in $FUNCTION
```

Placing this breakpoint action in the constructor of the Login() form of the ShipmentLocator application will be indicated by a diamond instead of a circle as seen in Figure 3-13.

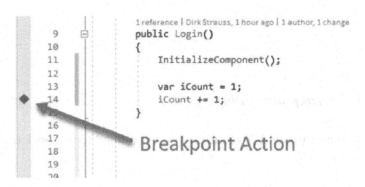

***Figure 3-13.*** *Breakpoint action*

When you run your application, you will see the expression output in the Output Window as seen in Figure 3-14.

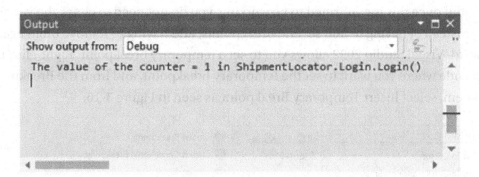

***Figure 3-14.*** *Action expression in Output Window*

This is great for debugging because if you don't select a condition, the Action will be displayed in the Output Window without hitting the breakpoint and pausing the code. The breakpoint action can be seen in Figure 3-15.

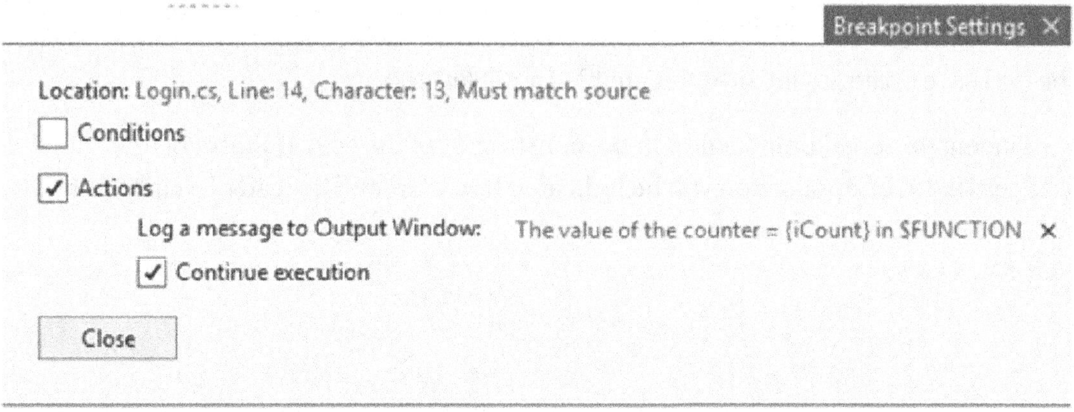

Breakpoint Settings ✕

Location: Login.cs, Line: 14, Character: 13, Must match source

☐ Conditions

☑ Actions

    Log a message to Output Window:    The value of the counter = {iCount} in $FUNCTION  ✕

    ☑ Continue execution

[ Close ]

***Figure 3-15.*** *The breakpoint action*

If you want to pause the code execution, then you need to uncheck the Continue execution checkbox.

# Temporary Breakpoints

There might be times when you only want a breakpoint hit once and never again. A scenario could exist where you need to check the change of a variable in several places, but once this is confirmed to be working, you do not need to check the variable again. Instead of having to add several breakpoints, and having to remove them again afterward, Visual Studio 2022 allows you to set a temporary breakpoint. Right-click the line of code where you want to set the temporary breakpoint, and from the Breakpoint menu item, select Insert Temporary Breakpoint as seen in Figure 3-16.

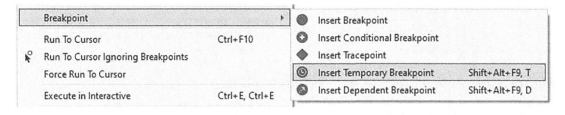

***Figure 3-16.*** *Insert Temporary Breakpoint*

You can also hold down Shift+Alt+F9, T to do the same thing.

# Dependent Breakpoints

If you look at Figure 3-16 again, you will notice an option to insert a dependent breakpoint. A dependent breakpoint is a fantastic addition to Visual Studio because it is a breakpoint that will only pause the debugger when another breakpoint is hit on which it has been marked as a dependent.

As seen in Figure 3-17, you can click the drop-down menu which will show you a list of other breakpoints to choose from. After selecting a dependent breakpoint, the debugger will only pause when the breakpoint you selected from the drop-down is hit.

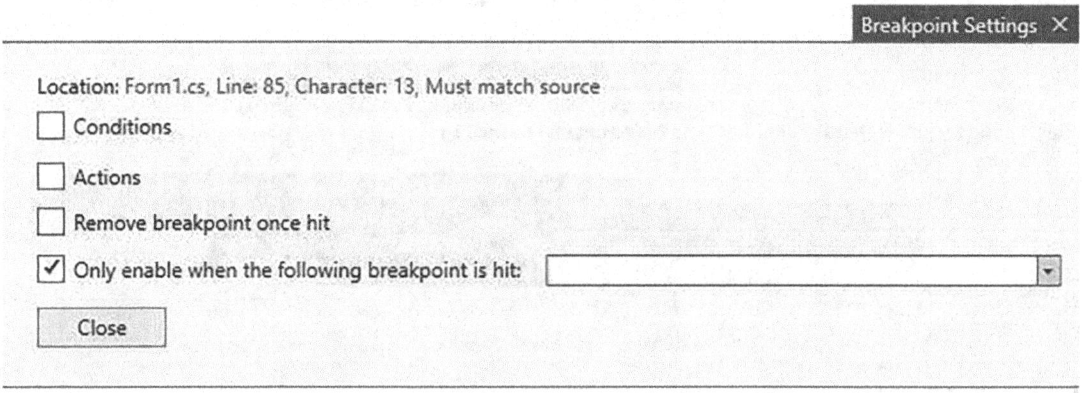

*Figure 3-17.* *Insert a dependent breakpoint*

# Dragging Breakpoints

You can also drag breakpoints to a different line of code. To do this, click and hold on the breakpoint and start dragging your mouse. You can now move it to another line.

# Manage Breakpoints with Labels

As you continue debugging your application, you will be setting many breakpoints throughout the code. Different developers have different ways of debugging. Personally, I add and remove breakpoints as needed, but some developers might end up with a lot of set breakpoints as seen in Figure 3-18.

```
 11
                        1 reference | Dirk Strauss, 18 hours ago | 1 author, 1 change
 12                     private void Form1_Load(object sender, EventArgs e)
 13                     {
 14                         var frmLogin = new Login();
 15                         _ = frmLogin.ShowDialog();
 16
●17                         txtWaybill.Text = GenerateWaybill(WBPartA(), WBPartB(100,2000));
 18                     }
 19

                        1 reference | Dirk Strauss, 18 hours ago | 1 author, 1 change
 20                     private void BtnTrack_Click(object sender, EventArgs e)
 21                     {
 22                         if (!(string.IsNullOrWhiteSpace(txtWaybill.Text)))
 23                         {
●24                             var waybillNum = txtWaybill.Text;
 25                             if (WaybillValid())
 26                             {
●27                                 var package = new Package(waybillNum);
 28                                 var packLoc = package.TrackPackage();
 29                                 if (packLoc != null)
 30                                 {
●31                                     txtLocationDetails.Text = $"Package location: " +
 32                                         $"{packLoc.LocationName} with coordinates " +
 33                                         $"Long: {packLoc.Long} and " +
 34                                         $"Lat: {packLoc.Lat}";
 35                                 }
 36                         }
```

***Figure 3-18.*** *Many breakpoints set*

This is where the Breakpoints window comes in handy. Think of it as mission control for managing complex debugging sessions. This is especially helpful in large solutions where you might have many breakpoints set at various code files throughout your solution.

The Breakpoints window allows developers to manage the breakpoints that they have set by allowing them to search, sort, filter, enable, disable, and delete breakpoints. The Breakpoints window also allows developers to specify conditional breakpoints and actions.

To open the Breakpoints window, click the Debug menu, Windows, and then Breakpoints. You can also press Ctrl+D, Ctrl+B. The Breakpoints window will now be displayed as seen in Figure 3-19.

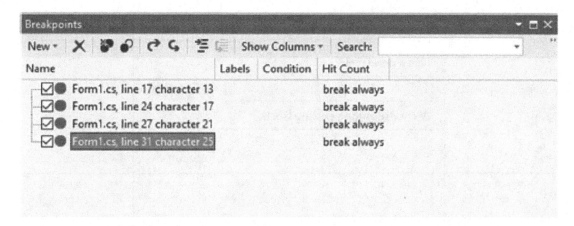

**Figure 3-19.** *Breakpoints window*

Compare the line numbers of the breakpoints listed in Figure 3-19 with the breakpoints displayed in Figure 3-18. You will see that this accurately reflects the breakpoints displayed in the Breakpoints window.

The only problem with this window is that it doesn't help you much in the way of managing your breakpoints. At the moment, the only information displayed in the Breakpoints window is the class name and the line number.

This is where breakpoint labels are very beneficial. To set a breakpoint label, right-click a breakpoint, and click Edit labels from the context menu as seen in Figure 3-20.

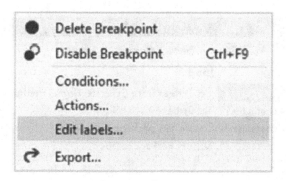

**Figure 3-20.** *Edit breakpoint labels*

The Edit breakpoint labels window is then displayed as seen in Figure 3-21.

**Figure 3-21.** *Add a new breakpoint label*

You can type in a new label or choose from any of the existing labels available. If you swing back to the Breakpoints window, you will see that these labels are displayed (Figure 3-22), making the identification and management of your breakpoints much easier.

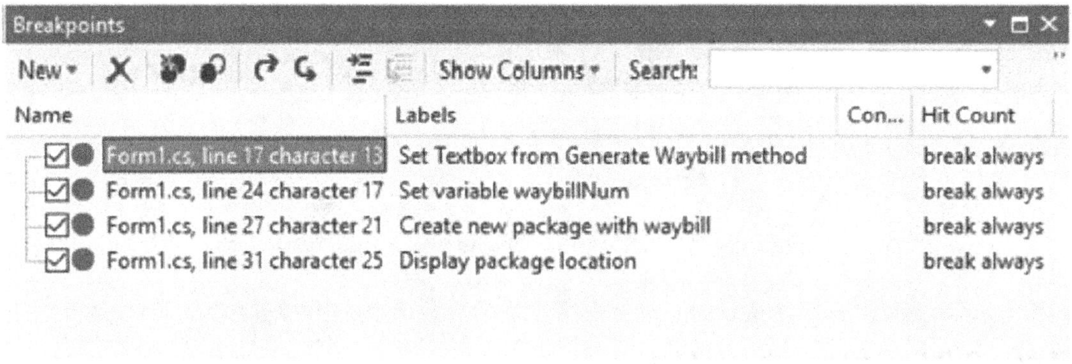

**Figure 3-22.** *Breakpoints window with labels set*

You are in a better position now with the breakpoint labels set to manage your breakpoints more effectively.

# Exporting Breakpoints

If you would like to save the current state and location of the breakpoints you have set, Visual Studio allows you to export and import breakpoints. This will create an XML file with the exported breakpoints that you can then share with a colleague.

---

I foresee the use of Visual Studio Live Share replacing the need to share breakpoints with a colleague just for the sake of aiding in debugging an application. There are, however, other situations I can see exporting breakpoints as being beneficial.

---

To export your breakpoints, you can right-click a breakpoint and click Export from the context menu, or you can click the export button in the Breakpoints window. You can also import breakpoints from the Breakpoints window by clicking the export or import button as highlighted in Figure 3-23.

***Figure 3-23.*** *Import or export breakpoints*

I'm not too convinced that the icons used on the import and export buttons are indicative of importing and exporting something, but that is just my personal opinion.

# Using DataTips

DataTips in Visual Studio allows developers to view information about variables during a debug session. You can only view DataTips in break mode, and DataTips only work with variables that are currently in scope.

This means that before you can see a DataTip, you are going to have to debug your code. Place a breakpoint somewhere in your code and start debugging. When you hit the breakpoint that you have set, you can hover your mouse cursor over a variable. The DataTip now appears showing the name of the variable and the value it currently holds. You can also pin this DataTip as seen in Figure 3-24.

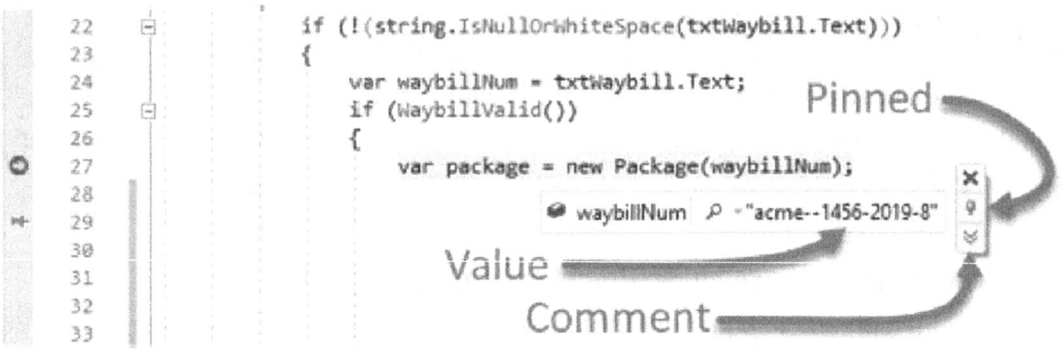

```
22      if (!(string.IsNullOrWhiteSpace(txtWaybill.Text)))
23      {
24          var waybillNum = txtWaybill.Text;
25          if (WaybillValid())
26          {
27              var package = new Package(waybillNum);
28
29                  ● waybillNum    ρ ▾ "acme--1456-2019-8"
30
31
32
33
```

Pinned

Value

Comment

*Figure 3-24.  Debugger DataTip*

When you pin a DataTip, a pin will appear in the gutter next to the line number. You can now move this DataTip around to another position on the screen. If you look below the pin icon on the DataTip, you will see a "double down arrow" icon. If you click this, you can add a comment to your DataTip as seen in Figure 3-25.

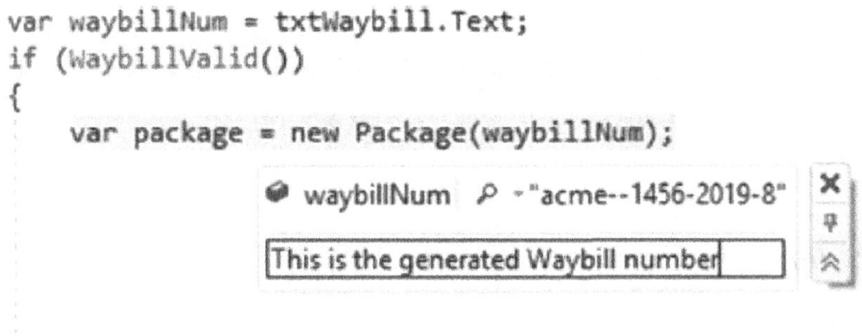

```
var waybillNum = txtWaybill.Text;
if (WaybillValid())
{
    var package = new Package(waybillNum);

        ● waybillNum   ρ ▾ "acme--1456-2019-8"    ✕
                                                   ⚲
        This is the generated Waybill number      ≫
```

*Figure 3-25.  DataTip comment*

DataTips also allow you to edit the value of the variable, as long as the value isn't read-only. To do this, simply select the value in the DataTip and enter a new value. Then press the Enter key to save the new value.

# Visualizing Complex Data Types

DataTips also allow you to visualize complex data in a more meaningful way. To illustrate this, we will need to write a little bit of code. We are going to create a class, then create a list of that class, and then create a data table from that list that we will view in the DataTip. I have just created a small Console Application. Start by creating the class in Listing 3-4.

***Listing 3-4.*** The Subject Class

```
public class Subject
{
    public int SubjectCode { get; set; }
    public string SubjectDescription { get; set; }
}
```

We are going to create a list of the Subject class. Before we do this, however, we need to write the code that is going to create a DataTable of the values in List<Subject>. This code is illustrated in Listing 3-5.

***Listing 3-5.*** Convert List to DataTable

```
static DataTable ConvertListToDataTable<T>(List<T> list)
{
    var table = new DataTable();
    var properties = typeof(T).GetProperties();
    foreach (var prop in properties)
    {
        _ = table.Columns.Add(prop.Name);
    }
    foreach (var item in list)
    {
        var row = table.NewRow();
        foreach (var property in properties)
        {
            var name = property.Name;
            var value = property.GetValue(item, null);
            row[name] = value;
        }
        table.Rows.Add(row);
    }
    return table;
}
```

In the Main method, add the code in Listing 3-6. We will then place a breakpoint on the call to the ConvertListToDataTable() method and step over that so that we can inspect the table variable's DataTip.

**Listing 3-6.** Create the List<Subject> and the DataTable

```
static void Main(string[] args)
{
    var lstSubjects = new List<Subject>();
    for (var i = 0; i <= 5; i++)
    {
        var sub = new Subject();
        sub.SubjectCode = i;
        sub.SubjectDescription = $"Subject-{i}";
        lstSubjects.Add(sub);
    }
    var table = ConvertListToDataTable<Subject>(lstSubjects);
}
```

When you hover over the table variable, you will see that the DataTip displays a magnifying glass icon as seen in Figure 3-26.

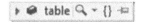

**Figure 3-26.**  *The table variable DataTip*

If you click the magnifying glass icon, you will see the contents of the table variable displayed in a nice graphical way as seen in Figure 3-27.

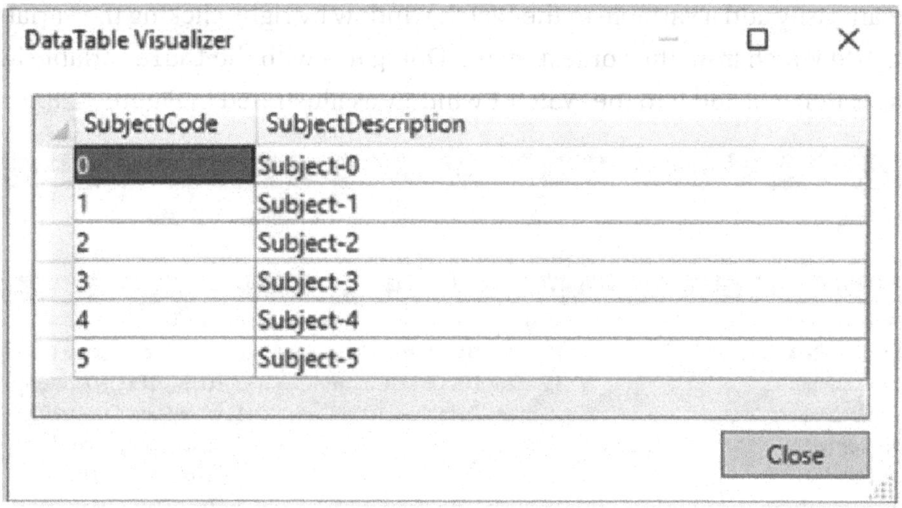

**Figure 3-27.** *DataTable Visualizer*

The magnifying glass icon tells us that one or more visualizers are available for the variable, in this example, the DataTable Visualizer.

## Bonus Tip

If you are feeling adventurous, pin the DataTip that is displayed when hovering over the table variable, and right-click the pinned DataTip. You can now copy the value, copy the expression, add a new expression, and remove the expression previously added. Go ahead and add the expression in Listing 3-7.

**Listing 3-7.** Add a DataTip Expression

```
table.Rows.Count
```

This is great if you forgot to add a variable watch or just want to see some additional info regarding the variable in the DataTip.

## Using the Watch Window

The Watch window allows us to keep track of the value of one or more variables and also allows us to see how these variable values change as one steps through the code.

You can easily add a variable to the Watch window by right-clicking the variable and selecting Add Watch from the context menu. Doing this with the `table` variable in the previous section will add it to the Watch 1 window as illustrated in Figure 3-28.

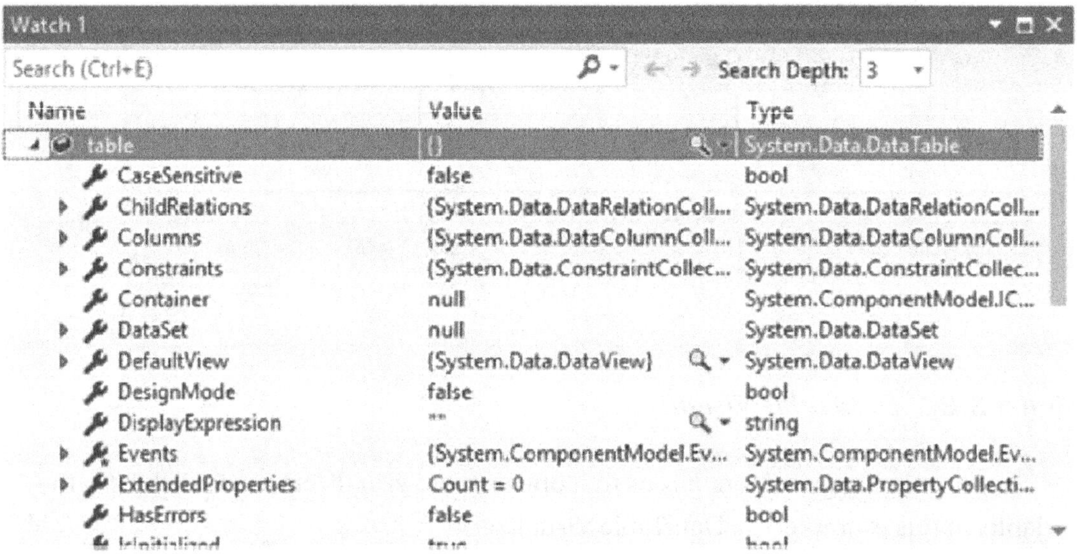

***Figure 3-28.***  *The Watch 1 window*

Here, you can open the visualizer by clicking the magnifying glass icon or expanding the `table` variable to view the other properties of the object. I use the Watch window often as it is a convenient way to keep track of several variables at once.

# The DebuggerDisplay Attribute

In the previous section, we discussed how to add a variable to the Watch window in Visual Studio. We saw that we can view the value of a variable or variables easily from this single window.

Using the same code we wrote in the previous section, add the variable called `lstSubjects` to the Watch window, and expand the variable. You will see the values of the `lstSubjects` variable listed as `{VisualStudioDebugging.Subject}` in the Value column as seen in Figure 3-29.

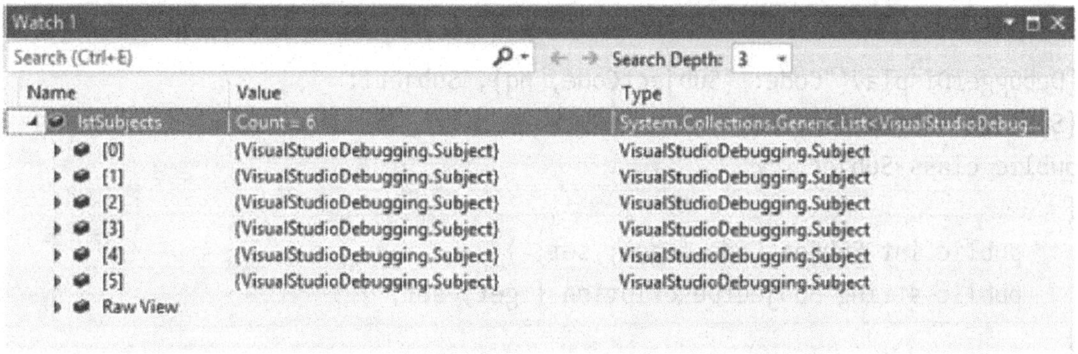

**Figure 3-29.** *The lstSubjects variable values*

To view the values of each item in the list, we need to expand the list item (Figure 3-30) and inspect the values.

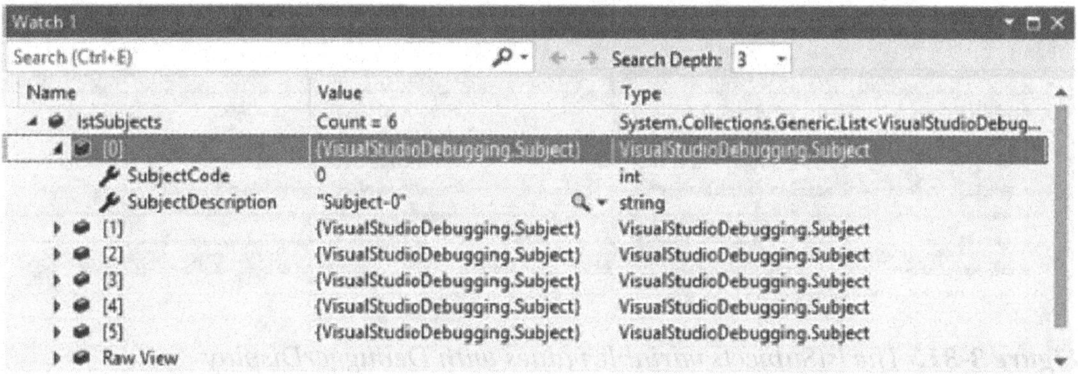

**Figure 3-30.** *View list item values*

This will quickly become rather tedious, especially when you are dealing with a rather large list, and you are looking for a specific value.

This is where the DebuggerDisplay attribute comes into play. We are going to modify the Subject class.

---

Ensure that you add the statement using System.Diagnostics to your code file.

---

Modify your Subject class as in Listing 3-8.

*Listing 3-8.* Modified Subject Class

```
[DebuggerDisplay("Code: {SubjectCode, nq}, Subject:
{SubjectDescription, nq}")]
public class Subject
{
    public int SubjectCode { get; set; }
    public string SubjectDescription { get; set; }
}
```

Start debugging your code again and have a look at your Watch window after adding the DebuggerDisplay attribute. Your item values are more readable as seen in Figure 3-31.

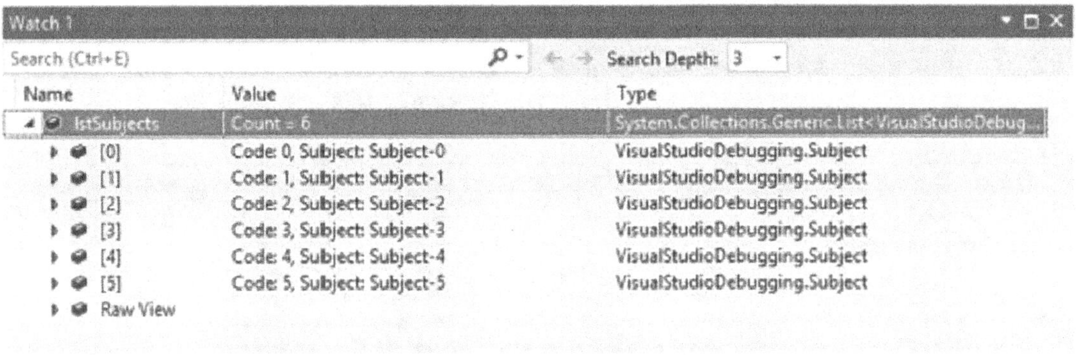

*Figure 3-31.* *The lstSubjects variable values with DebuggerDisplay*

The use of "nq" in the DebuggerDisplay attribute will remove the quotes when the final value is displayed. The "nq" means "no quotes."

# Evaluate Functions Without Side Effects

While debugging an application, we probably do not want the state of the application to change because of an expression we are evaluating. It is, unfortunately, a fact that evaluating some expressions might cause side effects.

To illustrate this, we will need to write some more code. We will be creating a class called Student that contains a List of Subject as seen in Listing 3-9.

***Listing 3-9.*** The Student Class

```
public class Student
{
    private List<Subject> _subjectList;
    public Student() { }
    public Student(List<Subject> subjects) => _subjectList = subjects;
    public bool HasSubjects() => _subjectList != null;
    public List<Subject> StudentSubjects
    {
        get
        {
            if (_subjectList == null)
            {
                _subjectList = new List<Subject>();
            }
            return _subjectList;
        }
    }
}
```

In this class, we have a HasSubjects() method that simply returns a Boolean indicating if the Student class contains a list of subjects. We also have a property called StudentSubjects that returns the list of subjects. If the list of subjects is null, it creates a new instance of List<Subject>.

It is here that the side effect is caused. If the HasSubjects() method returns false, calling the StudentSubjects property will change the value of HasSubjects().

This is better illustrated in the following screenshots. Create a new instance of Student and place a breakpoint right after that line of code (Figure 3-32).

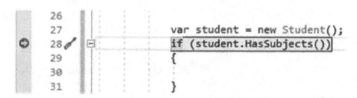

***Figure 3-32.*** *Place a breakpoint after Student*

If we now use the Watch window to look at the value returned by the HasSubjects() method, we will see that it returns false (Figure 3-33).

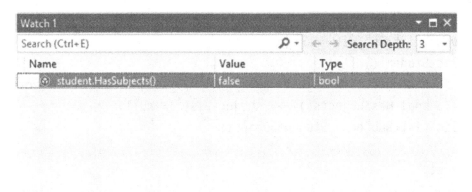

***Figure 3-33.*** *HasSubjects() method returns false*

When we call the StudentSubjects property, we see this side effect come into play in Figure 3-34. As soon as this property is called, the value of the HasSubjects() method changes.

This means that the state of our Student class has changed because of an expression that we ran in the Watch window.

This can cause all sorts of issues further down the debugging path, and sometimes the change might be so subtle that you don't even notice it. You could end up chasing "bugs" that never really were bugs to begin with.

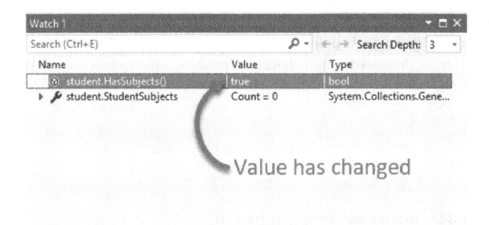

***Figure 3-34.*** *HasSubjects() method value has changed*

To prevent any side effects from an expression, just add nse to the end of the expression as seen in Figure 3-35.

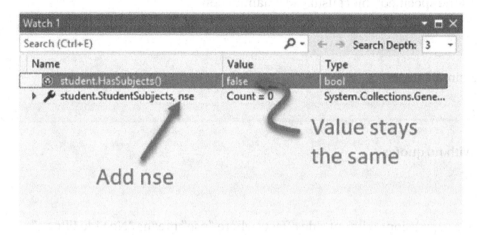

**Figure 3-35.**  *Adding nse to the expression to evaluate*

This time, the value of the HasSubjects() method remains the same, which means that the state of your class remains unchanged. As you have probably guessed by now, the nse added after the expression stands for "No Side Effects."

# Format Specifiers

Format specifiers allow you to control the format in which a value is displayed in the Watch window. Format specifiers can also be used in the Immediate and Command window. Using a format specifier is as easy as entering the variable expression and typing a comma followed by the format specifier you want to use. The following are the C# format specifiers for the Visual Studio debugger.

## ac

Force evaluation of an expression decimal integer

## d

Decimal integer

## dynamic

Displays the specified object using a Dynamic View

## h

Hexadecimal integer

## nq

String with no quotes

## nse

Evaluates expressions without side effects where "nse" means "No Side Effects"

## hidden

Displays all public and nonpublic members

## raw

Displays item as it appears in the raw node. Valid on proxy objects only

## results

Used with a variable that implements IEnumerable or IEnumerable<T>. Displays only members that contain the query result

You will recall that we used the "nq" format specifier with the DebuggerDisplay attribute discussed in a previous section.

# Diagnostic Tools

Visual Studio gives developers access to performance measurement and profiling tools. The performance of your application should, therefore, be high on your priority list. An application that suffers from significant performance issues is as good as broken (especially from an end user's perspective).

Visual Studio Diagnostic Tools might be enabled by default. If not, enable Diagnostic Tools by going to the Tools menu and clicking Options, Debugging, and then General. Ensure that Enable Diagnostic Tools while debugging is checked as seen in Figure 3-36.

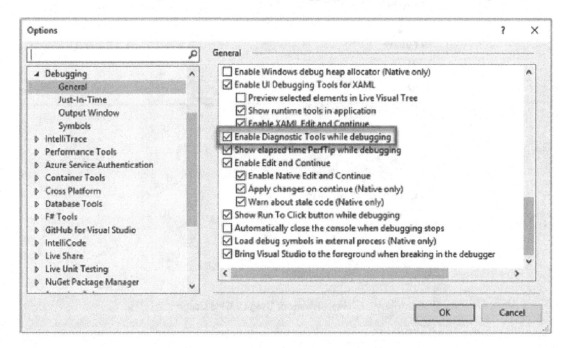

***Figure 3-36.*** *Enable Diagnostic Tools*

This will ensure that the Diagnostic Tools window opens automatically when you start debugging. When we start debugging our ShipmentLocator Windows Forms application, the Diagnostic Tools window will be displayed as seen in Figure 3-37.

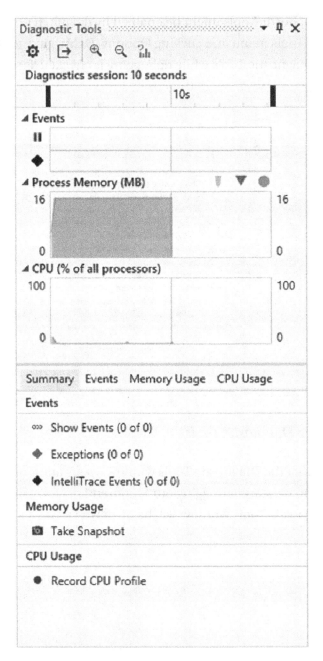

***Figure 3-37.*** *Diagnostic Tools*

With our Windows Forms application, you can use Diagnostic Tools to monitor memory or CPU usage as seen in Figure 3-38.

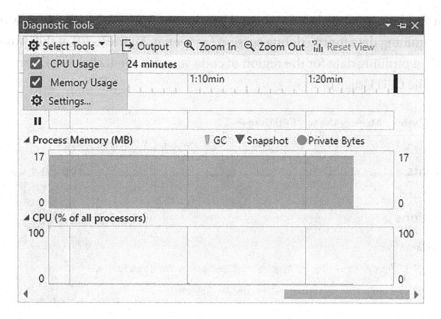

**Figure 3-38.** *Select what to analyze*

As you debug your application, you can see the CPU usage, memory usage, and other performance-related information.

# CPU Usage

A great place to start your performance analysis is the CPU Usage tab. Place two breakpoints in your Form1_Load at the start and end of the function (Figure 3-39) and start debugging.

```
11
                 1 reference | Dirk Strauss, 5 days ago | 1 author, 1 change
12               private void Form1_Load(object sender, EventArgs e)
13               {
14                   var frmLogin = new Login();
15                   _ = frmLogin.ShowDialog();
16
17                   txtWaybill.Text = GenerateWaybill(WBPartA(), WBPartB(100,2000));
18                   this.Text = $"Shipment Locator - {DateTime.Now.Year}";
19               }
```

**Figure 3-39.** *Setting breakpoints to analyze CPU usage*

When the debugger reaches the second breakpoint, you will be able to view the summary profiling data for the debug session (as seen in Figure 3-40) at that point. To view detailed profiling data for the region of code you analyzed, click the Open details link under the CPU Usage tab.

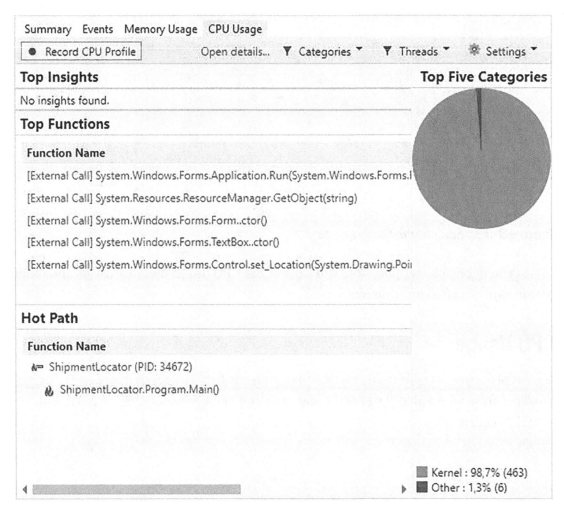

*Figure 3-40.* *CPU usage analysis results*

As seen in Figure 3-41, you can view the functions by changing the Current View to Functions in the drop-down.

| CPU Usage  ⊣ ✕  Package.cs          Login.cs          Form1.cs          Form1.cs [Design]        ▾ ⚙ |
|---|
| Current View:  Functions  ✕                                          Search                    🔎 ▾ |

| Function Name | Total CPU [unit, %] ▾ |
|---|---|
| [External Call] System.Windows.Forms.TextBox..ctor() | 12 (2,5 |
| [External Call] System.Windows.Forms.Control.set_Location(System.Drawing.Point) | 11 (2,3 |
| [External Call] System.Windows.Forms.Form+ControlCollection.Add(System.Windo... | 6 (1,2 |
| ShipmentLocator.Form1.Form1_Load(object, System.EventArgs) | 6 (1,2 |
| ShipmentLocator.Login.BtnLogin_Click(object, System.EventArgs) | 4 (0,8 |
| ShipmentLocator.Login.ctor() | 4 (0,8 |
| [External Call] System.DateTime.get_Now() | 2 (0,4 |
| ShipmentLocator.Form1.GenerateWaybill(string, int) | 2 (0,4 |
| [External Call] System.Windows.Forms.Application.EnableVisualStyles() | 1 (0,2 |
| [External Call] System.Windows.Forms.Application.EnableVisualStylesInternal(string,... | 1 (0,2 |
| ShipmentLocator.Login.InitializeComponent() | 1 (0,2 |

*Figure 3-41. The Current View filtered by functions*

If any of the functions in the CPU Usage pane seem to be problematic, double-click
the function and then change the Current View to Caller/Callee to view a more detailed
three-pane view of the analysis. As seen in Figure 3-42, the left pane will contain the
calling function, the middle will contain the selected function, and any called functions
will be displayed in the right pane.

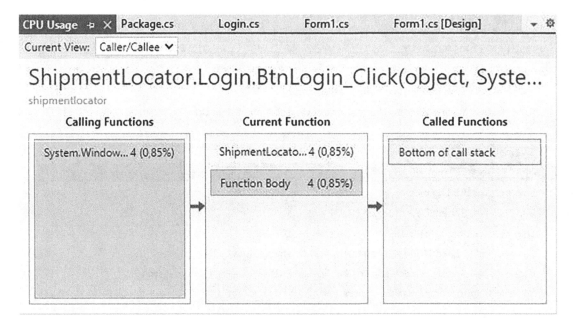

**Figure 3-42.** *Butterfly view of BtnLogin_Click*

In the Current Function pane, you will see the Function Body section which details the time spent in the function body. As seen in Figure 3-43, you will also see the code represented for this function.

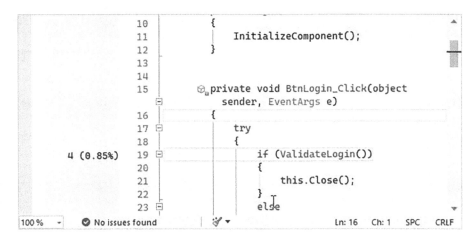

**Figure 3-43.** *The code for the function*

Because this excludes the calling and called functions, you get a better understanding of the function you are evaluating and can determine if it is the performance bottleneck or not.

# Memory Usage

Visual Studio Diagnostic Tools allows developers to see what the change in memory usage is. This is done by taking snapshots. When you start debugging, place a breakpoint on a method you suspect is causing a memory issue. Then you step over the method and place another breakpoint. An increase is indicated with a red up arrow as seen in Figure 3-44.

This is often the best way to analyze memory issues. Two snapshots will give you a nice diff and allow you to see exactly what has changed.

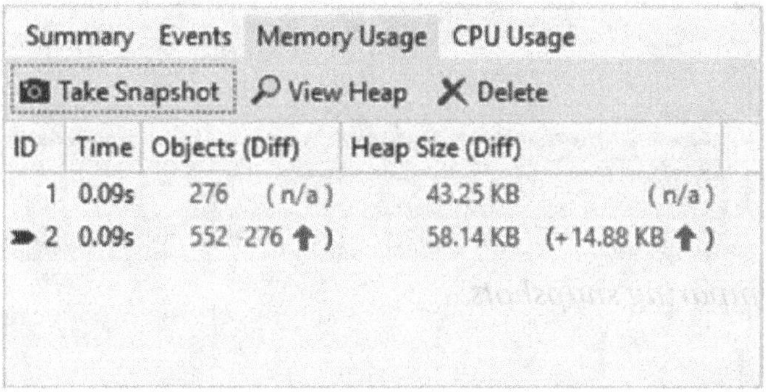

*Figure 3-44. Memory usage snapshots*

You can also compare two snapshots by clicking one of the links in the memory usage snapshots (Figure 3-44) and viewing the comparison in the snapshot window that opens (Figure 3-45). By selecting a snapshot in the Compare to drop-down list, you can see what has changed.

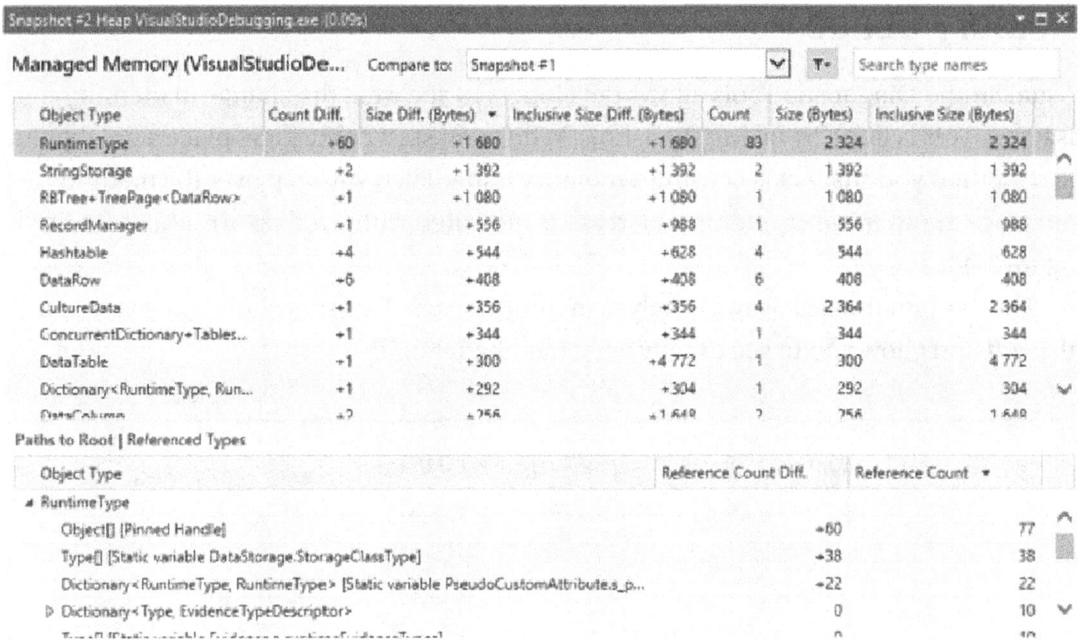

*Figure 3-45.* *Comparing snapshots*

# The Events View

As you step through your application, the Events view will show you the different events that happen during your debug session. This can be setting a breakpoint or stepping through code. It also shows you the duration of the event as seen in Figure 3-46.

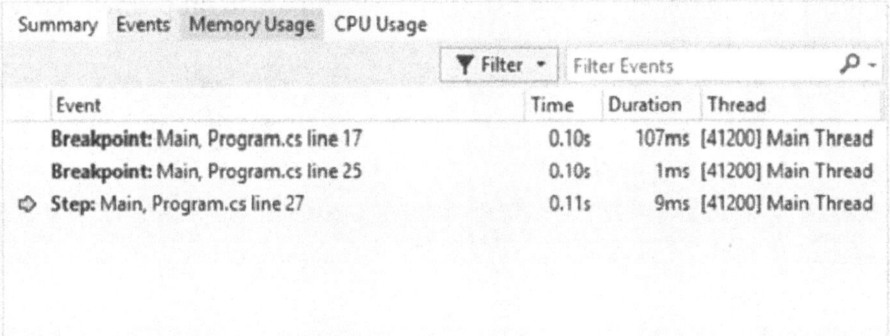

*Figure 3-46.* *The Events view*

This means that as you step through your code, the Events tab will display the time the code took to run from the previous step operation to the next. You can also see the same events displayed as PerfTips in the Visual Studio code editor as seen in Figure 3-47.

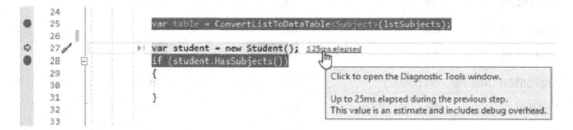

***Figure 3-47.*** *PerfTips in the code editor*

IntelliTrace events are available in this tab if you have Visual Studio Enterprise.

---

For a comparison of the Visual Studio 2022 Editions, head on over to `https://visualstudio.microsoft.com/vs/compare/` and see what each edition has to offer.

---

PerfTips allows developers to quickly identify potential issues in your code.

# The Right Tool for the Right Project Type

Table 3-1 shows which tools Visual Studio offers and the project types that can make use of these tools.

*Table 3-1.*  *Performance Tools for Project Types*

| Performance Tool | Windows Desktop | UWP | ASP.NET/ASP.NET Core |
|---|---|---|---|
| CPU Usage | Yes | Yes | Yes |
| Memory Usage | Yes | Yes | Yes |
| GPU Usage | Yes | Yes | No |
| Application Timeline | Yes (XAML) | Yes | No |
| PerfTips | Yes | Yes | Yes |
| Performance Explorer | No | No | No |
| IntelliTrace | .NET with VS Enterprise only | .NET with VS Enterprise only | .NET with VS Enterprise only |
| Events viewer | Yes | Yes | Yes |
| .NET Async | Yes (.NET only) | Yes | Yes |
| .NET Counters | Yes (.NET Core only) | No | Yes (ASP.NET Core only) |
| Database | Yes (.NET Core only) | No | Yes (ASP.NET Core only) |
| .NET Object Allocation | Yes (.NET only) | Yes | Yes |

# Immediate Window

The Immediate Window in Visual Studio allows you to debug and evaluate expressions, execute statements, and print the values of variables. If you don't see the Immediate Window, go to the Debug menu, and select Windows, and click Immediate or hold down Ctrl+D, Ctrl+I.

Let's place a breakpoint in one of our for loops as seen in Figure 3-48.

```
15              {
16                  var lstSubjects = new List<Subject>();
17                  for (var i = 0; i <= 5; i++)
18                  {
19                      var sub = new Subject();
20                      sub.SubjectCode = i;
21                      sub.SubjectDescription = $"Subject-{i}";
22                      lstSubjects.Add(sub);
23                  }
```

**Figure 3-48.** *Breakpoint hit*

Opening up the Immediate Window and typing in sub.SubjectDescription will display its value as seen in Figure 3-49.

You can also use ? sub.SubjectDescription to view the value of the variable.

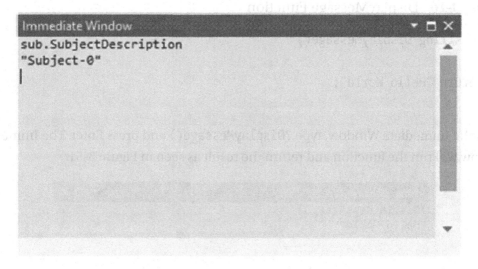

**Figure 3-49.** *Immediate Window*

If you had entered sub.SubjectDescription = "Math", you would be updating the value from "Subject-0" to "Math" as seen in Figure 3-50.

```
for (var i = 0; i <= 5; i++)
{
    var sub = new Subject();
    sub.SubjectCode = i;
    sub.SubjectDescription = $"Subject-{i}";
    lstSubjects.Add(sub);
} ≤1ms
```

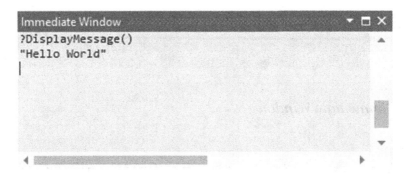

*Figure 3-50.* *Variable value changed*

You can also execute a function at design time (i.e., while not debugging) using the Immediate Window. Add the code in Listing 3-10 to your project.

*Listing 3-10.* DisplayMessage Function

```
static string DisplayMessage()
{
    return "Hello World";
}
```

In the Immediate Window, type `?DisplayMessage()` and press Enter. The Immediate Window will run the function and return the result as seen in Figure 3-51.

```
Immediate Window                              ▾ ☐ ✕
?DisplayMessage()
"Hello World"
|
```

*Figure 3-51.* *Execute the DisplayMessage function*

Any breakpoints contained in the function will break the execution at the breakpoint. Use the debugger to examine the program state.

# Attaching to a Running Process

Attaching to a process allows the Visual Studio Debugger to attach to a running process on the local machine or a remote computer. With the process you want to debug already running, select Debug and click Attach to Process as seen in Figure 3-52. You can also hold down Ctrl+Alt+P to open the Attach to Process window.

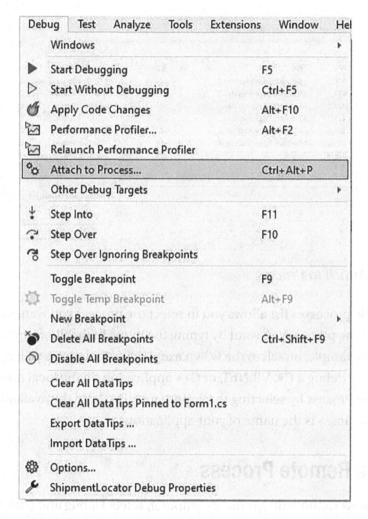

*Figure 3-52.* *Attach to Process*

The Attach to Process window is then displayed (Figure 3-53). The connection type must be set to Default, and the connection target must be set to your local machine name.

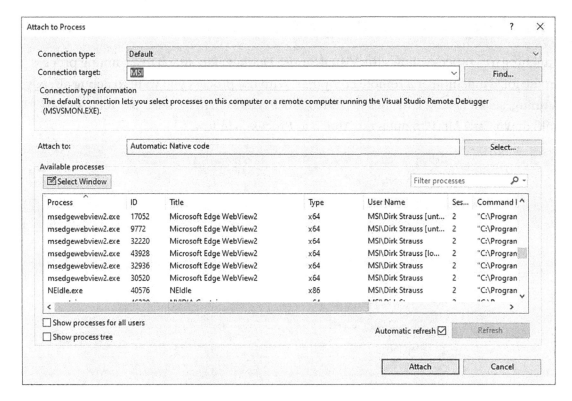

**Figure 3-53.** *Attach to Process*

The available processes list allows you to select the process you want to attach to. You can quickly find the process you want by typing the name in the filter process text box.

You can, for example, attach to the w3wp.exe process to debug a web application running on IIS. To debug a C#, VB.NET, or C++ application on the local machine, you can use the Attach to Process by selecting the <appname>.exe from the available processes list (where <appname> is the name of your application).

## Attach to a Remote Process

To debug a process running on a remote computer, select Debug and click Attach to Process menu, or hold down Ctrl+Alt+P to open the Attach to Process window. This time, select the remote computer name in the Connection target by selecting it from the drop-down list or typing the name in the connection target text box and pressing Enter.

If you are unable to connect to the remote computer using the computer name, use the IP and port address.

## Remote Debugger Port Assignments

The port assignments for the Visual Studio Remote Debugger are as follows:

- Visual Studio 2022: 4026

- Visual Studio 2019: 4024

- Visual Studio 2017: 4022

- Visual Studio 2015: 4020

- Visual Studio 2013: 4018

- Visual Studio 2012: 4016

The port assigned to the Remote Debugger is incremented by two for each release of Visual Studio.

# Reattaching to a Process

Starting with Visual Studio 2017, you can quickly reattach to a process you previously attached to. To do this, you can click the Debug menu and select Reattach to Process or hold down Shift+Alt+P. The debugger will try to attach to the last process you attached by matching the previous process ID to the list of running processes. If that fails, it tries to attach to a process by matching the name. If neither is successful, the Attach to Process window is displayed and lets you select the correct process. The option to reattach to a process you previously attached will only be available if you had previously attached to it.

# Remote Debugging

Sometimes, you need to debug an application that has already been deployed to a different computer. Visual Studio allows you to do this via remote debugging. To start, you need to download and install remote tools for Visual Studio 2022 on the remote computer.

Remote tools for Visual Studio 2022 enables app deployment, remote debugging, testing, profiling, and unit testing on computers that don't have Visual Studio 2022 installed.

# System Requirements

The supported operating systems for the remote computer must be one of the following:

- Windows 11

- Windows 10 (not phone)

- Windows 8 or 8.1 (not phone)

- Windows 7 SP 1

- Windows Server 2016

- Windows Server 2012 or Windows Server 2012 R2

- Windows Server 2008 SP 2, Windows Server 2008 R2 Service Pack 1

The supported hardware configurations to enable remote debugging are detailed in the following list:

- 1.6 GHz or faster processor

- 1 GB of RAM (1.5 GB if running on a VM)

- 1 GB of available hard disk space

- 5400 RPM hard drive

- DirectX 9-capable video card running at 1024 x 768 or higher display resolution

The remote computer and your local machine (the machine containing Visual Studio) must both be connected over a network, workgroup, or homegroup. The two machines can also be connected directly via an Ethernet cable.

---

Take note that trying to debug two computers connected through a proxy is not supported.

---

It is also not recommended to debug via a dial-up connection (do those still exist?) or over the Internet across geographical locations. The high latency or low bandwidth will make debugging unacceptably slow.

# Download and Install Remote Tools

Connect to the remote machine and download and install the correct version of the remote tools required for your version of Visual Studio. The link to download the remote tools compatible with all versions of Visual Studio 2022 is `https://visualstudio.microsoft.com/downloads#remote-tools-for-visual-studio-2022`.

---

If you are using Visual Studio 2017, for example, download the latest update of remote tools for Visual Studio 2017.

---

Also, be sure to download the remote tools with the same architecture as the remote computer. This means that even if your app is a 32-bit application, and your remote computer is running a 64-bit operating system, download the 64-bit version of the remote tools.

Install the remote tools and click Install after agreeing to the license terms and conditions (Figure 3-54).

***Figure 3-54.*** *Remote tools for Visual Studio 2022*

# Running Remote Tools

After the installation has been completed on the remote machine, run the Remote Debugger application as Administrator if you can. To do this, right-click the Remote Debugger app, and click Run as Administrator.

At this point, you might be presented with a Remote Debugging Configuration dialog box as seen in Figure 3-55.

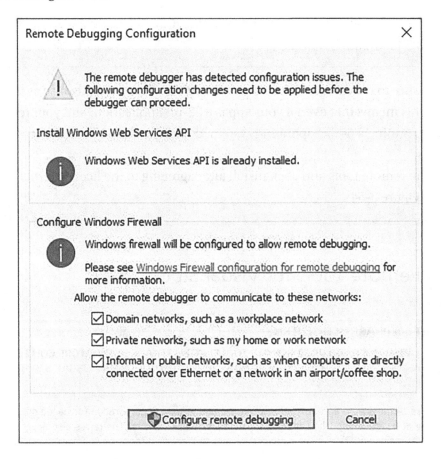

*Figure 3-55.* *Remote Debugging Configuration*

If you encounter this window, it possibly means that there is a configuration issue that you need to resolve. The Remote Debugging Configuration dialog box will prompt you to correct configuration errors it picks up. Do this by clicking the Configure remote debugging button.

You will then see the Remote Debugger window as seen in Figure 3-56.

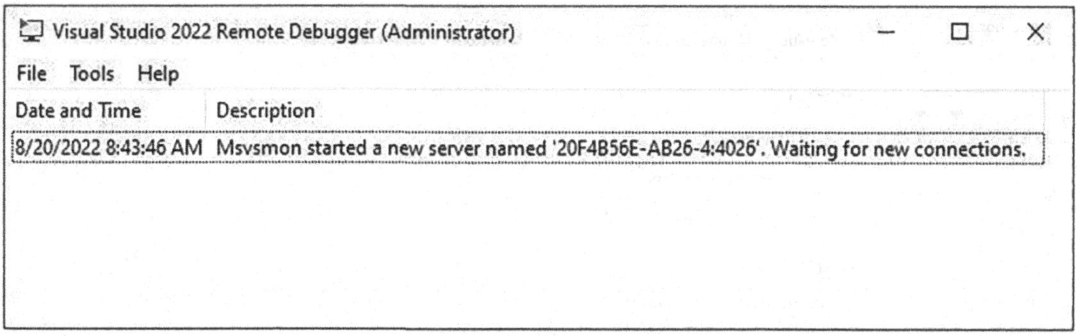

*Figure 3-56.*  *Visual Studio 2022 Remote Debugger*

You are now ready to start remote debugging your application.

## Start Remote Debugging

The great thing about the Remote Debugger on the remote computer is that it tells you the server name to connect to. In Figure 3-56, you can see that the server is named 20F4B56E-AB26-4:4026 where 4026 is the port assignment for Visual Studio 2022. Make a note of this server name and port number.

In your application, set a breakpoint somewhere in the code such as in a button click event handler. Now right-click the project in the Solution Explorer and click Properties. The project properties page opens as seen in Figure 3-57.

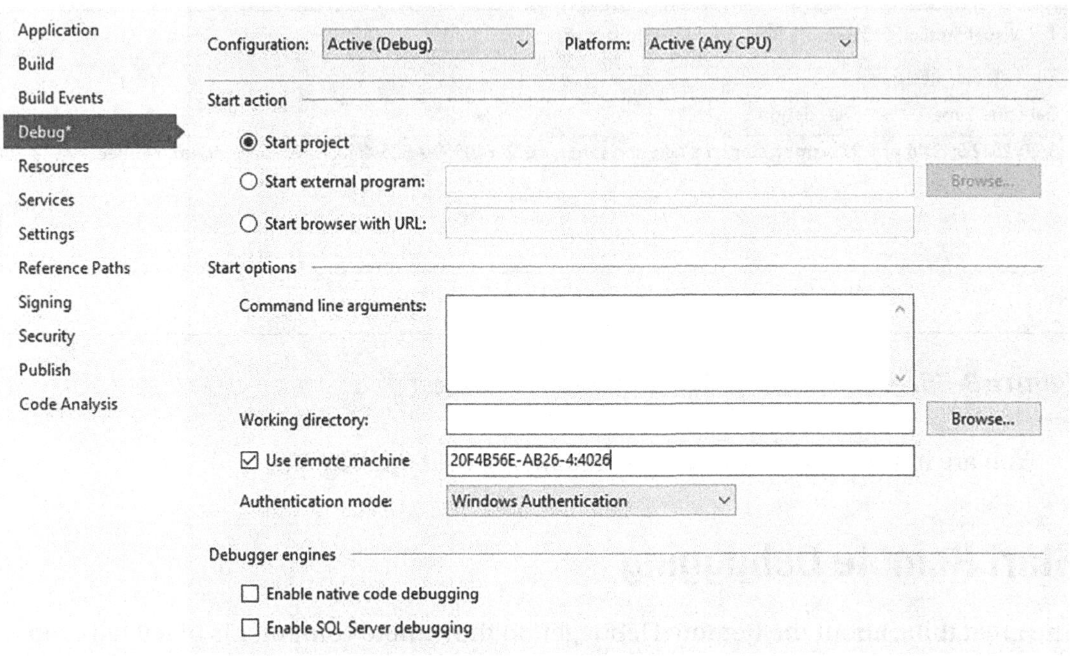

**Figure 3-57.** *Project properties page*

Now, perform the following steps to remotely debug your application:

1. Click the Debug tab, check the Use remote machine checkbox, and enter the remote machine name and port noted earlier. In our example, this is `20F4B56E-AB26-4:4026`.

2. Make sure that you leave the Working directory text box empty and do not check Enable native code debugging.

3. When all this is done, save the properties and build your project.

4. You now need to create a folder on the remote computer that is the same path as the Debug folder on your local machine (the Visual Studio machine). For example, the path to the project Debug folder on my local machine is `<source path> ShipmentLocatorApp\VisualStudioRemoteDebug\bin\Debug`. Create this same path on the remote machine.

5. Copy the executable that was just created by the build you performed in step 3 to the newly created Debug folder on the remote computer.

Be aware that any changes to your code or rebuilds to your project will require you to repeat step 5.

6. Ensure that the Remote Debugger is running on the remote computer. The description (Figure 3-56) should state that it is waiting for new connections.

7. On your local machine, start debugging your application, and if prompted, enter the credentials for the remote machine to log on. Once logged on, you will see that the Remote Debugger on the remote computer displays that the remote debug session is now active (Figure 3-58). A point to note here is that if you trust the network that you are debugging across, and you are having problems logging on, you can specify that no authentication is done. In the project properties, change the Authentication mode from Windows Authentication to No Authentication (Figure 3-57). Then, on the remote machine, click the Remote Debugger and click the Tools menu, and select Options. Here, you can specify that no authentication is done and that any user can debug.

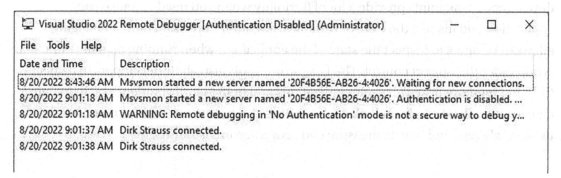

*Figure 3-58.* *Remote debug session connected*

8. After a few seconds, you will see your application's main window displayed on the remote machine (Figure 3-59). Yep, breakfast is the most important meal of the day.

***Figure 3-59.*** *Application main screen*

9.  On the remote machine, take whatever action is needed to hit the breakpoint you set earlier. I simply set a breakpoint behind the Start button click event handler. When you hit the breakpoint, it will be hit on your local machine (Visual Studio machine).

If you need any project resources to debug your application, you will have to include these in your project. The easiest way is to create a project folder in Visual Studio and then add the files to that folder. For each resource you add to the folder, ensure that you set the Copy to Output Directory property to Copy always.

# Summary

In this chapter, we saw that Visual Studio provides a rich set of debugging tools for developers. Breakpoints provide a lot of flexibility when you need to pause your application and inspect the state of variables and other objects. Remote debugging allows developers to inspect the state of the application when running on a machine that is not under their direct control. The Diagnostic Tools also allow developers to inspect CPU and memory usage for their applications and help identify bottlenecks. In the next chapter, we will take a closer look at unit testing and how to create and run unit tests, using IntelliTest, and how to measure code coverage in Visual Studio.

# CHAPTER 4

# Unit Testing

Many developers will have strong opinions on unit testing. If you are considering using unit tests in your code, then start by understanding why unit tests are useful and sometimes necessary.

Breaking down your code's functionality into smaller, testable units of behavior allows you to create and run unit tests. Unit tests will increase the likelihood that your code will continue to work as expected, even though you have made changes to the source code. In this chapter, we will have a look at

- Creating and running unit tests
- Using live unit tests
- Using IntelliTest to generate unit tests
- How to measure Code Coverage in Visual Studio

Unit tests allow you to maintain the health of your code and find errors quickly, before shipping your application to your customers. To introduce you to unit testing, we will start off with a very basic example of creating a unit test.

## Creating and Running Unit Tests

Assume that you have a method that calculates the temperature in Fahrenheit for a given temperature in Celsius. The code that we want to create a unit test for will look as in Listing 4-1.

*Listing 4-1.* Convert Celsius to Fahrenheit

```
public static class ConversionHelpers
{
    private const double F_MULTIPLIER = 1.8;
```

© Dirk Strauss 2023
D. Strauss, *Getting Started with Visual Studio 2022*, https://doi.org/10.1007/978-1-4842-8922-8_4

```
private const int F_ADDITION = 32;
public static double ToFahrenheit(double celsius)
{
    return celsius * F_MULTIPLIER + F_ADDITION;
}
}
```

We have constant values for the multiplier and addition to the conversion formula. This means that we can easily write a test to check that the conversion is an expected result.

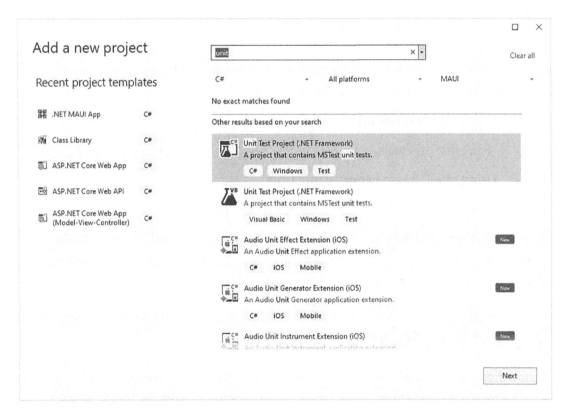

***Figure 4-1.*** *Add a new Unit Test project*

Start off by adding a new Unit Test project to your solution. You will see (Figure 4-1) that you have the option to add a Unit Test project template for the test framework you prefer to use.

Once you have added your Unit Test project to your solution, it will appear in the solution with a different icon indicating that it is a Unit Test project (Figure 4-2).

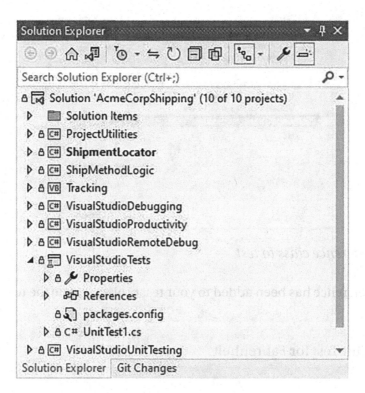

***Figure 4-2.***  *Unit Test project added to the solution*

To effectively test the class that contains the method that converts Celsius to Fahrenheit, we need to reference that class in our Unit Test project. Right-click the Unit Test project and add a reference to the project containing the class we need to test (Figure 4-3).

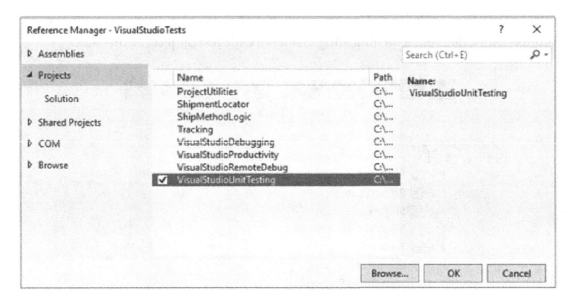

**Figure 4-3.** *Reference class to test*

When the reference has been added to your test project, create the test as seen in Listing 4-2.

**Listing 4-2.** Unit Test for Fahrenheit

```
[TestClass]
public class ConversionHelperTests
{
    [TestMethod]
    public void Test_Fahrenheit_Calc()
    {
        // arrange - setup
        var celsius = -7.0;
        var expectedFahrenheit = 19.4;
        // act - test
        var result = ConversionHelpers.ToFahrenheit(celsius);
        // assert - check
        Assert.AreEqual(expectedFahrenheit, result);
    }
}
```

When you look at the code in Listing 4-2, you will notice that we do three things in each test. These are

- Arrange – Where we set up the test

- Act – Where we test the code to get a result

- Assert – Where we check the actual result against the expected result

From the Test menu, select Test Explorer, or hold down Ctrl+E, T. In Test Explorer, click the green play button to run the test and see the test results displayed (Figure 4-4).

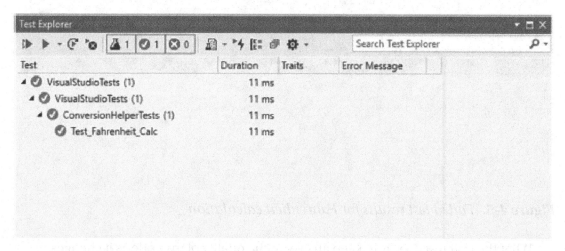

***Figure 4-4.*** *Running your Unit Test*

From the results displayed in the Test Explorer, you can easily see which tests failed and which have passed. From our rather simple test in Listing 4-2, you can see that the test passed easily and that the result we expected was indeed the actual result of the test. Note that our test compares two type double values for exact equality. The Assert. AreEqual method has an overload that accepts an error tolerance parameter.

To see what happens when a test fails, modify the Integer value for the constant F_ADDITION variable as seen in Listing 4-3.

***Listing 4-3.*** Modify the Fahrenheit Constant

```
private const double F_MULTIPLIER = 1.8;
private const int F_ADDITION = 33;
public static double ToFahrenheit(double celsius)
{
```

```
    return celsius * F_MULTIPLIER + F_ADDITION;
}
```

Running the tests again after the change will result in a failed test as seen in Figure 4-5. The change we made was a small change, but it's easy to miss this if we work in a team and on a big code base.

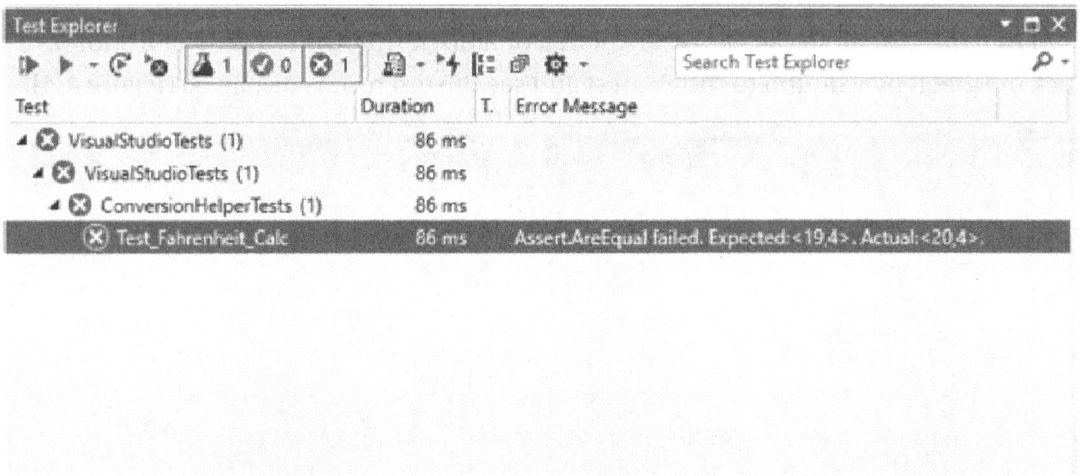

***Figure 4-5.*** *Failed test results for Fahrenheit calculation*

What the unit test does is to keep an eye on the quality of the code as it changes throughout development. This is especially important when working in a team. It will allow other developers to see if any code changes they have made have broken some intended functionality in the code.

---

In Visual Studio 2022, you can also run the tests by right-clicking the test project and selecting Run Tests from the context menu.

---

The Test Explorer offers a lot of functionality, and you can see this from looking at the labels on the image in Figure 4-6.

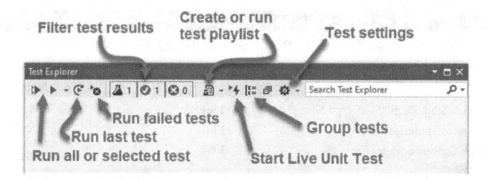

***Figure 4-6.*** *Test Explorer menu*

From the Test Explorer, you can

- Run all tests or just the last test

- Only run failed tests (great if you have many tests in your project)

- Filter the test results

- Group tests

- Start Live Unit Testing (more on this later)

- Create and run a test playlist

- Modify test settings

Let's have a look at creating a test playlist.

## Create and Run a Test Playlist

If your project contains many tests, and you want to run those tests as a group, you can create a playlist. To create a playlist, select the tests that you want to group from the Test Explorer, and right-click them. From the context menu that pops up, select Add to Playlist ➤ New Playlist as seen in Figure 4-7.

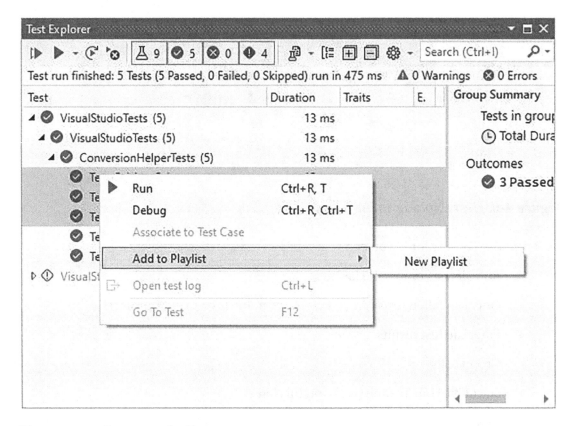

***Figure 4-7.*** *Create a playlist*

This will open a new Test Explorer window where you can run the tests and save the tests you selected under a new playlist name. This will create a .playlist file for you.

I created a new playlist called Temperature_Tests.playlist from the Celsius and Fahrenheit temperature conversion tests. The playlist file it creates is simply an XML file that in my example looks as in Listing 4-4.

***Listing 4-4.*** Temperature_Tests.playlist File Contents

```
<Playlist Version="1.0">
<Add Test="VisualStudioTests.ConversionHelperTests.Test_Fahrenheit_Calc" />
<Add Test="VisualStudioTests.ConversionHelperTests.Test_Celsius_Calc" />
</Playlist>
```

To open and run a playlist again, click the Create or run test playlist button and select the playlist file you want to run.

# Testing Timeouts

The speed of your code is also very important. If you are using the MSTest framework, you can set a timeout attribute to set a timeout after which a test should fail. This is convenient because as you write code for a specific method, you can immediately identify if the code you are adding to a method is causing a potential bottleneck. Consider the Test_Fahrenheit_Calc test we created earlier.

***Listing 4-5.*** Adding a Timeout Attribute

```
[TestMethod]
[Timeout(2000)]
public void Test_Fahrenheit_Calc()
{
    // arrange - setup
    var celsius = -7.0;
    var expectedFahrenheit = 19.4;
    // act - test
    var result = ConversionHelpers.ToFahrenheit(celsius);
    // assert - check
    Assert.AreEqual(expectedFahrenheit, result);
}
```

As seen in Listing 4-5, I have added a timeout of 2000 milliseconds. If you run your tests now, it will pass because the calculation it performs is all it does. To see the timeout attribute in action, swing back to the ToFahrenheit method in the ConversionHelpers class and modify it by sleeping the thread for 2.5 seconds as seen in Listing 4-6.

***Listing 4-6.*** Sleeping the Thread

```
public static double ToFahrenheit(double celsius)
{
    Thread.Sleep(2500);
    return celsius * F_MULTIPLIER + F_ADDITION;
}
```

Run your tests again and see that, this time, your test has failed because it has exceeded the specified timeout value set by the Timeout attribute (Figure 4-8).

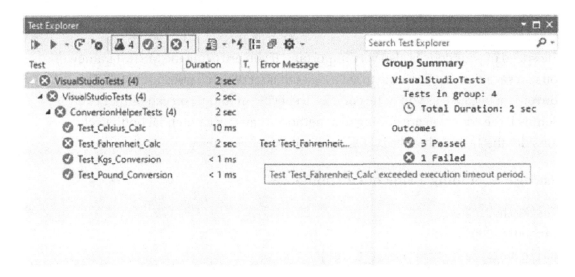

***Figure 4-8.*** *Test timeout exceeded*

Identifying critical methods in your code and setting a specific timeout on that method will allow developers to catch issues early on when tests start exceeding the timeout set. You can then go back and immediately refactor the code that was recently changed to improve the execution time.

# Using Live Unit Tests

First introduced in Visual Studio 2017, Live Unit Testing runs your unit tests automatically as you make changes to your code. You can then see the results of your unit tests in real time.

---

Live Unit Testing is only available in Visual Studio Enterprise edition for C# and Visual Basic projects targeting the .NET Framework or .NET Core. For a full comparison between the editions of Visual Studio, refer to the following link: `https://visualstudio.microsoft.com/vs/compare/`.

---

The benefits of Live Unit Testing are as follows:

- You will immediately see failing tests, allowing you to easily identify breaking code changes.

- It indicates Code Coverage, allowing you to see what code is not covered by any unit tests.

Live Unit Testing persists the data of the status of the tests it ran. It then uses the persisted data to dynamically run your tests as your code changes. Live Unit Testing supports the following test frameworks:

- xUnit.net – Minimum version xunit 1.9.2

- NUnit – Minimum version NUnit version 3.5.0

- MSTest – Minimum version MSTest.TestFramework 1.0.5-preview

Before you can start using Live Unit Testing, you need to configure it by going to Tools ➤ Options and selecting Live Unit Testing in the left pane (Figure 4-9).

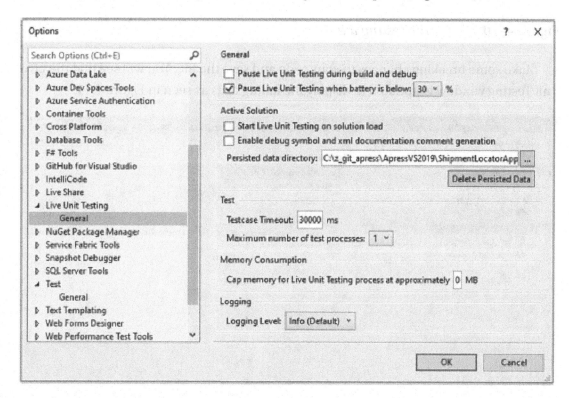

***Figure 4-9.***  *Configure Live Unit Testing*

Once you have configured the Live Unit Testing options, you can enable it from Test ➤ Live Unit Testing ➤ Start. To see the Live Unit Testing window, click the Live Unit Testing button as seen in Figure 4-6.

The Live Unit Testing window is displayed as seen in Figure 4-10.

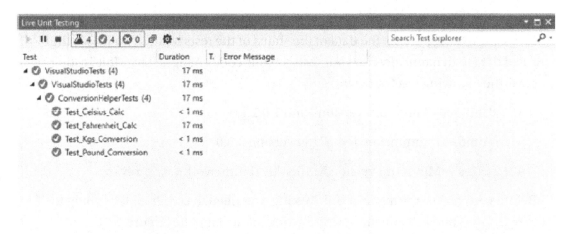

***Figure 4-10.*** *Live Unit Testing window*

Make some breaking changes to your code and save the file. You will see that the Live Unit Testing window is updated to display the failing tests as seen in Figure 4-11.

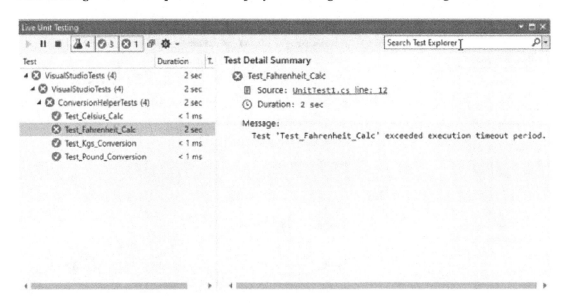

***Figure 4-11.*** *Live Unit Testing results updated*

Live Unit Testing gives you a good insight into the stability of the code you write, as you write the code. Let's go a little further. Add the class in Listing 4-7 to your project under test.

***Listing 4-7.*** Container Class Implementing ICloneable

```csharp
public class Container : ICloneable
{
    public string ContainerNumber { get; set; }
    public string ShipNumber { get; set; }
    public double Weight { get; set; }
    public object Clone() => throw new NotImplementedException();
}
```

Don't add any implementation to the Clone method. Swing back to the test project and add a Unit Test for the Container class as in Listing 4-8.

***Listing 4-8.*** Unit Test for the Container Class

```csharp
[TestMethod]
public void Test_Container()
{
    var containerA = new Container();
    var containerB = containerA.Clone();
    var result = (containerA == containerB);
    Assert.IsFalse(result);
}
```

Start Live Unit Testing, and you will notice that your test fails as seen in Figure 4-12.

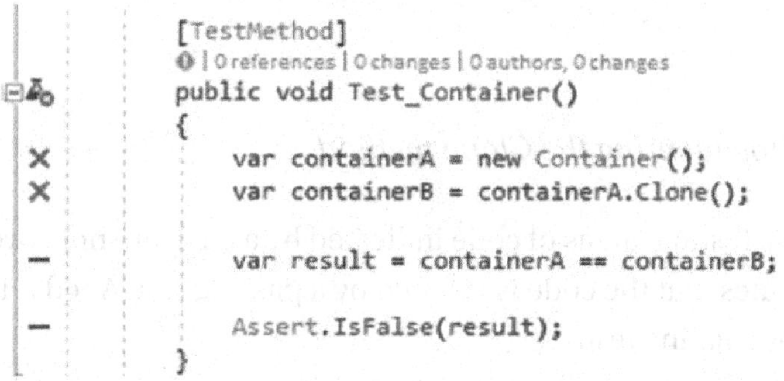

***Figure 4-12.*** *Live Unit Test results failed*

Have a look at the Container class, and you will notice that Live Unit Testing has also updated the code file with the faulting method (Figure 4-13).

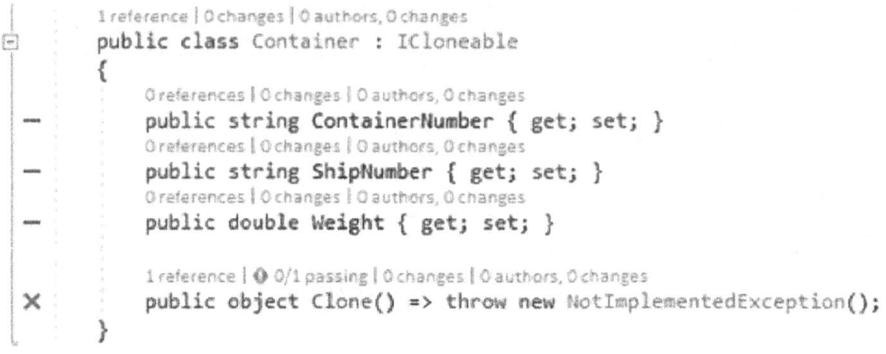

```
        1 reference | 0 changes | 0 authors, 0 changes
  ⊟     public class Container : ICloneable
        {
            0 references | 0 changes | 0 authors, 0 changes
  ─         public string ContainerNumber { get; set; }
            0 references | 0 changes | 0 authors, 0 changes
  ─         public string ShipNumber { get; set; }
            0 references | 0 changes | 0 authors, 0 changes
  ─         public double Weight { get; set; }

            1 reference | ◑ 0/1 passing | 0 changes | 0 authors, 0 changes
  ✕         public object Clone() => throw new NotImplementedException();
        }
```

*Figure 4-13.* *Container class Live Unit Test results*

As soon as you add implementation to the Clone method, your Live Unit Test results are updated as seen in Figure 4-14.

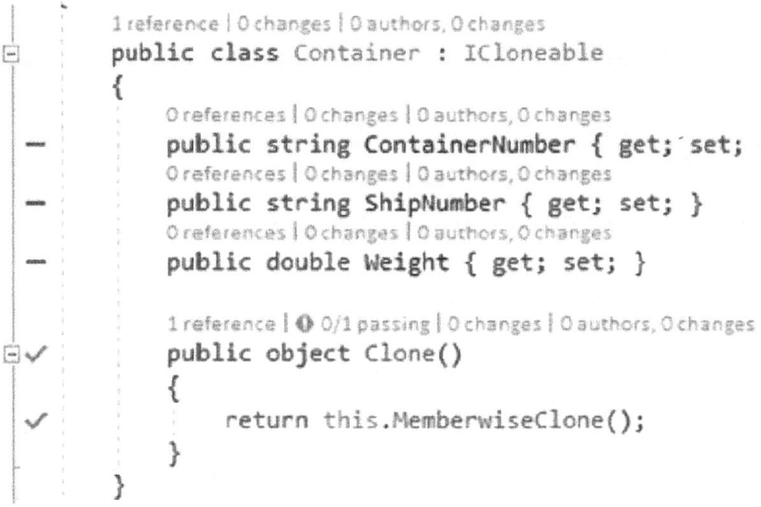

```
        1 reference | 0 changes | 0 authors, 0 changes
  ⊟     public class Container : ICloneable
        {
            0 references | 0 changes | 0 authors, 0 changes
  ─         public string ContainerNumber { get; set; }
            0 references | 0 changes | 0 authors, 0 changes
  ─         public string ShipNumber { get; set; }
            0 references | 0 changes | 0 authors, 0 changes
  ─         public double Weight { get; set; }

            1 reference | ◑ 0/1 passing | 0 changes | 0 authors, 0 changes
  ⊟✓        public object Clone()
            {
  ✓             return this.MemberwiseClone();
            }
        }
```

*Figure 4-14.* *Implementing the Clone method*

With Live Unit Testing, areas of code indicated by a dash are not covered by any tests. A green tick indicates that the code is covered by a passing test. A red X indicates that the code is covered by a failing test.

# Using IntelliTest to Generate Unit Tests

IntelliTest helps developers generate and get started using Unit Tests. This saves a lot of time writing tests and increases code quality.

---

IntelliTest is only available in Visual Studio Enterprise edition.

---

The default behavior of IntelliTest is to go through the code and try to create a test that gives you maximum Code Coverage. To illustrate how IntelliTest works, I will create a simple class that calculates shipping costs as seen in Listing 4-9.

***Listing 4-9.*** Calculate ShippingCost Method

```
public class Calculate
{
    public enum ShippingType { Overnight = 0, Priority = 1, Standard = 2 }
    private const double VOLUME_FACTOR = 0.75;
    public double ShippingCost(double length, double width, double height,
    ShippingType type)
    {
        var volume = length * width * height;
        var cost = volume * VOLUME_FACTOR;
        switch (type)
        {
            case ShippingType.Overnight:
                cost = cost * 2.25;
                break;
            case ShippingType.Priority:
                cost = cost * 1.75;
                break;
            case ShippingType.Standard:
                cost = cost * 1.05;
                break;
            default:
                break;
        }
```

```
        return cost;
    }
}
```

To run IntelliTest against the `ShippingCost` method, right-click the method, and click IntelliTest ➤ Run IntelliTest from the context menu. The results will be displayed in the IntelliTest window that pops up as seen in Figure 4-15. You can also see the details of the generated unit test in the Details pane.

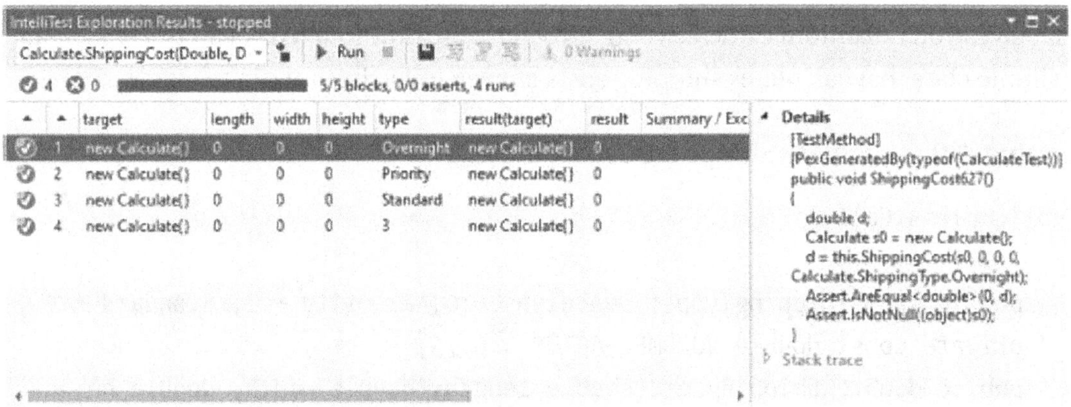

*Figure 4-15.* *IntelliTest results*

IntelliTest has taken each parameter going to the method and generated a parameter value for it. In this example, all the tests succeeded, but there is still a problem. This is evident from the result value which is always zero.

We can never allow a parcel to be shipped with zero shipping cost, no matter how small it is. What becomes clear here is that we need to implement minimum dimensions. We, therefore, need to modify the `Calculate` class as in Listing 4-10.

*Listing 4-10.* Modified Calculate Class

```
public class Calculate
{
    public enum ShippingType { Overnight = 0, Priority = 1, Standard = 2 }
    private const double VOLUME_FACTOR = 0.75;
    private const double MIN_WIDTH = 1.5;
    private const double MIN_LENGTH = 2.5;
    private const double MIN_HEIGHT = 0.5;
```

```
public double ShippingCost(double length, double width, double height,
ShippingType type)
{
    if (length <= 0.0) length = MIN_LENGTH;
    if (width <= 0.0) width = MIN_WIDTH;
    if (height <= 0.0) height = MIN_HEIGHT;
    var volume = length * width * height;
    var cost = volume * VOLUME_FACTOR;
    switch (type)
    {
        case ShippingType.Overnight:
            cost = cost * 2.25;
            break;
        case ShippingType.Priority:
            cost = cost * 1.75;
            break;
        case ShippingType.Standard:
            cost = cost * 1.05;
            break;
        default:
            break;
    }
    return cost;
}
}
```

Running IntelliTest again yields a completely different set of results as seen in Figure 4-16.

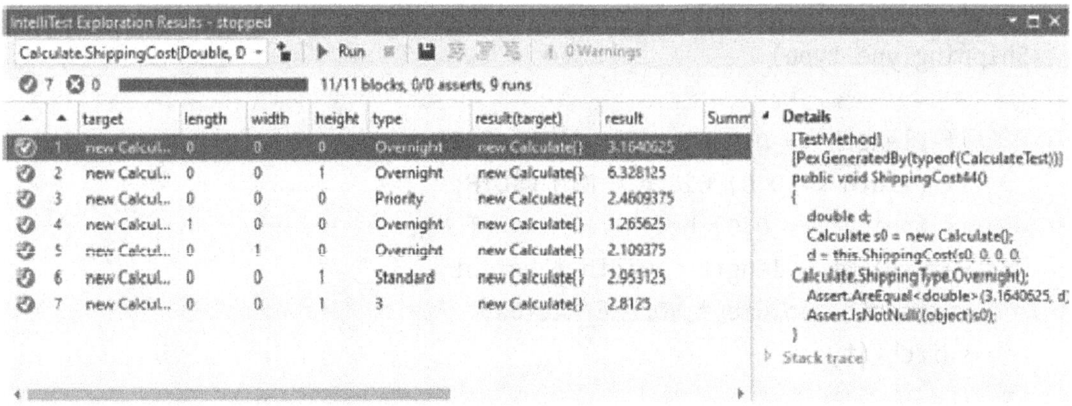

**Figure 4-16.** *IntelliTest results on the modified class*

This time, you can see that no matter what the value of the parcel dimensions is, we will always have a result returned for the shipping costs. To create the unit tests generated by IntelliTest, click the Save button in the IntelliTest window.

This will create a new Unit Test project for you in your solution as seen in Figure 4-17.

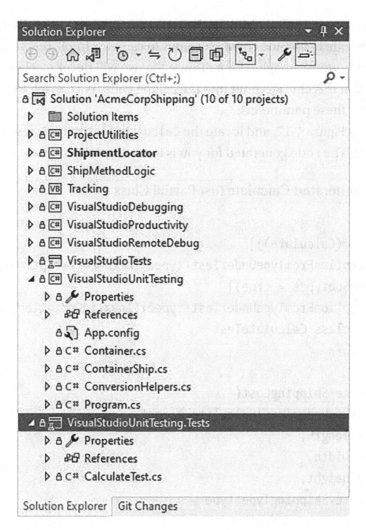

***Figure 4-17.*** *Generated Unit Tests*

You can now run the generated Unit Tests as you normally would with Test Explorer. As you continue coding and adding more logic to the `Calculate` class, you can regenerate the Unit Tests by running IntelliTest again. IntelliTest will then crawl through your code again and generate new Unit Tests for you to match the logic of your code at that time.

---

The underlying engine that IntelliTest uses to crawl through your code and generate the Unit Tests is Pex. Pex is a Microsoft Research project that was never productized or supported until IntelliTest started using it.

---

For a moment, I want you to think back to the code in Listing 4-10. Remember how we modified the code to include constant values to cater for IntelliTest setting the default parameter values to zero? Imagine for a minute that we will never receive a zero as a parameter and that this check is built into the calling code. We can tell IntelliTest to assume values for these parameters.

Have a look at Figure 4-17, and locate the `CalculateTest` partial class generated for you by IntelliTest. The code generated for you is in Listing 4-11.

***Listing 4-11.*** Generated CalculateTest Partial Class

```
[TestClass]
[PexClass(typeof(Calculate))]
[PexAllowedExceptionFromTypeUnderTest(typeof(ArgumentException),
AcceptExceptionSubtypes = true)]
[PexAllowedExceptionFromTypeUnderTest(typeof(InvalidOperationException))]
public partial class CalculateTest
{
    [PexMethod]
    public double ShippingCost(
        [PexAssumeUnderTest]Calculate target,
        double length,
        double width,
        double height,
        Calculate.ShippingType type
    )
    {
double result = target.ShippingCost(length, width, height, type);
        return result;
        // TODO: add assertions to method CalculateTest.
            ShippingCost(Calculate, Double, Double, Double, ShippingType)
    }
}
```

We are now going to tell the Pex engine that we want to assume certain values for the parameters. We do this by using `PexAssume`.

---

PexAssume is a static helper class containing a set of methods to express preconditions in parameterized Unit Tests.

---

Modify the code in the CalculateTest partial class' ShippingCost method by adding PexAssume.IsTrue as a precondition for each parameter as illustrated in Listing 4-12.

***Listing 4-12.*** Modified CalculateTest Partial Class

```
[PexMethod]
public double ShippingCost(
    [PexAssumeUnderTest]Calculate target,
    double length,
    double width,
    double height,
    Calculate.ShippingType type
)
{

    PexAssume.IsTrue(length > 0);
    PexAssume.IsTrue(width > 0);
    PexAssume.IsTrue(height > 0);
    double result = target.ShippingCost(length, width, height, type);
    return result;
    // TODO: add assertions to method CalculateTest.ShippingCost(Calculate,
        Double, Double, Double, ShippingType)

}
```

By doing this, I can now modify my Calculate class to remove the constant values ensuring that the length, width, and height parameters are greater than zero. The Calculate class will now look as in Listing 4-13.

***Listing 4-13.*** Modified Calculate Class

```
public class Calculate
{
    public enum ShippingType { Overnight = 0, Priority = 1, Standard = 2 }
    private const double VOLUME_FACTOR = 0.75;
```

```
public double ShippingCost(double length, double width, double height,
ShippingType type)
{
    var volume = length * width * height;
    var cost = volume * VOLUME_FACTOR;
    switch (type)
    {
        case ShippingType.Overnight:
            cost = cost * 2.25;
            break;
        case ShippingType.Priority:
            cost = cost * 1.75;
            break;
        case ShippingType.Standard:
            cost = cost * 1.05;
            break;
        default:
            break;
    }
    return cost;
}
}
```

Run IntelliTest again, and see that the parameter values passed through are never zero (Figure 4-18).

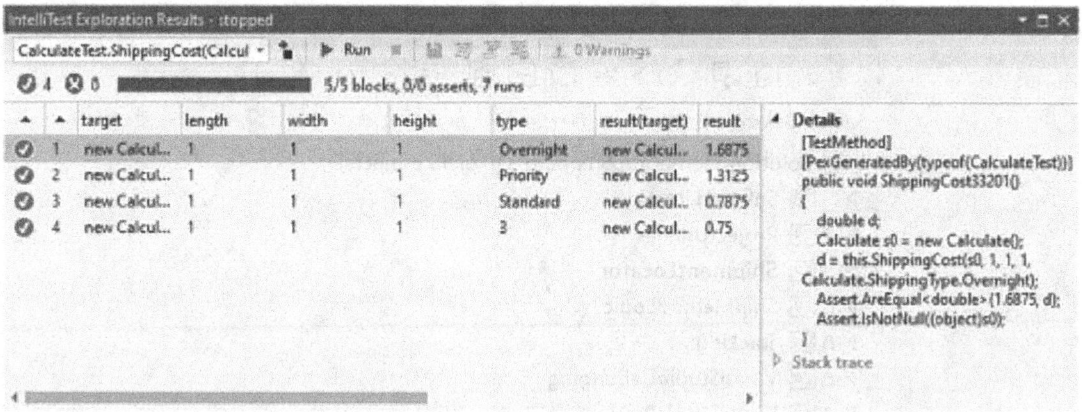

**Figure 4-18.** *IntelliTest results with PexAssume*

You can modify the `CalculateTest` partial class by adding assertions to the `ShippingCost` method. When you expand CalculateTest in the Solution Explorer (Figure 4-19), you will see several `ShippingCost` test methods listed.

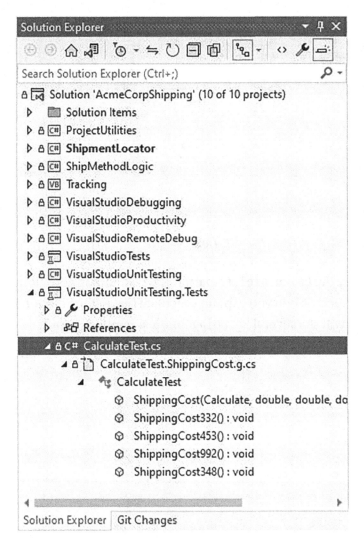

***Figure 4-19.*** *ShippingCost generated tests*

These correspond to the IntelliTest results as seen in Figure 4-18. Do not modify these code files, as your changes will be lost when IntelliTest is run again and it regenerates those tests.

# Focus IntelliTest Code Exploration

Sometimes, IntelliTest needs a bit of help focusing code exploration. This can happen if you have an Interface as a parameter to a method and more than one class implements that Interface. Consider the code in Listing 4-14.

***Listing 4-14.*** Focusing Code Exploration

```
public class ShipFreight
{
    public void CalculateFreightCosts(IShippable box)
    {
    }
}
class Crate : IShippable
{
    public bool CustomsCleared { get; }
}
class Package : IShippable
{
    public bool CustomsCleared { get; }
}
public interface IShippable
{
    bool CustomsCleared { get; }
}
```

If you ran IntelliTest on the CalculateFreightCosts method, then you will receive warnings as can be seen in Figure 4-20.

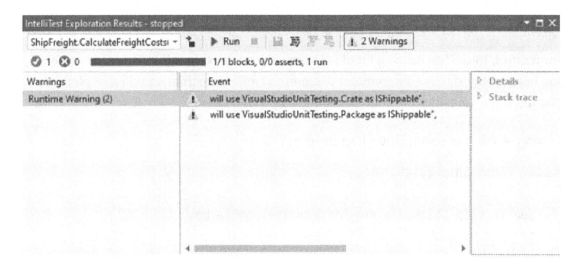

**Figure 4-20.** *Focus code exploration*

You can tell IntelliTest which class to use to test the interface. Assume that I want to use the Package class to test the Interface. Now, just select the second warning and click the Fix button on the menu as seen in Figure 4-21.

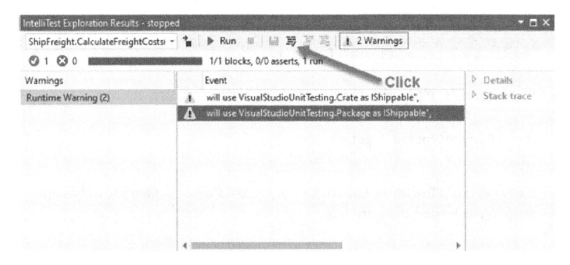

**Figure 4-21.** *Tell IntelliTest which class to use*

IntelliTest now updates the PexAssemblyInfo.cs file by adding [assembly:
PexUseType(typeof(Package))] to the end of the file to tell IntelliTest which class to use. Running IntelliTest again results in no more warnings being displayed.

# How to Measure Code Coverage in Visual Studio

Code Coverage indicates what portion of your code is covered by Unit Tests. To guard against bugs, it becomes obvious that the more code is covered by Unit Tests, the better tested it is.

---

IntelliTest is only available in Visual Studio Enterprise edition.

---

The Code Coverage feature in Visual Studio will give you a good idea of your current Code Coverage percentage. To run the Code Coverage analysis, open up Test Explorer, and click the drop-down next to the play button (Figure 4-22).

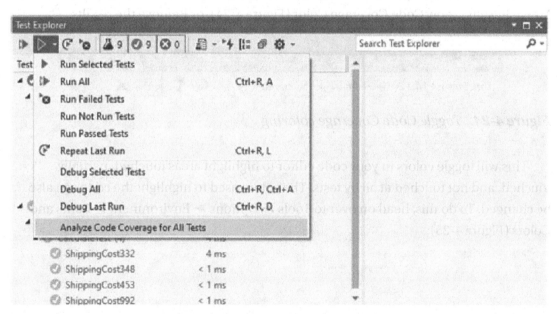

*Figure 4-22.  Analyze Code Coverage*

Click Analyze Code Coverage for All Tests in the menu.

---

You can also go to the Test menu, click Windows, and click Test Explorer.

---

The Code Coverage Results are then displayed in a new window (Figure 4-23). You can access this window from the Test menu and then select Windows ➤ Code Coverage Results or hold down Ctrl+E, C on the keyboard.

241

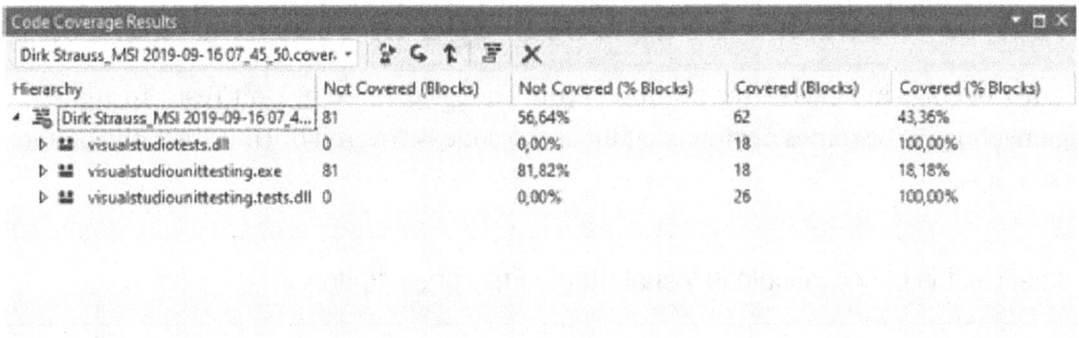

| Hierarchy | Not Covered (Blocks) | Not Covered (% Blocks) | Covered (Blocks) | Covered (% Blocks) |
|---|---|---|---|---|
| ▲ 🗇 Dirk Strauss_MSI 2019-09-16 07_4... | 81 | 56,64% | 62 | 43,36% |
| ▷ 👥 visualstudiotests.dll | 0 | 0,00% | 18 | 100,00% |
| ▷ 👥 visualstudiounittesting.exe | 81 | 81,82% | 18 | 18,18% |
| ▷ 👥 visualstudiounittesting.tests.dll | 0 | 0,00% | 26 | 100,00% |

**Figure 4-23.** *Code Coverage Results*

In the Code Coverage Results window, you can Export the results, Import Results, Merge Results, Show Code Coverage Color (Figure 4-24), or Remove the results.

**Figure 4-24.** *Toggle Code Coverage coloring*

This will toggle colors in your code editor to highlight areas touched, partially touched, and not touched at all by tests. The colors used to highlight the code can also be changed. To do this, head on over to Tools ➤ Options ➤ Environment ➤ Fonts and Colors (Figure 4-25).

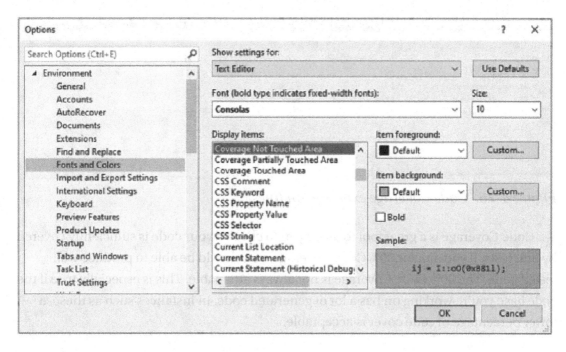

***Figure 4-25.*** *Change Fonts and Colors*

This should give you a good understanding of how much code is covered by unit tests. Developers should typically aim for at least 80% Code Coverage. If the Code Coverage is low, then modify your code to include more tests. Once you are done modifying your code, run the Code Coverage tool again as the results are not automatically updated as you modify your code.

Code Coverage is typically measured in blocks. A block of code is a section of code that has exactly one entry point and one exit point. If you prefer to see the Code Coverage in terms of lines covered, you can change the results by choosing Add/Remove Columns in the results table header (Figure 4-26).

| Code Coverage Results | | | | ▾ ☐ ✕ |
|---|---|---|---|---|

Dirk Strauss_MSI 2019-09-16 07_45_50.cover. ▾    🔁 ⤵ ↑ ▤ ✕

| Hierarchy | Not Covered (Lines) | Not Covered (% Lines) | Covered (Lines) | Covered (% Lines) |
|---|---|---|---|---|
| ◢ ⛏ Dirk Strauss_MSI 2019-09-16 07_4... | 68 | 43,31% | 89 | 56,69% |
| ▷ 📇 visualstudiotests.dll | 0 | 0,00% | 30 | 100,00% |
| ▷ 📇 visualstudiounittesting.exe | 68 | 70,83% | 28 | 29,17% |
| ▷ 📇 visualstudiounittesting.tests.dll | 0 | 0,00% | 31 | 100,00% |

***Figure 4-26.*** *Code Coverage expressed in lines*

Code Coverage is a great tool to allow you to check if your code is sufficiently covered by unit tests. If you aim for 80% Code Coverage, you should be able to produce well-tested code. The 80% Code Coverage is not always attainable. This is especially true if the code base you're working on has a lot of generated code. In instances such as these, a lower percentage of code cover is acceptable.

# Summary

Unit testing in Visual Studio helps developers maintain the health of their code and find errors quickly, before shipping their applications to their customers. While some features are not available in all editions of Visual Studio, the free Visual Studio Community does offer developers some unit test functionality. This is enough to get them by. In the next chapter, we will be looking at a feature that all developers should be very familiar with. Source control management is essential to any project. We will explore this and some new features of Visual Studio 2022 such as multi-repo support, comparing branches, Checkout Commit, and line staging but to name a few. Let's look at source control next.

# CHAPTER 5

# Source Control

If you have worked on projects in a team environment, or if you need a place to keep your own code safe, then you'll agree that using a source control solution is essential. It doesn't matter if it's a large enterprise solution or a small Pet project, Visual Studio makes it extremely easy for developers to use Git and GitHub.

---

Git is a tool that developers install locally on their machine. GitHub is an online service that stores code safely that has been pushed to it from computers using the Git tool.

---

In 2018, Microsoft acquired GitHub for $7.5 billion in Microsoft stock. This acquisition of GitHub brought about changes to their pricing tiers. Previously, developers could only create public repos on the free tier. In January 2019, however, GitHub announced that developers can now create unlimited private repositories on the free tier.

This is great, especially if you are working on a side project that you do not want to share with anyone just yet. In this chapter, we will be looking at using Git and GitHub inside Visual Studio 2022. We will see how to

- Create a GitHub account
- Create and clone a repository
- Commit changes to a repository
- Create a branch from your code
- Create and handle pull requests

These are all things that developers will do on a daily basis when working with Git and GitHub. While the process might change slightly if you use a different source control strategy, the concepts remain the same.

© Dirk Strauss 2023

D. Strauss, *Getting Started with Visual Studio 2022*, https://doi.org/10.1007/978-1-4842-8922-8_5

# Create a GitHub Account

Let's start off with creating a GitHub account. Point your browser to `www.github.com`, as shown in Figure 5-1, and create an account by clicking the signup button.

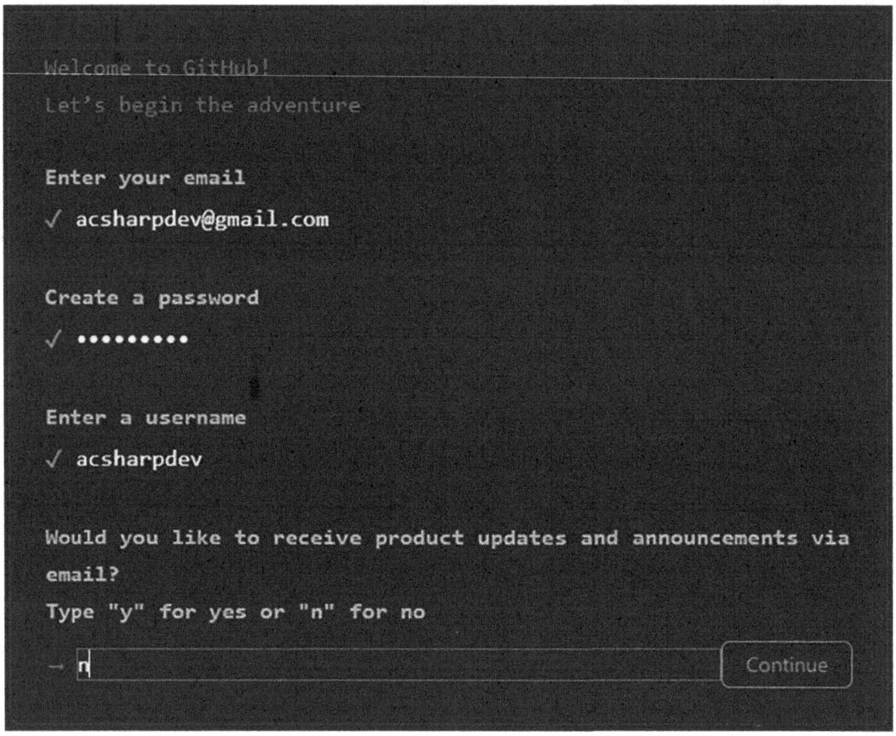

```
Welcome to GitHub!
Let's begin the adventure

Enter your email
✓ acsharpdev@gmail.com


Create a password
✓ •••••••••


Enter a username
✓ acsharpdev


Would you like to receive product updates and announcements via
email?
Type "y" for yes or "n" for no

→ n                                                    Continue
```

***Figure 5-1.***  *Sign up for GitHub*

Enter a username (Figure 5-1), email address, and password. GitHub then checks your password to verify that it does not appear on a list of known compromised passwords. If all checks out, a confirmation code is sent to your email address. After verifying your email address, GitHub will take you through a short personalization process before finally offering you an option to sign up for the Team account or continuing with the free account.

After entering your details, you will be taken to your dashboard. You can continue using the free account, but there is also the option to upgrade to a Pro account. The free subscription offers the basics suitable for most developers, while the pro subscription offers several more features. The free subscription is very generous and will appeal to most developers. The free subscription includes the following, among others:

- Unlimited public and private repositories

- Three collaborators for private repositories

- Issues

- Project tables and boards

- Pages and wikis for public repos

- GitHub Actions (2000 minutes/month) or free for public repos

The pro subscription, on the other hand, offers more which includes

- Unlimited public and private repositories

- Unlimited collaborators

- Issues

- Project tables and boards

- Repository insights

- Automatic code review assignment

- GitHub Actions (3000 minutes/month) or free for public repos

GitHub Team on the other hand allows a team of developers to collaborate on projects, and GitHub bills for GitHub Team on a per-user basis.

---

For more info on all GitHub's products, browse to the following URL:
`https://docs.github.com/en/get-started/learning-about-github/`
`githubs-products.`

---

After creating your account on GitHub, you will be sent a welcome email with additional information and links to get you started. GitHub uses repositories to store your code, and you would create a repository for each project you want to work on. Clicking the Create repository button will take you to the Create a new repository page. If not, you can access your repositories from the menu under your profile image. This will take you to your repositories page from where you can create your first repository as seen in Figure 5-2.

***Figure 5-2.***   *Create a new repository*

The next logical step is to create a repository for your new project. Let's have a look at that in the next section.

## Create and Clone a Repository

Visual Studio 2022 makes it extremely easy to create a repository on GitHub. I have created a simple Windows Forms application called PetProject in Visual Studio that just contains some boilerplate code. This is only temporary. Before I start writing actual code, I want to set up my GitHub repo. From the menu in Visual Studio, select Git and click Create Git Repository as seen in Figure 5-3.

***Figure 5-3.*** *Create Git Repository*

You will then be presented with the Create a Git repository window as seen in Figure 5-4. The window will default the local path to the path that your project is currently saved in. I always add a README file to my repos and keep the rest set to the default options regarding the license template and .gitignore template.

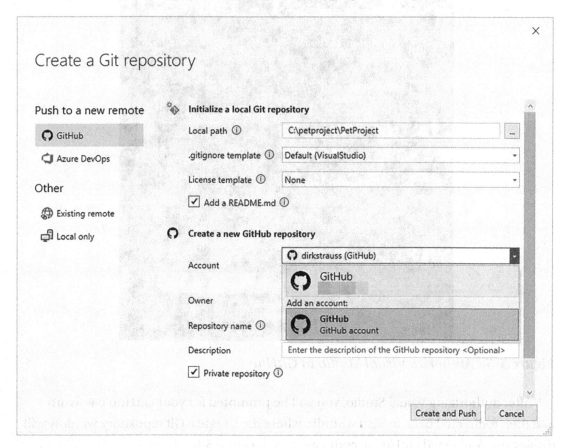

***Figure 5-4.*** *Create a Git repository*

Because I already have a GitHub account, the Account drop-down will default to that account. If you do not have a GitHub account, you can add a GitHub account from the drop-down. When you click Add a GitHub account, you will be taken to your account on GitHub to authorize Visual Studio as seen in Figure 5-5.

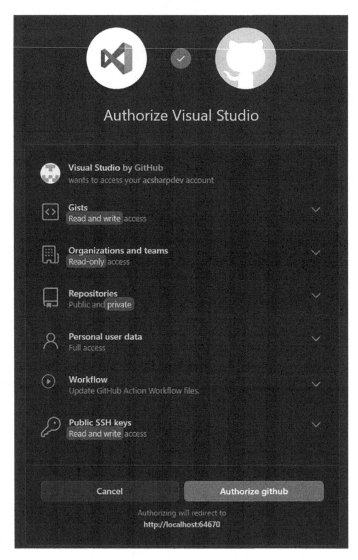

*Figure 5-5. Authorize Visual Studio in GitHub*

After authorizing Visual Studio, you will be prompted for your GitHub password and then redirected back to Visual Studio where the Create a Git repository window will display the connected GitHub account as seen in Figure 5-6.

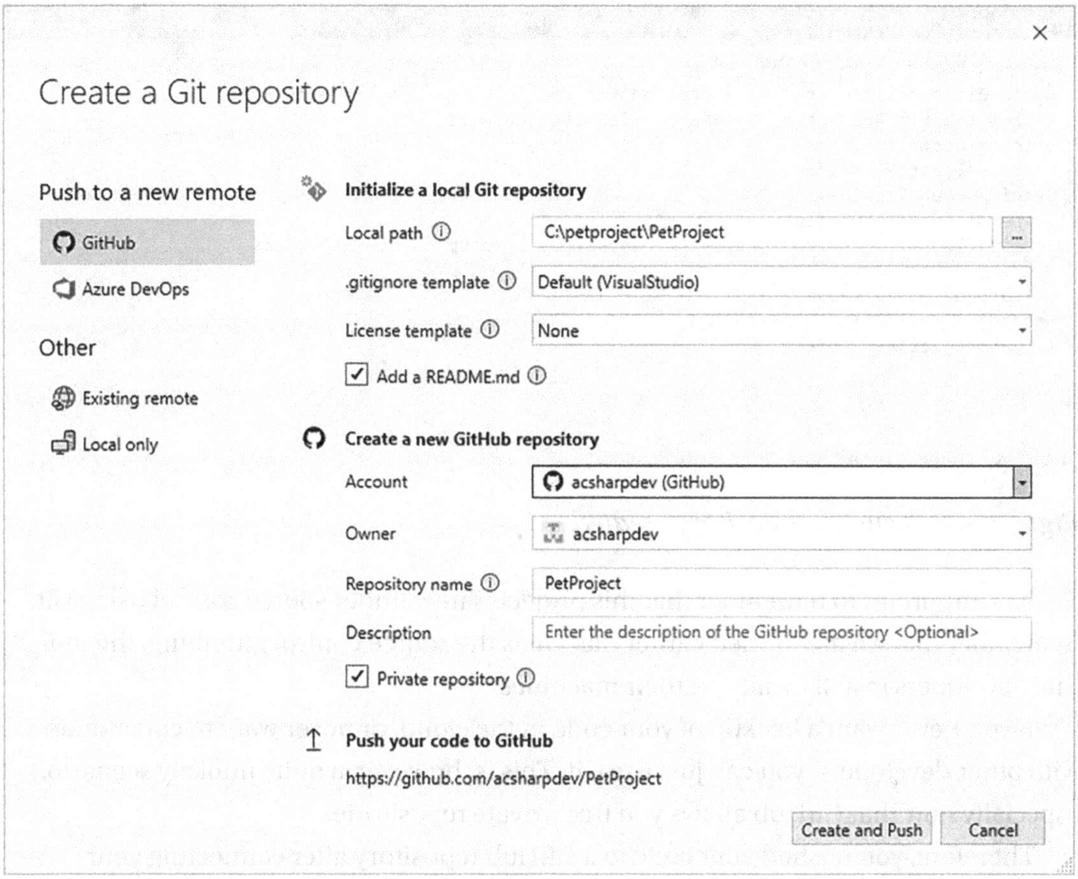

*Figure 5-6.*  *Create and push your code*

You can now click the Create and Push button that will create the repo on GitHub for you. This will also create a new local Git repository for your solution. Open up the Output Window (Ctrl+Alt+O) from the View menu and click Output. Here, you will see that a new local Git repository has been created (Figure 5-7).

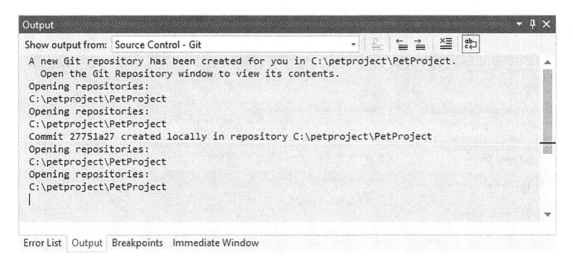

***Figure 5-7.*** *New Git repository created*

It is important to remember that this project is now under source control using Git. Remember that we mentioned earlier that Git is the source control plumbing, the tool that developers install locally on their machines.

If you never want a backup of your code in the cloud, or never want to collaborate with other developers, you can just use Git. This is, however, a quite unlikely scenario, especially now that GitHub allows you free private repositories.

Therefore, you pushed your code to a GitHub repository after connecting your account. You can see that the repository has been created for you by going to your GitHub account as seen in Figure 5-8.

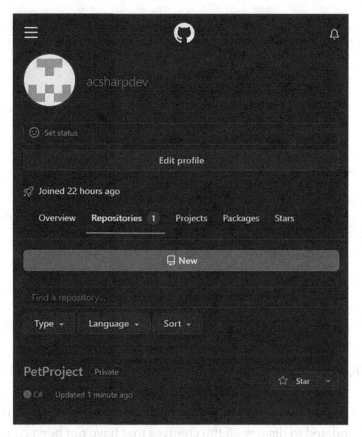

***Figure 5-8.*** *The created repository on GitHub*

There you will see the Private PetProject repo you just pushed from Visual Studio.

Next to the Solution Explorer, you will see the Git Changes tab as seen in Figure 5-9. Currently, there are no changes in our project to commit.

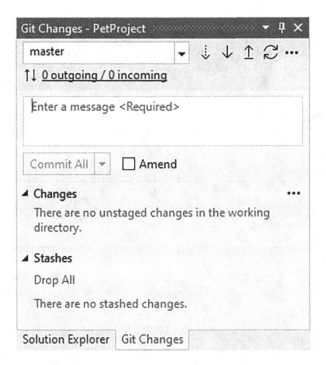

***Figure 5-9.*** *The Git Changes*

Make some UI or code changes to your project, and you will see that the Git Changes window will be updated to display all the changes that have not been committed to your Git repo as seen in Figure 5-10.

***Figure 5-10.*** *Git Changes showing changes files*

Enter a commit message as seen in Figure 5-11 and then click the drop-down arrow next to the Commit All button.

***Figure 5-11.*** *Entering a commit message*

Here, you can see the options for committing your code as seen in Figure 5-12. You can simply commit all your changes, commit and push to the remote repo, commit to the remote repo and do a sync, or stash your code.

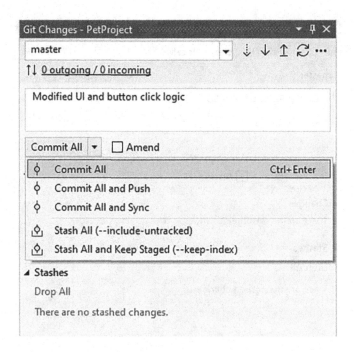

*Figure 5-12.* *Commit options*

We are just going to commit the changes without pushing to the remote repo.

---

Remember, the Commit All will create the changes locally. Nothing will be created on the remote GitHub repo yet.

---

After clicking the Commit All option, the Git Changes tab will tell you that the changes were committed locally and display the commit ID (in this case, c3371328) as seen in Figure 5-13.

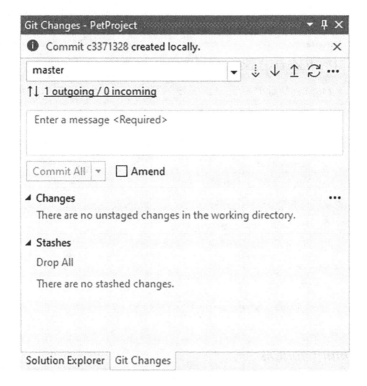

***Figure 5-13.*** *Commit the changes locally*

You might want to commit locally while working on code, and you are not quite ready to push the changes to the remote. This is a nice workflow to follow. Make some changes, commit locally with a specific commit message, make some more changes, commit again with another commit message, and so on.

---

**Note**    Each commit message and ID will also be visible on GitHub along with the files that have changed.

---

When you have completed the changes, and committed everything locally, you can push these changes to the remote repo by clicking the Push arrow as seen in Figure 5-14.

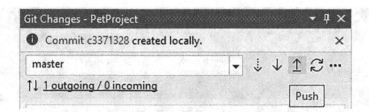

*Figure 5-14.  Push changes to the remote repo*

Doing this will push the changes to GitHub, and you will be notified in the Git Changes tab that your changes have been pushed to the remote repo on GitHub as seen in Figure 5-15.

*Figure 5-15.  Successful push to the remote repo*

If you go to your GitHub repository, you will see that the code you pushed is displayed in your repo (Figure 5-16) along with the commit message entered earlier in Figure 5-11.

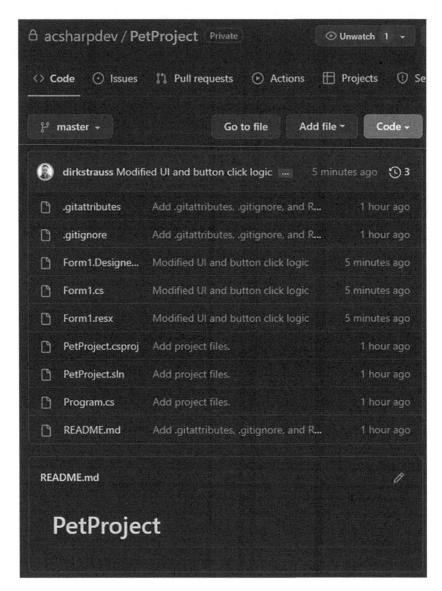

*Figure 5-16.* *The pushed changes in GitHub*

It is also nice to remember that if you have made changes to a file that you have not committed yet and want to change the file back to the state it was since the last commit, you can undo these changes easily. As seen in Figure 5-17, I have made some changes to the README file that I no longer want.

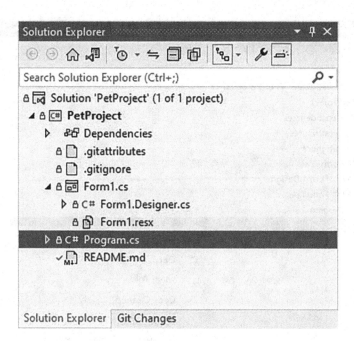

*Figure 5-17.* *Changed files you want to undo*

By right-clicking the file as seen in Figure 5-18 and selecting Git ➤ Undo Changes from the context menu, you can revert the file back to the state it was after the last commit.

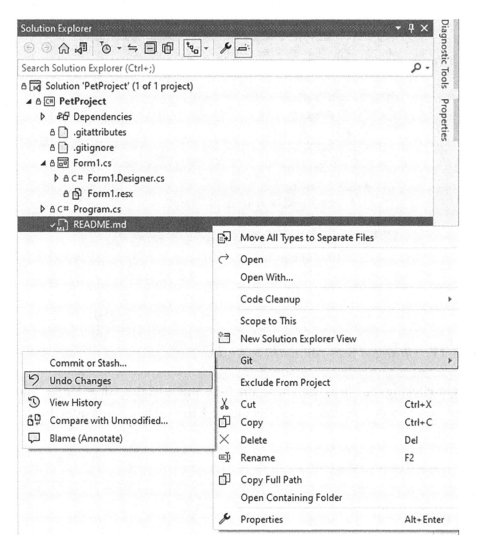

***Figure 5-18.*** *The Undo Changes option*

This is nice, especially when you have made some debug-specific changes to a config file that you do not want to commit to source control.

## Cloning a Repository

What I want to do now is have another colleague of mine contribute to my project. Seeing as this is a private repository, I need to invite him to collaborate. In GitHub, go to the settings tab in your repository. Then click Collaborators as seen in Figure 5-19.

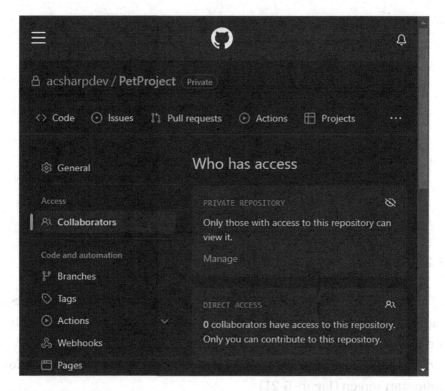

***Figure 5-19.*** *Add collaborators*

The free account can have three collaborators, so this will be using one of your allotted collaborators. You can now add collaborators to your repository by searching for their GitHub username and adding them as a collaborator. In this example, I will add myself as a collaborator. I will now receive a notification in my inbox that @acsharpdev wants me to work on his project with him (Figure 5-20).

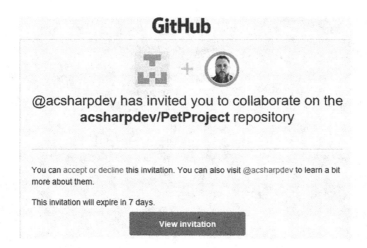

*Figure 5-20. Invitation to collaborate*

Once I accept the invitation, I will have push access to the project. The @acsharpdev user will now see me as a collaborator under the collaborator's tab in GitHub. To start working on the code, I need to clone the repository to my local machine. Start Visual Studio, and then click the Clone a repository option under the Get started section of the Visual Studio start screen (Figure 5-21).

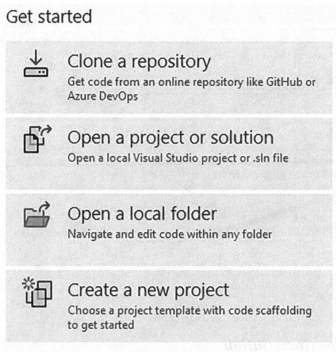

Figure 5-21. *Clone or check out code*

This will take you to the Clone a repository screen as seen in Figure 5-22.

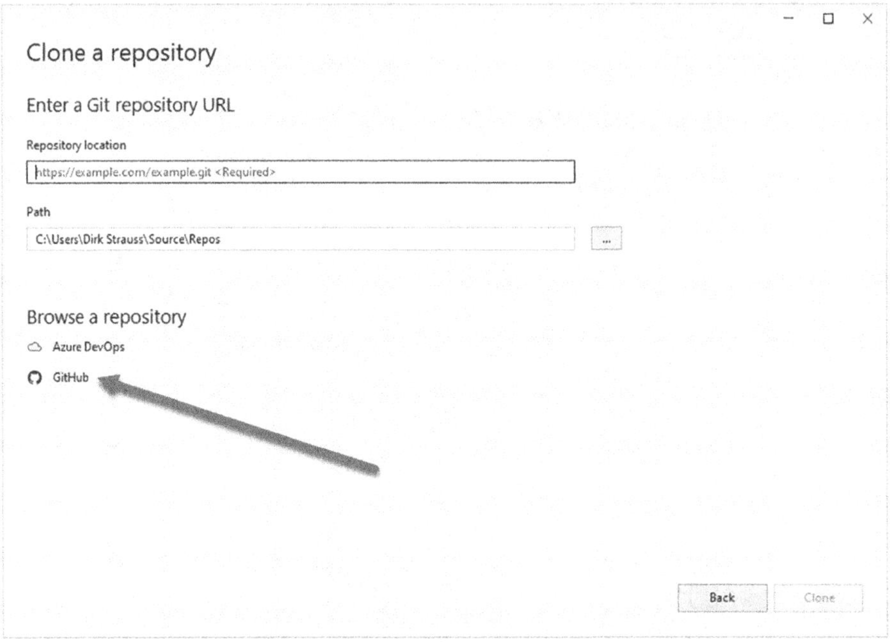

***Figure 5-22.*** *Clone from GitHub*

From this screen, you can enter the repository location to get the code from, but because I am a collaborator on this GitHub project, I can simply click the GitHub option (Figure 5-22).

This will display the Open from GitHub screen (Figure 5-23).

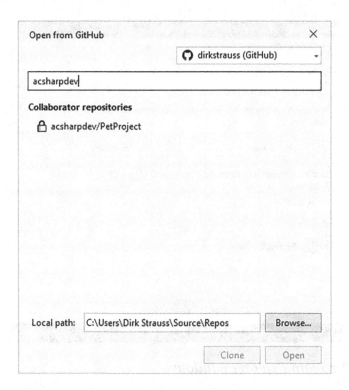

**Figure 5-23.** *Open from GitHub*

It is here that I will see the project that I have been invited to under the Collaborator repositories. Select the project, ensure that the local path is correct, and click the Clone button. The Visual Studio project is then cloned to my local machine. In previous versions of Visual Studio, you would see the repo in the Team Explorer window. Opening Team Explorer in Visual Studio 2022, you will see that the Git features have moved to their own window (Figure 5-24).

***Figure 5-24.*** *The Team Explorer window*

I now have cloned the repository to my local machine, and I can now collaborate with @acsharpdev on his project and share my changes with him easily.

# Create a Branch from Your Code

A new feature needs to be added to the Pet project. It would be better for me to work on the changes to the project in an isolated manner. To do this, I can create a branch in Git. A branch allows me to make changes to the code without changing the code in the main branch, also called the master branch. In Visual Studio, I can see that I am currently working on the master branch if I look at the bottom-right status bar in Visual Studio (Figure 5-25).

***Figure 5-25.*** *Working in the master branch*

To create a new branch, click the current branch to open the Branches view (Figure 5-26).

***Figure 5-26.*** *Branches view*

I will now create a local branch in Visual Studio. To do this, click the New Branch button in the Branches view.

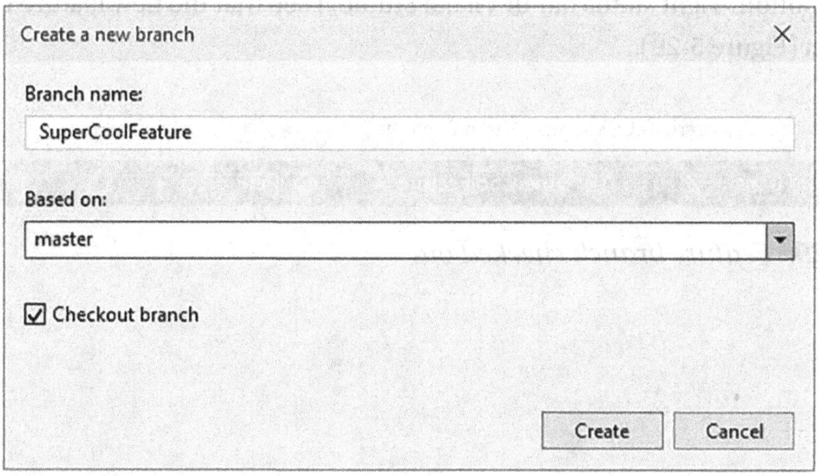

***Figure 5-27.*** *Create a new branch*

I can now give my new branch a suitable name (Figure 5-27) and tell it to create the branch from the master branch. I keep the Checkout branch selected to check out my new branch and click the Create button.

***Figure 5-28.*** *Feature branch created*

As seen in Figure 5-28, my new local branch is created and checked out. When I look at the bottom-right status bar in Visual Studio, I see that the new feature branch is checked out (Figure 5-29).

***Figure 5-29.*** *Feature branch checked out*

This means that from now on, all changes made to the code will stay in this branch. Let's add some new code to the project.

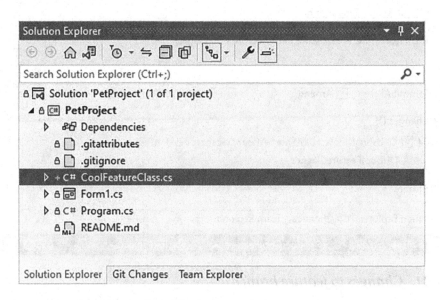

**Figure 5-30.** *New feature code added*

As seen in Figure 5-30, I have added a new class called CoolFeatureClass that contains the new code I added. I must now commit the changes to my branch. In the Git Changes tab, I can see the code that I have changed in my branch (Figure 5-31).

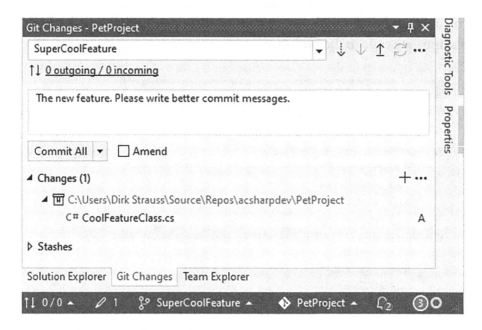

***Figure 5-31.*** *Changes to feature branch*

You can see that the SuperCoolFeature branch is still selected. Under the changes section, you will see all the files that I have changed. Before you commit your code, you need to add a suitable commit message. Then I can click the drop-down next to the Commit All button and select Commit All and Push (Figure 5-32).

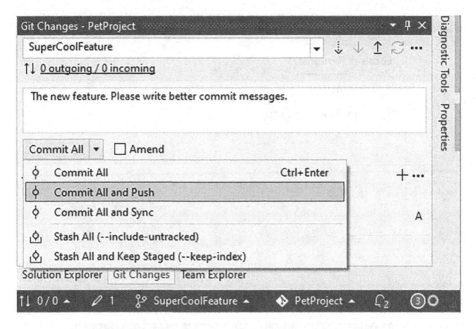

***Figure 5-32.*** *Commit All and Push*

This will commit the changes to the local repo and then push them to the remote repo. If you click the SuperCoolFeature branch and view the Remotes tab, you will see that your feature branch has been pushed to GitHub (Figure 5-33).

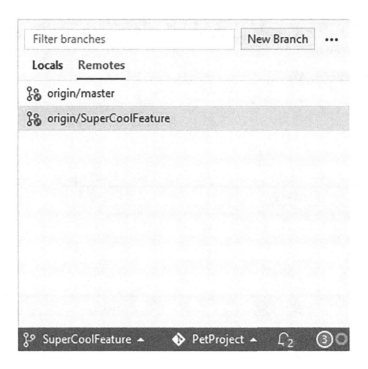

**Figure 5-33.** *Branch pushed to the server*

The code is now safely on the GitHub repo. How do I get my changes into the master branch? For this, we will be creating a pull request.

# Creating and Handling Pull Requests

The term pull request might sound strange to some folks that aren't used to working with a source control system. The "pull" means to request that your code be pulled into the main working branch of the source code. Some developers also refer to a pull request as a merge request.

In Visual Studio, we can easily create a pull request. By doing this, we are telling the team that our code is ready to be peer-reviewed and, if it's good, merged into the main master branch.

You will remember that in the previous section, we created a branch and added all our new features to the branch. Then we committed those changes to Git (locally) before pushing them up to GitHub.

To create a pull request, click the Git menu in Visual Studio and select GitHub ➤ New Pull Request.

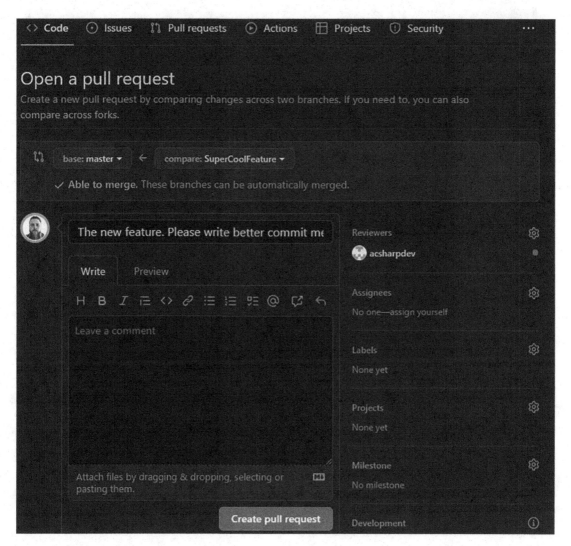

***Figure 5-34.*** *Create a pull request*

You will see that (Figure 5-34) you are taken to GitHub where you can now create a pull request by clicking the "Create pull request" button. Before doing that, select a reviewer (in this case, the acsharpdev user) and enter some pull request details (Figure 5-35).

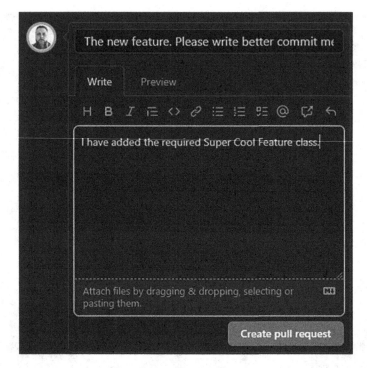

***Figure 5-35.*** *Pull request details*

When you have added all the required details, you click the Create pull request button. This pull request will now go to the acsharpdev user where he can review my code, add comments, and hopefully approve my changes.

When the pull request is successfully created, you will see the pull request by going to the Pull requests tab on GitHub (Figure 5-36).

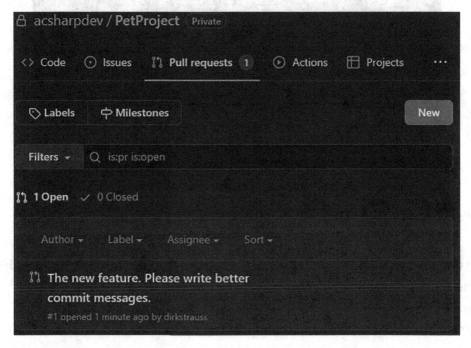

***Figure 5-36.*** *Pull request created*

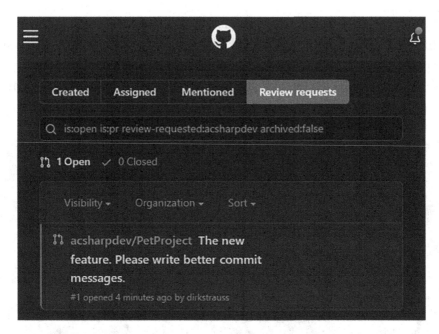

***Figure 5-37.*** *New pull request notification*

On the other side of the continent, the acsharpdev user has just finished working on some code and sees my pull request on GitHub under the Review requests tab (Figure 5-37).

He can now click the pull request that I created to view the details (Figure 5-38).

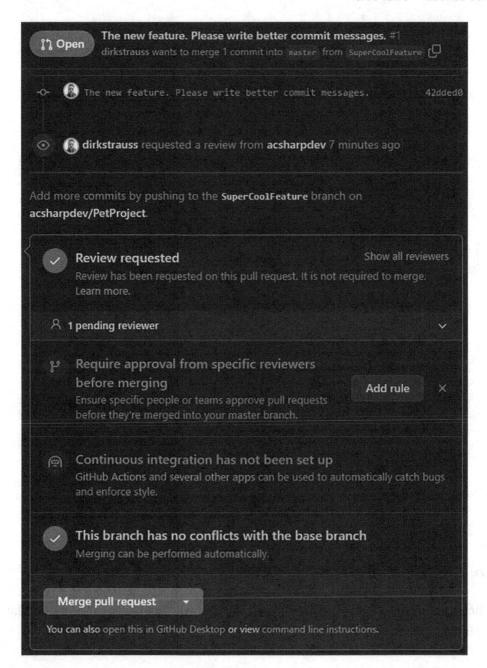

*Figure 5-38. View pull request details*

By clicking the Files changed tab (Figure 5-39), he can see that I only added a new class called CoolFeatureClass.

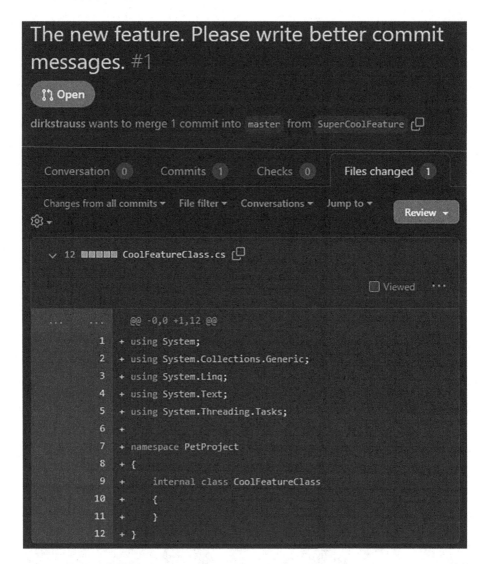

*Figure 5-39.* *View differences*

Clicking the new class I added, John will not see a diff (because this is a new class), but he is still able to review the code.

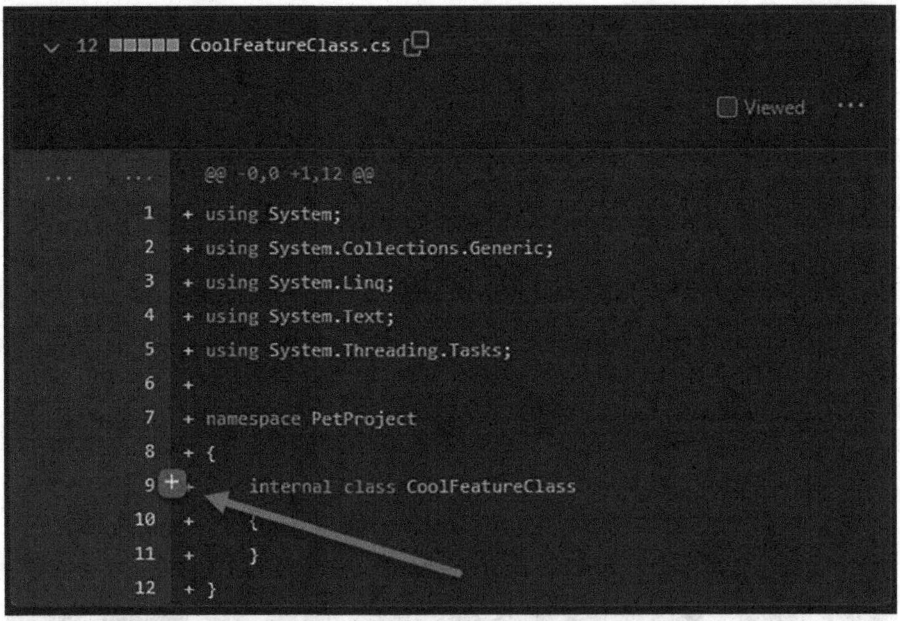

*Figure 5-40.* *Review code in pull request*

Hovering your mouse over the code, you will see a plus sign appear (Figure 5-40).

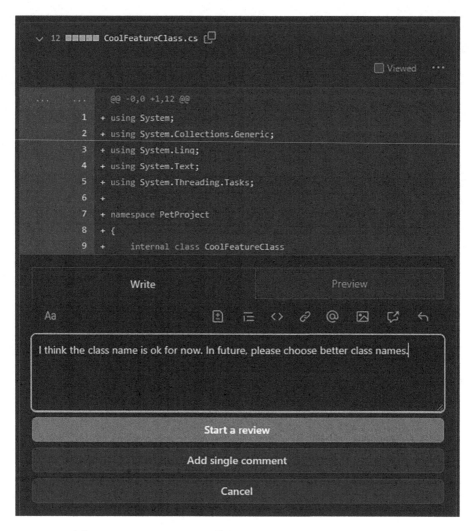

*Figure 5-41.* *Adding comments to pull requests*

Clicking the plus sign will allow him to add a comment to the code I have added (Figure 5-41). Once the comments have been added, I can see these in the pull request I created on GitHub (Figure 5-42).

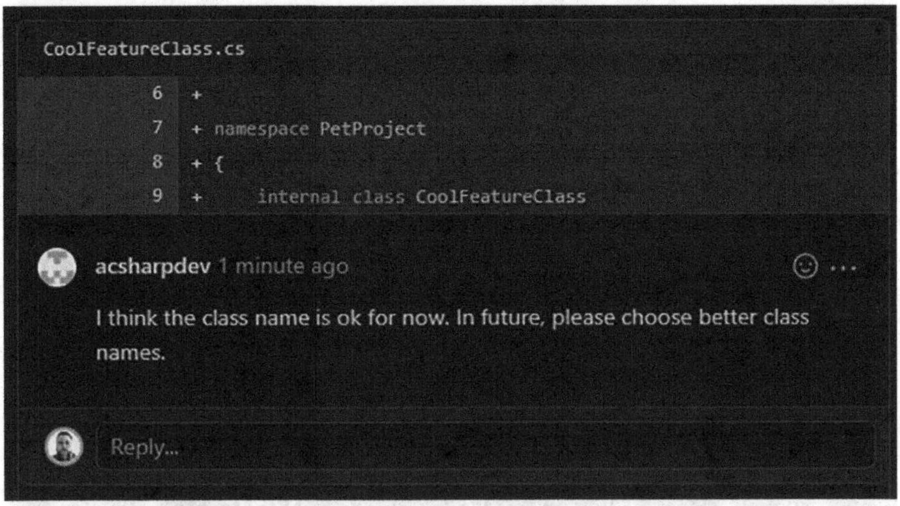

*Figure 5-42.* *View pull request comments*

This allows me to see the comments John added and take any action if needed. I can now reply to the comment as seen in Figure 5-43.

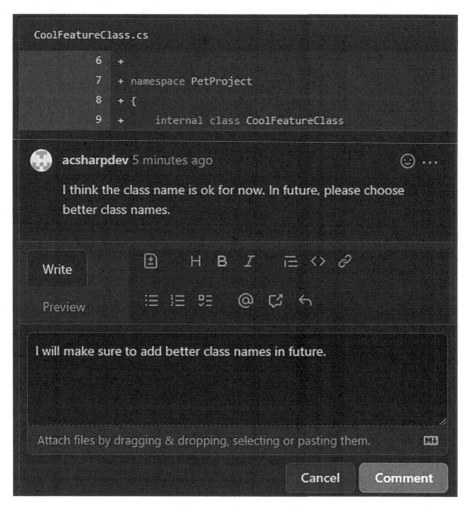

***Figure 5-43.*** *View review comments*

He can now click the Resolve conversation button under the Conversation tab and then approve the pull request (Figure 5-44).

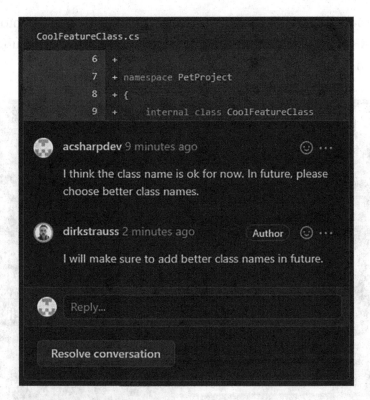

***Figure 5-44.*** *Approving a pull request*

When the conversation is resolved, the pull request can be merged into the master branch. For this, we need to click the Merge pull request button on GitHub to do the merge as seen in Figure 5-45.

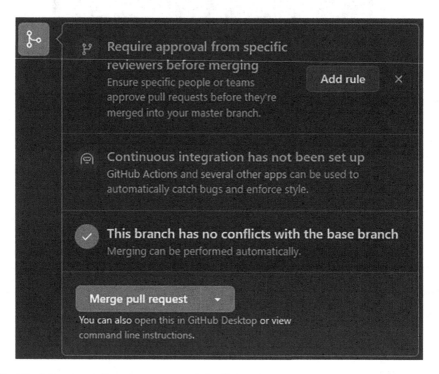

***Figure 5-45.***  *Merge pull request on GitHub*

Looking at Figure 5-46, you will see that we have three options when clicking the Merge pull request drop-down. These are

- Create a merge commit

- Squash and merge

- Rebase and merge

The default option is Create a merge commit and will take the commits from the pull request and merge them into the master branch creating a new commit in a merge commit. Squashing is a lot like rebasing a branch, because you can take a multiple commit pull request and squash it down into a single commit. Rebasing, on the other hand, provides a way to keep the Git history clean by taking the feature branch and "transplant" the commits on top of the master branch.

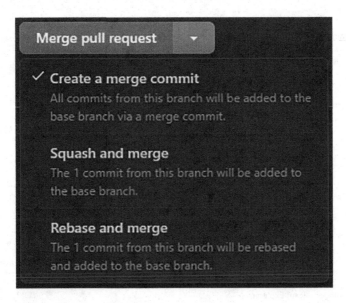

***Figure 5-46.*** *Merge pull request*

After the merge is complete in GitHub, I can safely delete my SuperCoolFeature branch as seen in Figure 5-47.

***Figure 5-47.*** *Pull request merged into the master branch*

I can now switch to my master branch and pull the changes to get the new feature into my local master branch. Switch to your master branch by clicking the branch name in the bottom-right toolbar of Visual Studio and selecting master from there.

Then, click the Fetch arrow in the Git Changes tab and then on the incoming link. There I will see all the incoming commits as seen in Figure 5-48.

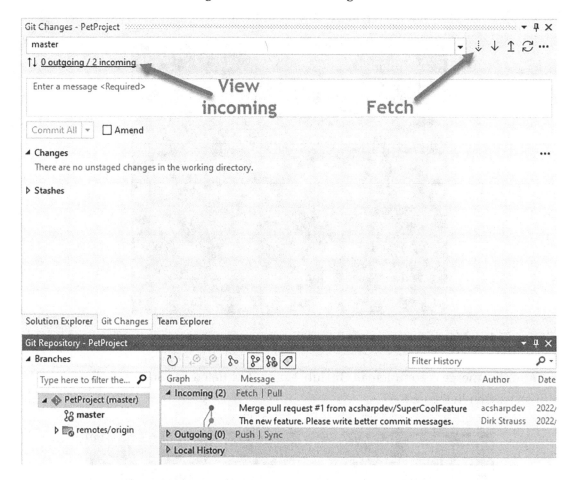

***Figure 5-48.***  *View incoming commits*

Notice that the branch displayed under Branches is the master branch. This is because we switched to our local master branch in Git. The new feature was merged with the remote master branch on GitHub by the acsharpdev user a few minutes ago. I need to pull those changes into my local master branch to get it up to date. To do this, I click the Pull arrow next to the Fetch arrow in the Git Changes tab.

Fetch only downloads the changes from the remote repository (GitHub) but does not integrate the code into your local branch. Fetch just really shows you what changes there are that need to be merged into your local branch.

Pull is used to update your local branch with the latest changes on the remote repository. This merge might potentially result in merge conflicts that you need to resolve before continuing.

After the pull has completed and the changes have been merged into my local master branch, my Solution Explorer will show the new class I added earlier to my feature branch, in my local master (Figure 5-49).

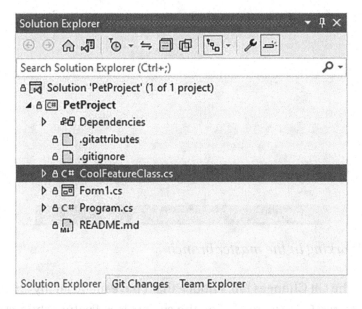

***Figure 5-49.*** *Local master branch merged*

At this point, because the changes have been merged into the master branch, and my local master branch has been updated, I can safely delete the feature branch I created earlier.

Using pull requests allows developers to have a lot more control over the code that gets merged into the main working branch of the project. Using branches allows me to make changes to the code in an isolated manner without risking the stability of the master branch.

# Working with Stashes

Sometimes, you might be working on some changes, and you continue to make a whole range of changes without noticing that you are working on the wrong branch.

In Figure 5-50, you can see that we are currently working on the master branch. I should be making all my changes on the NewFeatures branch. This is a very easy mistake to make (perhaps not with the master branch), especially if you are working in several different branches in your code.

***Figure 5-50.*** *Working in the master branch*

Switching to the Git Changes tab, I notice that I have made all my changes on the master branch (Figure 5-51) instead of on the correct NewFeatures branch.

Enter a world of pain, because I now need to backtrack everything I did and remove the code and then go and apply these to the correct branch. This is where stashes come in very handy.

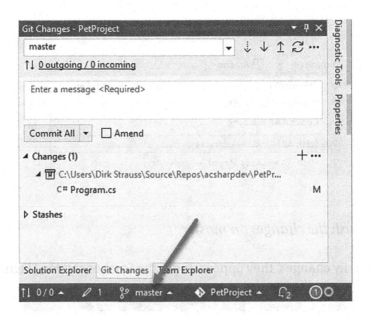

***Figure 5-51.*** *Changes in the incorrect branch*

Stashing takes all the changes I have made and puts them away locally (Figure 5-52). It then reverts all the changes I had made to the master branch. This means that I have my master branch back to the way it was before the changes were made.

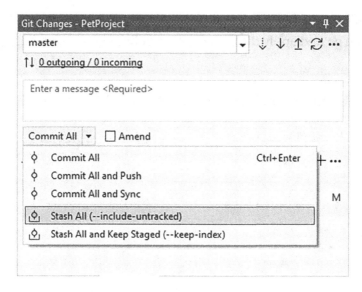

*Figure 5-52.* *Stash the changes on master*

When I stash my changes, they appear under the Stashes section (Figure 5-53).

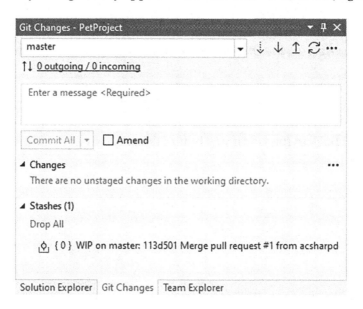

*Figure 5-53.* *Changes stashed*

I can then go and switch to the correct branch as seen in Figure 5-54.

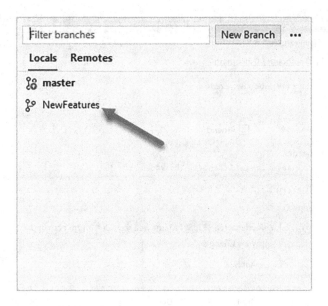

***Figure 5-54.*** *Change to correct branch*

With my correct branch selected (Figure 5-55), I can view the changes, apply them, pop them, or drop the changes. The options are

- Apply – Apply the changes to the branch and keep the stash.

- Pop – Apply the changes to the branch and drop the stash.

- Drop – This will delete the stash without applying anything.

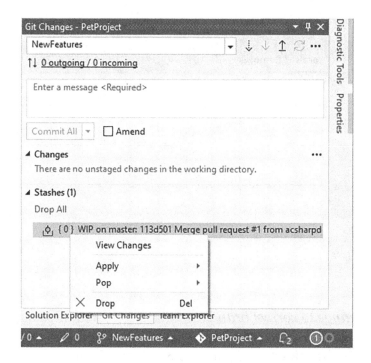

***Figure 5-55.***  *Apply, pop, or drop the stash*

Stashing allows me to pause the changes I was working with and carry on with something else for a while. Another great example of using stashes is when I am working on a branch, and I need to make a bug fix. I can stash my changes which will revert the code in my branch. Then I can make the bug fix and push that up to the remote repo before popping my stash back to my branch. Stashing allows developers to be very flexible when working with code changes.

# Multi-repo Support

A new feature in Visual Studio 2022 is multi-repo support. You can now work in a single solution, with projects hosted in different Git repositories.

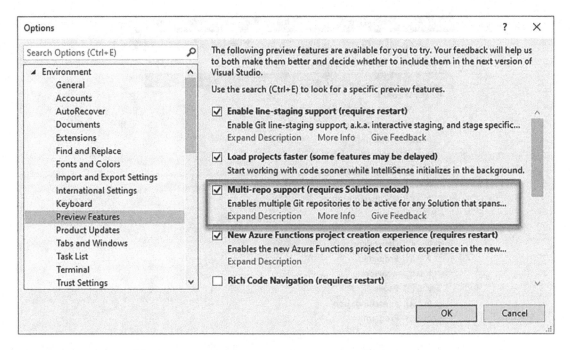

*Figure 5-56. Enable Preview Features*

At the time of writing this book, multi-repo support had to be enabled from the Preview Features section in the Options window as seen in Figure 5-56.

*Figure 5-57. Multiple GitHub repos*

I have two repositories in GitHub: one for my web application and a second for a Web API project as seen in Figure 5-57. With the multi-repo support option enabled, I can now open my web application in Visual Studio 2022 and then add an existing project by right-clicking the solution and selecting Add ➤ Existing Project and selecting my Web API project.

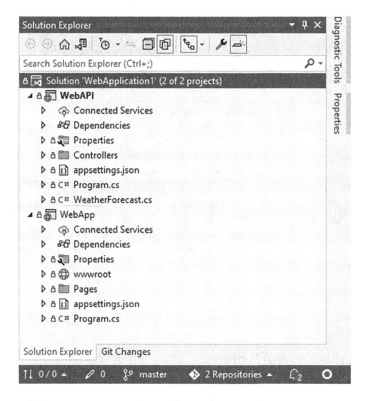

***Figure 5-58.*** *Multi-repos open in Visual Studio*

As seen in Figure 5-58, both my projects across both repositories are loaded in Visual Studio, and the repo in the status bar shows that I am working with two repositories.

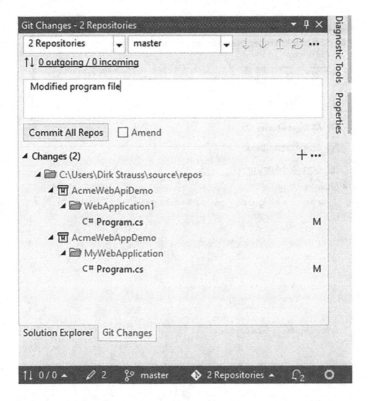

***Figure 5-59.*** *Changes in both repositories*

As seen in Figure 5-59, I can make changes in both repositories and commit all these changes locally by clicking the Commit All Repos button.

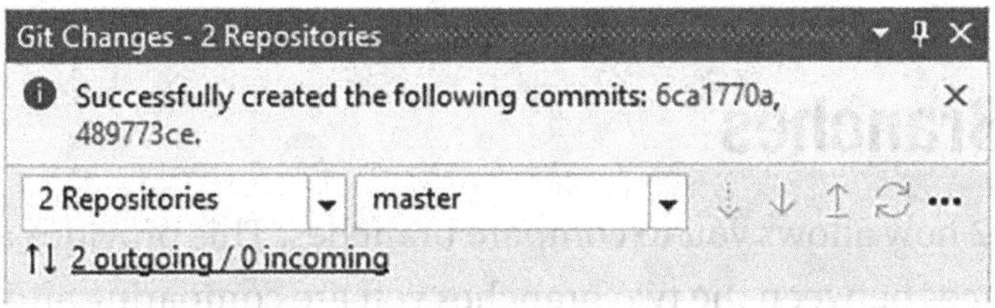

***Figure 5-60.*** *Changes committed locally*

Once these changes are committed locally, I can't just push them as seen in Figure 5-60. To accomplish this, I need to select the repos individually from the Repos drop-down (Figure 5-61) and push the changes one by one.

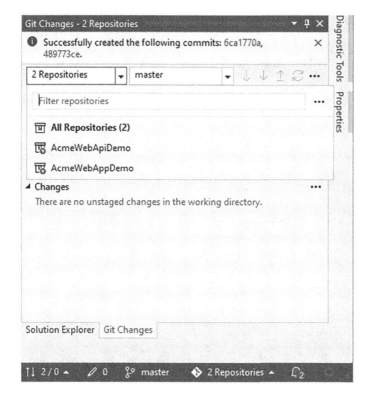

***Figure 5-61.*** *Select the repo to push*

Having the ability to work with multiple repositories in Visual Studio is convenient because I no longer need to open a separate instance of Visual Studio to work on a different repository.

# Compare Branches

Visual Studio 2022 now allows you to compare branches. This provides a convenient way to see the differences between the two branches you are comparing and will be helpful before creating a pull request, before merging, or even when choosing to delete a branch.

***Figure 5-62.*** *View the branches to compare*

As seen in Figure 5-62, when I click the currently checked out branch (NewFeatures), I can see that I also have a branch called master. To compare the NewFeatures branch with the master branch, right-click the master branch and select Compare with Current Branch from the context menu as seen in Figure 5-63.

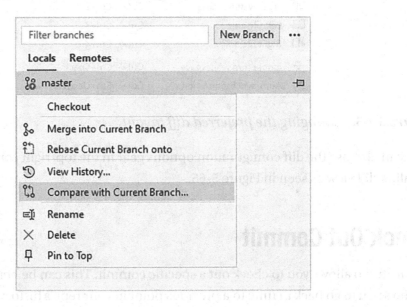

***Figure 5-63.*** *Compare to master branch*

Visual Studio will then display a diff between the two branches you selected to compare as seen in Figure 5-64.

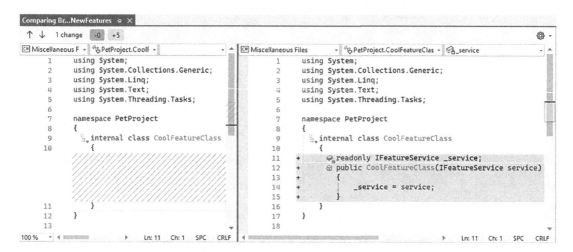

**Figure 5-64.** *The branch diff*

I am now able to see exactly what is different between the two branches without leaving Visual Studio.

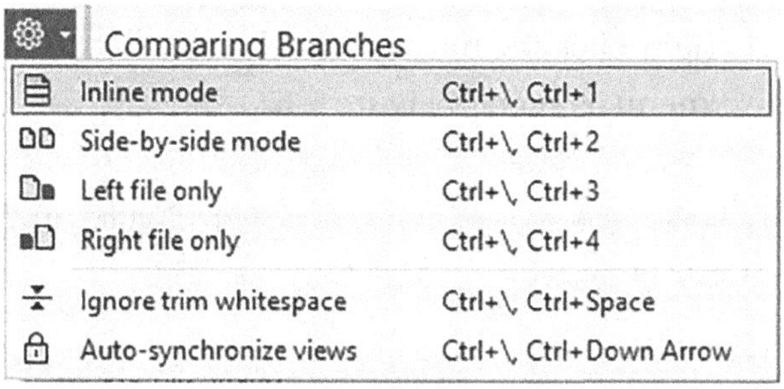

**Figure 5-65.** *Changing the preferred diff layout*

I can also use the diff configuration options gear in the top-right corner to switch to an inline diff view as seen in Figure 5-65.

# Check Out Commit

Visual Studio allows you to check out a specific commit. This can be beneficial because it allows you to go back in time to a previous point in your repo's history if you need to test a specific section of code. You can also do this for a remote branch, and it saves you from having to create a local branch if you are not planning on adding any new code to it. To do this, open the Git Repository window by selecting the View menu and clicking Git Repository as seen in Figure 5-66.

| View | Git | Project | Build | Debug | Test | Analy |
|------|-----|---------|-------|-------|------|-------|
| ⊠ Solution Explorer | | | | Ctrl+Alt+L | | |
| ⧉ Git Changes | | | | Ctrl+0, Ctrl+G | | |
| ⧉ Git Repository | | | | Ctrl+0, Ctrl+R | | |
| ⍜ Team Explorer | | | | Ctrl+\, Ctrl+M | | |
| ⊟ Server Explorer | | | | Ctrl+Alt+S | | |
| ⧉ SQL Server Object Explorer | | | | Ctrl+\, Ctrl+S | | |
| ⧉ Test Explorer | | | | Ctrl+E, T | | |

**Figure 5-66.** *View the Git Repository*

You can also hold down Ctrl+O, Ctrl+R to open the Git Repository which can be seen in Figure 5-67.

| Graph | Message | | Author | Date | ID |
|-------|---------|---|--------|------|-----|
| | Filter History | 🔍 ▾ | | | |
| ▷ Incoming (0) | Fetch \| Pull | | | | |
| ▷ Outgoing (0) | Push \| Sync | | | | |
| ⊿ Local History | | | | | |
| ● | Added code stub for FeatureService impl... | NewFeatures | Dirk Strauss | 2022/08/... | 83cee094 |
| ● | Added feature service and Interface | | Dirk Strauss | 2022/08/... | 60352f47 |
| ● | Merge pull request #1 from acsharpdev/Super... | master | acsharpdev | 2022/08/... | 113d5011 |
| ● | The new feature. Please write better commit messages. | | Dirk Strauss | 2022/08/... | 42dded0e |
| ● | Modified UI and button click logic | | Dirk Strauss | 2022/08/... | c3371328 |
| ● | Add project files. | | Dirk Strauss | 2022/08/... | 27751a27 |
| ● | Add .gitattributes, .gitignore, and README.md. | | Dirk Strauss | 2022/08/... | c7c61efb |

**Figure 5-67.** *The Git Repository window*

To check out a specific commit, right-click the commit in the Git Repository window as seen in Figure 5-68 and select Checkout (--detach) from the context menu.

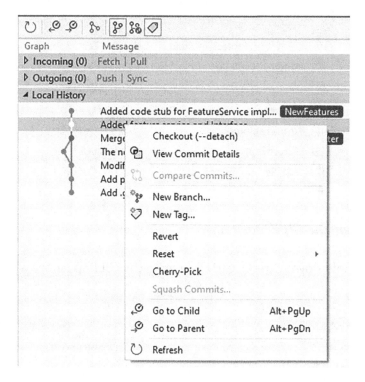

***Figure 5-68.*** *Check out a commit*

Visual Studio now displays a confirmation window (Figure 5-69) to inform you that by checking out this commit, you will be in a detached HEAD state. In other words, your repo's HEAD will be pointing to a specific commit instead of a branch.

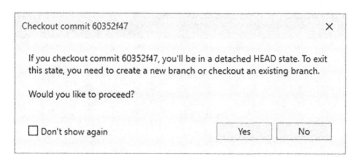

***Figure 5-69.*** *The checkout commit confirmation*

The status bar of Visual Studio will now show that you are currently pointed to a specific commit instead of to a branch (Figure 5-70).

*Figure 5-70.* *The Visual Studio status bar*

You can now run your tests and modify code as required. You can even commit your code if required. To get back to your branch, simply select it from the branch selector in the Visual Studio status bar.

# Line Staging

Also known as interactive staging, line-staging support is helpful when splitting changes across different commits. To enable this Preview Feature, ensure that the Enable line-staging option is enabled from the Preview Features section in the Options window as seen in Figure 5-71.

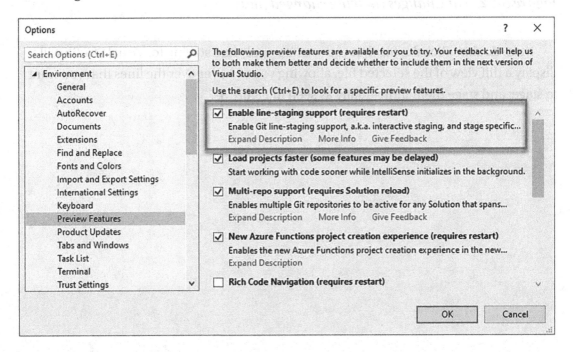

*Figure 5-71.* *Enable line-staging support*

To see line staging in action, make some changes to one of your files, and then view the file in the Git Changes window as seen in Figure 5-72.

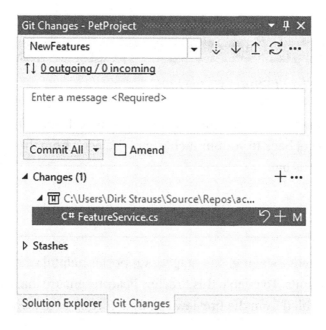

***Figure 5-72.*** *Git Changes showing changed files*

Next, double-click the file that you want to apply line staging to. Visual Studio will display a diff view of the selected file, allowing you to hover over the lines that you want to stage, and stage them individually as seen in Figure 5-73.

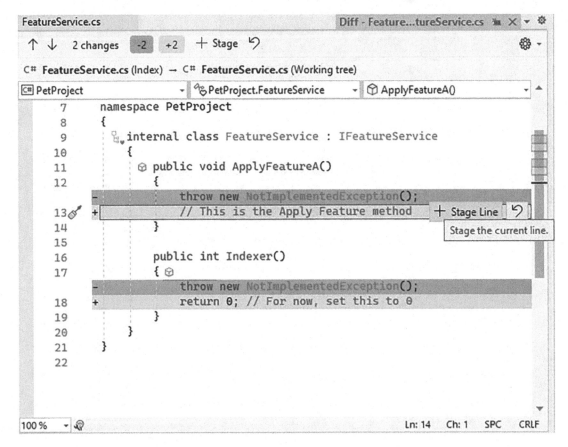

***Figure 5-73.*** *Staging a specific line of code*

Line staging also supports side-by-side and inline diff modes. Being able to stage specific lines of code is a nice feature and allows developers to be quite flexible when committing code.

# Summary

Microsoft has added a lot of new features and enhancements to Visual Studio 2022. We had a look at cloning repositories, creating branches, and handling pull requests. Multi-repo support is a fantastic new feature, and being able to compare commits, check out specific commits, and stage specific lines of code without leaving Visual Studio makes for a welcome productivity enhancement. I hope that you will continue exploring Visual Studio and embracing the rich set of features it provides.

# Index

## A

Action expression, 174, 175
AddScoped, 94
AddTransient, 94
ASP.NET Web Application, 73, 79
Attach to Process window
    connection type, 205, 206
    reattach to process, 207
    remote process, 206, 207
    w3wp.exe process, 206

## B

Bonus Tip, 185
Bookmarks, 132–136
Breakpoints
    action expression, 174, 175
    actions, 172–176
    conditional, 172–176
    context menu, 172
    debug toolbar, 166, 167
    dependent, 177
    dragging, 177
    exporting, 181
    filter condition, 173, 174
    Force Run to Cursor, 171, 172
    hit count condition, 173
    with labels, 177–180
    Run to Click, 169, 170
    Run to Cursor, 170, 171
    set breakpoints, 177, 178
    setting, 166

specific business rules, 167–169
Start button, 166
Step button, 167
Step Out button/Shift+F11, 167
Step Over button/F10, 167
temporary, 176
window, 178, 179

## C

CalculateFreightCosts method, 239
C# format specifiers
    ac, 191
    d, 191
    dynamic, 192
    h, 192
    hidden, 192
    nq, 192
    nse, 192
    raw, 192
    results, 192
Class Coupling, 155
Clone method, 227, 228
Code Coverage, 225, 229, 241–244
Code shortcuts, 135–137
Code snippets
    Ctrl+K, Ctrl+X, 127
    custom try-catch, 128, 129
    insert code, 125
    manager, 126
    namespace, 131
    try-catch block, 126

© Dirk Strauss 2023
D. Strauss, *Getting Started with Visual Studio 2022*, https://doi.org/10.1007/978-1-4842-8922-8

# T

# U

# V

# W, X, Y, Z

Printed in the United States
by Baker & Taylor Publisher Services